Integrated Case Studies in Accounting and Information Systems

Mohsen Sharifi
Eastern Michigan University

Badie Farah
Eastern Michigan University

Prentice-Hall, Inc., Englewood Cliffs, New Jersey 07632

Library of Congress Cataloging-in-Publication Data

Sharifi, Mohsen. (date)
  Integrated case studies in accounting and information systems.

   1. Accounting—Data processing.   2. Information
storage and retrieval systems—Accounting.
I. Farah, Badie.   II. Title.
HF5679.S4754 1986   657'.028'5   86-30297
ISBN 0-13-469016-8

Editorial/production supervision and
   interior design: Nancy Benjamin
Cover design: Ben Santora
Manufacturing buyer: Ray Keating

To my family—M.S.

In memory of my parents—B.F.

Printed in the United States of America

10 9 8 7 6 5 4 3 2 1

ISBN 0-13-469016-8 01

Acknowledgment
Line Printer Spacing Chart and Punch Card
Layout Form reproduced courtesy Burroughs
Corporation.

Prentice-Hall International (UK) Limited, *London*
Prentice-Hall of Australia Pty. Limited, *Sydney*
Prentice-Hall Canada Inc., *Toronto*
Prentice-Hall Hispanoamericana, S.A., *Mexico*
Prentice-Hall of India Private Limited, *New Delhi*
Prentice-Hall of Japan, Inc., *Tokyo*
Prentice-Hall of Southeast Asia Pte. Ltd., *Singapore*
Editora Prentice-Hall do Brasil, Ltda., *Rio de Janeiro*

Contents

6 DESIGN OF A SYSTEM FOR FIXED ASSETS AND GENERAL LEDGER | 150

7 DESIGN OF A SYSTEM FOR MANAGEMENT PLANNING AND CONTROL | 185

Preface

Theory and applications of and research about accounting information systems are well established and documented. Many, if not all, of the major principles of this subject are covered in undergraduate and graduate courses in the various programs offered by colleges of business. In these courses students acquire exposure to the accounting principles needed for the analysis and design of accounting information systems. The field, however, remains applied in nature. Hence, a practical approach and training in systems analysis and design are desirable.

Both accounting systems analysis and design principles are necessary for developing meaningful accounting information systems. Therefore, a merger between the methods of teaching these subjects is important for producing a good understanding and a solid foundation for this subject. This merged teaching method should stress practical exposure to the analysis and development of accounting information systems as its main goal. By utilizing a case study approach to teaching, this objective can be attained.

The case studies offered in this book provide applications that students need to exercise the principles of accounting systems analysis and design. The cases presented are general; that is, they can be tailored to a specific situation by some minor modifications. The cases include all the ingredients of the particular system they describe.

One of the features of this book is that all major transaction cycles are treated in a single source. A thorough study of each case should help the student to better grasp the processing and control activities within each cycle and the important relationships connecting them. This is accomplished by relating information requirements for each cycle to the resulting system configuration and file structure.

The cases cover the spectrum of accounting applications encountered in most businesses. In each of these cases the accounting application under study is described. The firm used to illustrate development of the application is then described. The relationships among the various departments of the firm are fully discussed with relation to information transfer and controls. Then a systems analysis and design of the accounting application, with details of activities and data, are developed. The system design can be used as a blueprint for the development of similar systems for the same kind of accounting application.

Some of these cases represent modifications of systems designed at operating companies that engaged our students in the development of accounting information systems. Other cases were class tested to advance the principles of accounting information systems development.

This text could be used in information systems analyses and design courses in colleges of business or in industrial engineering programs at the advanced undergraduate or the graduate level. In accounting programs this text is intended to be used in conjunction with a main text such as *Accounting Information Systems* by Page and Hooper.

This casebook would be most appropriate for accounting information systems courses taught with a systems analysis and design perspective. The casebook can be viewed as providing a set of typical configurations for the various cycles that might be used as a basis for developing or evaluating other design alternatives. And when used as a supplement, it can strengthen the student's understanding of these cycles and control concepts, particularly for nonaccounting majors.

This book could also play a useful role in AIS courses taught from an audit perspective. Most current AIS texts do not provide adequate depth regarding transaction processing and control functions. In addition, the various applications could be used as models for programming assignments in a programming-oriented AIS course or COBOL, PL/I, and APL programming courses.

Each of the cases is a self-contained unit; therefore, the instructor need not follow any particular order in their discussion. We recommend that the cases be assigned as a reading reference as soon as the instructor starts systems development. The different aspects of the systems methodology can be explored by referring to the case materials. At the same time the instructor may want to assign the problems at the end of each chapter or modify the existing cases according to his or her teaching approach, depending on the stages of systems development discussed. Furthermore, some or all of the chapters may be assigned to a given course depending on the amount of time available. The authors welcome and appreciate comments, suggested modifications, and criticism in relation to the individual cases, their coverage, or the scope of the text.

We wish to express our deep gratitude to the students at the College of Business, Eastern Michigan University, who participated in testing some of these cases. Many people have contributed to this effort; without them it would have been impossible. Our heartfelt thanks and appreciation go especially to Mrs. Mary Shipley, who typed the manuscript. We also acknowledge the reviewers for their helpful and valuable comments. Special thanks are due the consulting editor, Professor Willard R. Jarchow, whose constructive criticism and comments are incorporated in this book. Our special thanks as well to graduate students Brian Glass, Richard Hitt, Mark Morsfield, and Philippe Sammour, who were extremely helpful in the preparation of the manuscript.

As we acknowledge all those who helped us complete the project, we also claim responsibility for all errors, inconsistencies, and inadequacies that exist between these covers.

Mohsen Sharifi
Badie Farah

Ypsilanti, Michigan

Note: All names of people and companies in the cases presented in this book are fictional.

1 | **The Nature of Accounting Systems**

The capabilities of computers are summarized in two words: speed and accuracy. Both capabilities are crucial for the accounting profession. Public accountants have always been providers of useful, reliable, and accurate information. Numerous social and economic changes, which have resulted in increased complexity, for organizations necessitate the dissemination of this information faster than ever.

With the advent of the computer, there has been a measurable change in the nature of accounting tasks traditionally performed by accountants. Among the more noticeable changes are the following three.

1. Accountants are now more involved with decision-oriented functions such as cash-flow budgets and lease-or-buy decisions, in addition to traditional routine recordkeeping functions.

2. Reports are more timely because the time elapsed between an event and the reporting of results is shortened or eliminated.

3. Added demand is imposed on new entrants into the accounting profession, and their education is now broader based so that they can assist in systems analysis and design.

Although the routine recording and reporting of accounting events may eventually be handled by other functional departments such as information processing, information services, or similar departments, accountants will still play a major role in design development of information systems. They must be able to understand, evaluate, and contribute constructively to the system design endeavor.

It is the objective of this book and the cases it incorporates to provide guidelines for future accountants and for professionals already in the field by demonstrating the process of design of various financial and managerial accounting systems.

THE NATURE OF ACCOUNTING SYSTEMS

Traditionally, accounting has been defined by the American Institute of Certified Public Accountants as

the art of recording, classifying, and summarizing in a significant manner and in terms of money, transactions and events which are, in part at least, of a financial character, and interpreting the results thereof.[1]

About a decade later, the Committee on Accounting and Information Systems presented a functional model for an information system. This model is depicted in Fig. 1-1. It encompasses all the activities of the firm which involve collecting, processing, storing, and reporting of information related to common goals, resources, and resource management. In this context, the committee considers accounting a system with its own set of goals, activities, and resources, and thus a subpart of the firm's information system.[2]

Based on the model presented, it would be difficult to distinguish between accounting and nonaccounting systems. Nevertheless the committee defines the "Accounting Information System to be that portion of the formal information system concerned with the measurement and prediction of income, wealth, and other economic events of the organization and its subparts or entities."[3] This view is congruent with the American Accounting Association's definition of accounting: "the process of identifying, measuring and communicating economic information to permit informed judgments and decisions."[4]

Accounting systems provide periodic information about the activities of an enterprise. This information may be generated from historical data based on traditional accounting systems, or it may include plans and expectations for the future such as budgets and standard costs. In recent years, we have observed some emphasis on efforts to provide futuristic long-range information for strategic planning in organizations.

Accounting systems in a traditional form satisfied most management informational needs for many years. But as the business environment became more complex, traditional systems no longer served management to the fullest extent. Management was compelled to develop other systems to supplement financial accounting. In this text accounting information systems are divided into three subsystems: financial accounting systems, managerial accounting

---

[1] American Institute of Certified Public Accountants, *Accounting Terminology Bulletin No. 1.* New York: AICPA, 1961, p. 9.

[2] "Report of the Committee on Accounting and Information Systems," *The Accounting Review Supplement* (Sarasota, Fla.: American Accounting Association, 1971), p. 289.

[3] Ibid., pp. 289–90.

[4] *A Statement of Basic Accounting Theory* (Sarasota, Fla.: American Accounting Association, 1966), p. 1.

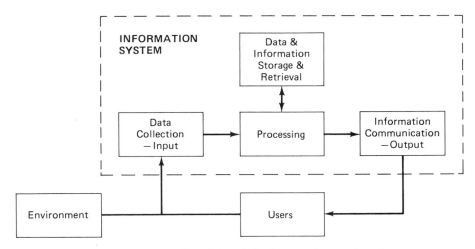

FIGURE 1-1   A Functional Model of an Information System

systems, and more advanced systems. (The latter includes decision support systems.)

Financial Accounting Systems

Financial accounting is the process of providing financial information of an entity to those users of the information who are normally referred to as "outsiders." Outsiders typically include stockholders and other investors, creditors (lending institutions and private individuals), government agencies, unions, and the general public. Procedures used to prepare financial information are closely linked to treatment of transactions affecting assets, liabilities, owners' equity, revenue, and expenses. Financial information may also include "consolidated" and partnership information.

Information of this kind must be prepared within the Financial Accounting Standards Board (FASB) guidelines known as Generally Accepted Accounting Principles (GAAP). In applying these principles, certain qualitative characteristics (relevance and reliability), assumptions (economic entity, going concern and periodicity), concepts, and elements must be taken into consideration.

Computerization of financial accounting is generally thought to result in improved efficiency. However, the benefits derived from automation of financial accounting functions may not substantially outweigh the cost of producing this information. Processing in the financial accounting area consists of the steps generally known as recording of journals, posting from various types of journals, footing the general ledger, preparing the trial balance, adjusting the trial balance, and preparing financial statements. Automation of financial processing is totally different from automation or computerization of such transaction-recording functions as order taking or order processing.

Computers have had a wide impact on this area in recent years. Traditional forms for recording accounting information are disappearing as the journals and ledgers are stored in new physical form, on magnetic tapes and disks.

Management Accounting

The Committee on Management Accounting has defined management accounting as the "application of appropriate techniques and concepts in processing the historical and projected economic data of an entity to assist management in establishing plans for reasonable economic objectives and in the making of the rational decision with a view toward achieving these objectives."[5]

Management accounting encompasses a broader domain than financial accounting. It deals with management's internal use of information for strategic planning, management controls and operational controls.[6]

For the accountant, the main difference between financial accounting and managerial accounting is the application of GAAP to financial accounting. Managerial accounting information is prepared according to management-prescribed guidelines, regardless of its consistency with GAAP. Recently, the National Association of Accountants has attempted to provide a set of standards in management accounting practice in order to make this field conform to some kind of guidelines.

To attain a higher degree of specialization, management accounting has been divided into the two areas of responsibility accounting and profitability accounting. *Responsibility accounting* requires a specific type of reporting, which normally consists of a set of correlated reports connecting the lower level of management to the highest level. In this type of reporting, the higher the level of a manager, the more condensed the report prepared, and the more organizational units encompassed. *Profitability accounting* refers to a process of comprehensive budgeting, along with related aspects of organizational structure.[7]

The main role of computers in managerial accounting systems is to recognize and process the codes that are assigned to different responsibility centers or various profit centers. With rapidly growing knowledge in the fields of management accounting and computer science, more sophisticated applications and better utilization of computers will materialize in the years to come.

More Advanced Systems

Financial and managerial accounting information systems are not able to provide all the information management needs for decision making. To overcome this shortcoming, information systems specialists have suggested the concept of

---

[5] "Report of the Committee on Management Accounting," *The Accounting Review Supplement* (Sarasota, Fla.: American Accounting Association, 1970), p. 210.

[6] These areas are further explored in Chapter 7.

[7] For detailed discussion of this subject refer to a managerial accounting textbook.

a unified information processing or "total information" system. However, according to John Dearden, the entire information system of a company is too large for the classification to be meaningful. Moreover, Dearden points out, the design of different types of systems requires different types of skill and knowledge, which makes the design of a total system almost impossible. He suggests that there are three major information systems typical to any organization. These systems are financial information systems, personnel information systems, and logistic information systems. There are other minor systems within any organization that could, to some extent, be integrated with the major information systems. These minor systems process information on marketing, research and development, strategic planning, and executive observations. In order to respond to management's information needs, Dearden suggests integration of data into a single data base.[8]

In the most recent literature, strategic planning and executive observation systems are renamed *decision support systems* (DSS). In recent years, these systems have gained substantial popularity.

Computers are an indispensable part of the more advanced systems. This is because most DSS and integrated systems are dependent upon a well-organized and thoughtfully defined data structure. The efficient manipulation of data within any organization would never materialize without the support of powerful software, hardware, and data bases.

FINANCIAL ACCOUNTING SYSTEMS

Basic Financial Accounting Functions

Based on traditional definitions, the main functions of financial accounting are to handle routine transactions, to serve interested groups outside the firm's environment by following the Generally Accepted Accounting Principles, and to keep the entity in compliance with the regulations of various government agencies.

Handling Routine Transactions. Most of the effort of the financial accounting system is spent on handling routine transactions. The process starts as soon as an event of a financial nature occurs. Seven steps are involved in this process.

1. Prepare source documents such as purchase orders.
2. Enter the transaction in the different journals (journalization).
3. Post the events recorded in the journal to the ledger on a periodic basis.

---

[8] John Dearden, "How to Organize Information Systems," *Harvard Business Review,* March–April 1965. Copyright© 1965 by the President and Fellows of Harvard College, all rights reserved.

4. Maintain account balances in the ledger, and prepare a trial balance.
5. Prepare and post adjusted entries to the ledger.
6. Prepare the account balances in the ledger.
7. Close the accounts.

Service to Outsiders. The value of accounting information is twofold. First, it is useful to the firm, and second, it satisfies the need of outsiders. Various outsiders are normally interested in different forms of financial information.

- *Stockholders* are interested in investment decisions. They decide whether to add to or subtract from their existing equity on the basis of the performance information available in a firm's financial statements.
- *Creditors* are interested in estimating the present as well as future cash flow. They do this by referring to the entity's financial statements.
- *Labor unions* need to know about profitability of the firm so that they can demand a more favorable package in future negotiations. They are also interested in such issues as profitsharing plans and changes in pension plans as well as the long-range stability of the firm. This information normally is reflected in financial statements.
- *Customers* need to know whether a supplier is a reliable source. Profitability of the firm as a sign of prosperity and longevity of the firm as a reliable source are their most important concerns (other than good service, of course).
- *Government agencies* are interested in the profitability of the firm as a viable source of tax revenues (corporate tax, property tax, sales tax, income tax, unemployment tax). The agencies normally rely on financial statements to satisfy their information needs.

Compliance with Government Regulation. Various governmental units such as the Securities and Exchange Commission, the Federal Communication Commission, the Federal Power Commission, and the Federal Trade Commission are interested in still other information in order to verify the compliance of companies with their respective regulations. For instance, the Federal Power Commission is interested in cost information furnished by utilities, so it can establish rates. The source of most of the information for regulatory agencies is the financial statement.

Undoubtedly, routine transactions can be handled with more speed and accuracy by computers. However, the general systems design considerations of both manual and computerized systems are similar. For instance, in both types of systems, the designer is interested in form design and data manipulation.

In more advanced information systems, there is a tendency to eliminate source documents as much as possible. Having the source documents eliminated can create other types of complications for the systems analyst such as maintaining the audit trails and the integrity of data.

Elements of Financial Accounting Systems

In financial accounting systems, two types of decisions are prevalent. First, decisions about the type of events to be identified and captured, and second, decisions about the methods of measuring the events and reporting them. In financial accounting, only events having monetary implications are identified and recorded. Those events ought to be reported periodically to the users of financial accounting systems.

Whether the system is computerized or manual, several steps must be taken from the time of an event's occurrence to the time of the event's reporting. The sequence, generally referred to as the *accounting cycle*, has seven steps.

1. *Data collection.* Necessary before an event can be recorded.

2. *Recording.* Registers the collected data in books called journals. In computerized systems, data collection and recording may be handled in many different forms through so-called input devices. One of the oldest computer data entry devices is the punched-card reader; one of the newest is the automatic teller machine (ATM).

3. *Classifying.* Categorizing each group of transactions or events into different accounts. In a manual system, this process is referred to as *posting*. In computerized system, it may be called *sorting of files*.

4. *Summarizing.* Determining the balance of each account. In manual systems, this step of the process is rather cumbersome and the source of many clerical errors. In a computerized system, summarizing is fast and almost error-free.

5. *Updating accounts or adjusting.* This process is affected mostly by the "matching process" in accounting practice. One can see only minor differences between manual and computerized versions of this step.

6. *Preparing financial statements.* This step involves the preparation of the balance sheet, the income statement, and the statement of changes in financial position. The manual preparation of these statements is quite time-consuming. Computerized preparation is more efficient. The speed of computers has had a great impact on the preparation of financial statements. In many financial institutions, such as banks, financial statements are prepared daily.

7. *Closing the accounts.* This step is essential, due to the need to observe the periodicity assumption. This step, like adjusting entries, benefits only marginally from the computerization of the system.

The completion of the accounting cycle is materialized through ledgers, journals, and posting.

Ledger. A ledger is normally a collection of accounts. The number of accounts in a ledger is generally a function of management information needs. Depending on the nature of the system, the ledger could take the form of a bound book, looseleaf pages (in a manual system), a set of punched cards, or a group of electronic impulses on a reel of magnetic tape or disk pack (in a computerized system).

Journal. A journal is a chronologic record of accounting transactions showing certain features of a transaction such as the date, names of the accounts, amount (debit or credit), and a description of the transaction. In a manual system, a journal may take various forms generally referred to as specialized journals. In a computerized system, a journal can be in either of two forms: a punched cards file or a transaction file on magnetic tape or disk.

Posting. Transferring data from a journal to a ledger is called posting. Most of the errors in a manual system occur at this stage. In order to minimize these errors, specialized journals have been developed and used. In a computerized system, this process occurs with unmatched speed and accuracy. Computerized posting is handled in various ways such as by copying the transaction file into other files, updating different accounts, or simply changing a status code on a transaction file from ''journal'' to ''ledger.'' The application of changes in the status code is demonstrated in Chapter 7.

Closing. The process of closing is a systematic process of terminating different accounts by following certain steps, such as closing expense accounts into income summary accounts. Since closing is normally done only once at the end of each fiscal period, even in a modern system, little benefit is derived here from the computerization of the system.

Internal Controls

The control of accounting transactions should be viewed within the context of internal control, defined in the *Statement on Auditing Standards No. 1* as ''the plan of organization and all of the coordinated methods and measures adopted within a business to safeguard its assets, check the accuracy and reliability of its accounting data, promote operational efficiency, and encourage adherence to prescribed managerial policies.''[9]

To assure reliability of accounting data, a special set of controls must be established which are generally referred to as *accounting controls. Statement on Auditing Standards No. 1* also defines accounting control as the plan of organization and all methods and procedures that are concerned mainly with safeguarding assets and the reliability of financial records. Consequently they are designed to provide reasonable assurance that the transactions are executed and recorded in accordance with management's authorization and to permit preparation of financial statements in conformity with the Generally Accepted Accounting Principles.[10]

[9] American Institute of Certified Public Accountants, *Statement on Auditing Standards No. 1*, paragraph 320.08 (New York: AICPA, 1972).

[10] Ibid.

In order to accomplish the objectives of accounting controls, the manual system relies heavily on human assets—intelligence, integrity, and sense of responsibility. However, in a computer-based environment, most of the controls that require human intervention or judgment are programmed into the system. Furthermore, not as many individuals work on the computerized system as would be expected to work on a manual system. This means greater responsibility for some and elimination of others, due to the computerization of certain control functions. As a result, a specific set of standards has been developed under *Statement on Auditing Standards No. 3.* According to this statement, two groups of controls must be established in any computerized environment.

The first set are *general controls,* which relate to all electronic data processing (EDP) activities and

comprise (a) the plan of organization and operation of the EDP activity; (b) the procedures for documenting, reviewing, testing and approving systems or programs and changes thereto; (c) controls built into the equipment by the manufacturer [commonly referred to as *hardware controls*]; (d) control over access to equipment and data files; and (e) other data and procedural controls affecting overall EDP operations.[11]

The second set are *application controls,* which "relate to a specific task performed by EDP. Their function is to provide reasonable assurance that the recording, processing, and reporting of data are properly performed."[12] Application controls are classified into the three categories: input controls, processing controls, and output controls.

Both general controls and application controls affect financial accounting subsystems to the fullest extent. Effective implementation of these controls should make possible preparation of financial accounting statements as a useful and reliable source of information.

Listing each control feature available to the analyst is not necessary at this point. Because each application requires its own set of controls, their implementation in other applications may not be appropriate. However, in the following chapters, both general and application controls are discussed within the context of each chapter's case study.

MANAGERIAL ACCOUNTING SYSTEMS

Management accounting has been defined as

The process of identification, measurement, accumulation, analysis, preparation, interpretation, and communication of financial information used by management to plan,

---

[11] American Institute of Certified Public Accountants, *Statement on Auditing Standards No. 3,* paragraph 7 (New York: AICPA, 1974).

[12] Ibid., paragraph 8.

evaluate, and control within an organization and to assure appropriate use of and accountability for its resources. Management accounting also comprises the preparation of financial reports for non-management groups such as shareholders, creditors, regulatory agencies, and tax authorities.[13]

The terms used in the definition that are most significant for design of information systems for managerial accounting, are *measurement, analysis, communication, plan,* and *control*.[14] Note that the second part of the definition has a bearing on the financial accounting system, which was discussed in the first part of this chapter.

Basic Management Accounting Functions

The basic function of a manager is decision making. Two types of decisions are the most frequent: plans and controls.

Planning. Planning is a process that has been defined as delineating goals, predicting potential results under various ways of achieving the goals, and deciding how to attain them.[15] As implied in this definition, setting goals and objectives is the starting point of the planning process. Goals are normally set by the top management and adopted by all the members of an organization.

The planning process will not be effective if the social, economic, and political forces at work in the environment are not considered. Furthermore, in order to improve the quality of the decisions in this area, an information system must be designed specifically to provide all the planning informational needs.

Control. Control is the other side of the coin. It is perceived as action that implements the planning decision and as performance evaluation that provides feedback of the results.[16] When control through feedback is communicated to the decision maker, the process is referred to as *cybernetics*. In this context performance reports, variances, analysis and the principle of management by exception are the examples of cybernetics law of first- and second-order feedback.

Information systems are crucial to the control process. Timely information is an essential part of this system because lack of it can cost organizations millions of dollars.

---

[13] National Association of Accountants, *Statement on Management Accounting No. 1A,* New York, March 19, 1981, p. 4.

[14] Ibid, p. 5.

[15] Charles T. Horngren, *Cost Accounting: A Managerial Emphasis,* 5th ed. (Englewood Cliffs, N.J.: Prentice-Hall, 1982), p. 5.

[16] Ibid., p. 5.

Elements of Management Accounting Systems

Management accounting systems have two primary elements: identification and processing of managerial accounting information.

Identification is the recognition and evaluation of business transactions and economic events that are appropriate for accounting action.[17] An integral part of the identification process is the measurement of the economic impact of the transaction.

Processing of managerial accounting information starts with the accumulation of the identified transactions in a consistent manner. This process would not be complete without the preparation and interpretation of planning and control data in a logical and meaningful format. Furthermore, the results of the transactions identified, measured, and interpreted need to be communicated to management for appropriate decision/action.

Both the identification and processing elements depend on effective design of the managerial accounting information system.

Internal Controls

The management accounting information system in most organizations is a part of the corporate management information system. Therefore, it is subject to the same degree of scrutiny and control as is applied to the total corporate information system. However, the information generated by this system is more flexible in form and less subject to pronouncement of authoritative bodies such as the Financial Accounting Standards Board and regulatory bodies such as the Securities and Exchange Commission. This allows the systems analyst to be more innovative in design and to use resources in the most efficient manner. It should be emphasized that the same types of controls—general and application—should be considered in the design of managerial accounting information systems.

MORE ADVANCED SYSTEMS

Traditional accounting systems (both financial and managerial) were designed to produce historical information. Although historical information is useful to decision makers, it may not provide them with the forward look and insight that are essential to management planning and control. In order to compensate for this deficiency, systems designers usually attempt to integrate decisions into the systems.

---

[17] National Association of Accountants, *Statement on Management Accounting No. 1A.*

Integration of Decisions into the Systems

Integrated information systems are the offsprings of earlier versions of systems, integrated data processing systems. The main emphasis in later systems has been the integration of the computerized function, rather than providing the management with more relevant information. This has resulted in excessive duplication of data and programs within the system. The duplication problem is compounded when the data must be updated, and, soon, most of the files within the system become inconsistent with one another, raising questions of data integrity.

In order to overcome this problem, systems analysts have made an attempt to integrate *some* management functions into the integrated data processing function, thereby transferring routine decision-making functions to the computer. As a result, management has been relieved of many routine activities and found more time to spend on organizational problems. The power of the computer has a synergistic effect, especially when work can be performed "on-line" and in "real time." Management has gained capabilities, and the processing mode of systems has changed from a historical perspective to a forward-looking perspective.

Overzealous analysts, hoping to improve the system further, have suggested elimination of all duplication, and integration of all elements of the system (including goals) into one unified system called a "total system."

Because of many technological and conceptual problems, the goal of a total system has never materialized, and no system has ever been able to support all possible decisions. As a result, systems analysts have reassessed the goal of a total system and developed the reformed version, the decision support system (DSS).

Decision Support Systems

Decision support system is a new term that started to gain popularity in the late seventies. There are two prominent views about DSSs. Some systems analysts and academicians consider the DSS the product of evolution in the field of information processing. In this context, the individual EDP systems have advanced and become integrated data processing systems, management information systems (MISs), and eventually decision support systems. Proponents of the other view suggest that data processing systems are designed to facilitate transaction processing through automation of procedures, and attainment of efficiency of computer runs and storage allocation. But DSSs are created to aid or support management decisions. Therefore, DSSs are defined as *interactive* computer-based systems, which *help* decision makers utilize *data* and *models* to study and analyze *unstructured* decision problems.[18]

---

[18] Ralph H. Sprague, "A Framework for the Development of Decision Support Systems," *MIS Quarterly,* MIS Research Center, University of Minnesota, December 1980, p. 1.

The key words in the definition suggest that the focus of DSS is on aiding top management to formulate solutions to very complex and unstructured problems. Furthermore, in the DSS an attempt is made to combine the use of models with traditional access. However, such systems must be designed for easy use by persons who are not computer specialists.

All these features make the DSS a necessary tool for the top executive in the strategic planning type of decisions. Typical situations suitable for DSS analysis are "what is" problems, "what if" problems, and other ad hoc problems. One of the advantages cited of the DSS is the ability to carry out ad hoc analysis. It has also been suggested that the DSS, in addition to increasing the number of alternatives examined, provides fast response to unexpected situations.[19]

Since most of the problems suitable for DSS are unstructured, each organization could, in theory, create and design a custom-made DSS for its own particular use. However, some of the software manufacturers have been able to produce products that are useful to almost any environment. Although the cost of larger models is high enough that they are purchased only by large companies, smaller versions of these packages have made a DSS model affordable to smaller firms.

Since the outputs of DSSs are mostly estimates, their data integrity is not as crucial as is the case with financial accounting systems. However, in some cases DSS models may utilize financial accounting files as input. Since these data have been subject to many controls, the reliability of the DSS output need not be questioned because of lack of data integrity. However, some questions may still be raised about the assumptions used to construct the DSS. (The use of DSS models and strategic planning are discussed further in Chapter 7.)

AUDIT IMPLICATIONS OF COMPUTERIZED SYSTEMS

Audit of computerized systems is somewhat different from the audit of manual systems due to certain changes. These changes are in the environment in which the audit is being performed, the role that computers play in performing audit tasks, and increased risk exposure for irregularities.

These changes also may be attributed to changes in hardware technology, software advancement, and organizational structure. The changes in hardware technology brought substantial complexity to the audit process by requiring the auditor to learn new concepts and terminology. Changes in software development have created added pressure on the auditors from different perspectives. First, the auditor must be able to understand the software used in client systems. Second, in order to perform the audit task more effectively and efficiently,

---

[19] Peter G. W. Keen, "Value Analysis: Justifying Decision Support Systems," *MIS Quarterly,* MIS Research Center, University of Minnesota, March 1981.

the auditor ought to be familiar with generalized audit software (GAS) packages written in this area. Finally, the changes in organizational structure caused by the automation of many tasks have resulted in the elimination of many manually performed control steps. This has subjected the systems to more and varied risk exposures.

In this new atmosphere the systems designers normally invite the auditor to become a part of the design team. This brings more insight to the design process and more likelihood that the system will serve the purpose for which it has been designed.

The audit implication of a computerized system is independent of the capabilities of the hardware system. That is, similar considerations are appropriate whether the computer is a mainframe, minicomputer, or microcomputer. There are instances where a microcomputer has been utilized by the auditor to facilitate the more efficient audit process.[20]

In each of the following chapters, the audit implications for each of the cases are discussed and listed under two headings of general and application controls.

General Controls

The auditor is normally interested in the following general controls.

Organizational Controls. Organizational controls include the following:

1. Location of the information systems function in the organization
2. Qualification of information systems staff
3. Separation of duties among information systems staff
4. Separation of the departments that initiate changes in master file
5. Securing blank negotiable documents such as checks
6. Existence of documentation standards

Systems and Programming Controls. Systems and programming controls include:

1. Review of documentation for adequacy, completeness, and currency
2. Use of standardized programming techniques
3. Adequate procedures for authorization, approval, and testing of the program
4. Prevention of operator's access to the program details

---

[20] For more information, refer to G. Grundnitski, ''Generalized Audit Software Capabilities for Microcomputers,'' in J. Sardinas (ed.), *Proceedings of 1984 EDP Audit Symposium* (Amherst: University of Massachusetts, 1985).

Operations Controls. These consist of:

1. Control of the operator's adherence to prescribed procedures
2. Maintaining a machine log
3. Review of output reports before distribution
4. Control over distribution of the reports
5. Creation and maintenance of test data for new applications
6. Adequate procedures for storing tape, disk, and program documentation
7. Availability of alternate site in disaster circumstances
8. Procedures for use of backup facilities
9. Safeguarding important master files or program in safe location
10. Creation of preventive maintenance program

Application Controls

The application controls can be divided into three different areas: input controls, process controls, and output controls.

Input Controls. Input controls include:

1. Control of inputs submitted for processing by use of batch control, logging of batches, user's department approval, prenumbering of transactions, and cancellation of source documents after data entry step
2. Validation of input through edit such as check digit, comprehensive validation, limit, and reasonable tests
3. Correction of errors based on specific procedures such as creation of suspense files and manual logging of erroneous transactions
4. Proper securing of on-line data entry devices by locks and supervision at all time, control over passwords and dial-up facilities, restriction of access authorization table, maintaining an on-line access log, and correcting the errors at the time of entry

Process Controls. Process controls consist of:

1. Processing of authorized transaction and master file
2. Authorization of master file maintenance through prenumbered maintenance form and approval procedures
3. Integrity of the master file through control totals, record count, and report of master file before and after processing
4. Reasonable assurance that errors are detected and reported
5. Protection of data base management systems (DBMSs) through prevention of simultaneous updates, creation of audit trail of all changes to the data base, prevention of deletion of shared data, periodical footing of data base and procedure for recreation of the data base after systems failure

6. Minimizing the impact of failure for critical on-line applications
7. Dumping of the data base at regular intervals

Output Controls. These consist of:

1. Verification of accuracy of outputs through reconciliation of control totals, excluded data with master file
2. Security over master file and confidential reports
3. Control of report distribution by information systems staff
4. Existence of control over schema and subschema in data base environment

In each of the next six chapters only the most important considerations related to that particular case are listed under the general and application control headings. However, prior to designing any accounting information system, and depending on the system, all of the controls must be integrated into the design process.

IMPLICATIONS OF MICROCOMPUTERS

Certain issues of the development of accounting information systems are related to the type of machine used in the implementation of these systems. Due to the explosive growth of microcomputer use in today's businesses, some of these issues are discussed in relation to their influence in developing software for microcomputers. The more prominent issues are secondary storage, auxiliary equipment, main memory, and operating systems and utilities.

Secondary Storage

The devices available to handle secondary storage for microcomputers are somewhat limited in variety and capacity when compared to those available for mainframe computers. The most widely used device is the magnetic disk drive. Usually, a microcomputer has two disk drives associated with it. A hard disk drive is available for most machines, but because of its high cost, its usage is limited. Some older machines have magnetic tape drives as secondary storage devices. Because of the relatively slow speed and unreliable operation of tape drives, only a small number of them are still used in business operations.

The implication of the limited variety of secondary storage devices available for microcomputers is that a hierarchy of secondary storage for data is largely meaningless or at best limited. Because the price of disk drives and diskettes is very reasonable, the hierarchy of storage is between having diskettes on-line or off-line. In other words, less frequently used files are stored on diskettes that are kept off-line, whereas frequently accessed files are stored on diskettes that are kept on-line.

Another issue is the limited capacity of on-line secondary storage. This is due to the limited number of ports available for secondary storage devices and their cost. A solution to this problem might be found in data segmentation, which necessitates the partitioning of a unit of data (say, a file) into two or more segments. These segments are brought on-line separately and as needed, and are removed when they are not in use any longer. For example, data summaries such as weekly totals or monthly totals might need to be kept in a separate file on a diskette that is kept off-line until manipulating these summaries becomes necessary. Similarly, for long programs, a segmentation scheme is necessary; however, it might be more complex in this case. Usually, indexing and linking (sometimes called chaining) are used to facilitate segmentation. In larger computer systems, segmentation of data is not usually necessary and files are kept on-line in their entirety.

To facilitate chaining, several processing steps must be encoded. The number of these steps could vary from a simple and small subroutine to a larger and more complex program. These sets of instructions are executed whenever needed, thus consuming some processing power. In addition, the operator of the microcomputer needs to manipulate a number of diskettes, possibly a large number, by loading and unloading them in the drives. The frequent intervention of the operator, in turn, slows the operation of the total system and tends to introduce errors. The likelihood of error can be reduced by instituting rigorous and detailed procedures for systems operations.

Auxiliary Equipment

A variety of auxiliary equipment is usually available for mainframes—plotters, microfiche, and microfilm equipment, badge scanners, high-speed printers, and so on. In the case of most microcomputers, auxiliary equipment is limited to monitors and printers. The major concern here is the characteristics of these devices such as the quality of characters, number of characters per line, and number of lines per page. Today's monitors are very versatile, adequate for business operations, and reasonable in price. However, printers are more problematical. Some printers have insufficient printing speed, print quality, width of printed line, and reliability under extensive use. Because of this, some voluminous reports might need to be reduced in size and content or eliminated altogether.

Main Memory

The limited size of the microcomputer's main memory (even with expansions) tends to slow down processing. Large systems suffer more than others because of the amount of processing overhead needed to achieve chaining of programs and data files. Instead of one large system, it might be desirable to have separate microcomputers to process the various information needs of an organization. For example, one microcomputer may be used for the processing of accounts receivable, cash collections, and sales while another is used for inventory control. Another solution, less convenient yet less expensive, is to schedule the processing of the various systems at different hours. For example, sales might be processed in the morning and midday, followed by accounts receivable in the afternoon and cash at night.

Operating Systems and Utilities

Some of the operating systems that are available on microcomputers are limited in terms of the capabilities and extent of facilities they provide to the user. Furthermore, important utilities such as sort and merge may not be provided, or when provided they may be limited in their capabilities. Therefore, a close examination of these facilities is necessary to ensure that the needed components are available. Otherwise, these components have to be encoded within the system which might require resources that are not available.

In summary, the issues that are related to using microcomputers in the processing of accounting information systems are those of development and implementation rather than analysis and design. That is, the basic principles of systems analysis and design, used in the following case studies, are applicable regardless of the hardware employed in operating the accounting information system. Furthermore, the general specifications of systems components and their interactions provided in each case study remain the same for microcomputer implementations. Some of the details need to be changed, however, to reflect the reality of the limitations of microcomputers with relation to processing speed, secondary storage, main memory, capacity, printed output characteristics and quality, and the operating system and utilities available. These modifications may be limited or more encompassing depending on the accounting information system under consideration, the targeted hardware, and its associated software.

DATA BASE MANAGEMENT SYSTEMS

Data base management systems (DBMS) have been increasingly in use to assist in the development of the organization's data processing requirements. A DBMS can overcome most of the shortcomings that are inherent in a conventional data processing system. A generalized DBMS usually provides a number of facilities such as

- *Better tools* for programmers, including a high-level data manipulation language to facilitate accessing, storing, and updating of data
- *Complete validation* of input data before it is stored
- *Quick answers* to query questions that may be constructed by nontechnical staff. This is usually carried out in a simple-to-use query language. Using such a

language, data can be extracted from files, simple manipulations performed on it, and the results reported in a suitable format.

• *Modeling* complex relationships that may exist among the data entities in an organization's information systems. Programming languages used in business applications usually provide for modeling simple relationships such as sequential data organization.

• *A language* for describing the specific relationships among data entities in a particular system. This language is usually known as data description language (DDL). Although there are many commercially available DBMSs, they provide for constructing three general types of data models. These models are hierarchical, network, and relational.

Today's DBMSs fall into two different categories. The first category is oriented to providing data-interrogation facilities for the nontechnical user. These interrogation sessions are conducted in a structured question-and-answer dialogue, or in a fill-in-the-blanks format. This class is termed the *self-contained DBMS*. The other category is referred to a *host language DBMS*. This class allows the user to call these systems from programs written in the host language (such as COBOL and PL/I).

The case studies presented in the following chapters describe the accounting information needs of an organization in terms of its components and their interactions and without any specific implementation strategy in mind. Development considerations such as the selection of a programming language, whether to use DBMS technology or not, and if so which one, depend to a large degree on the currently operational information systems, the hardware available, the level of staff training, and other factors such as time and cost. These issues are outside the scope of this book and are not treated further.

SUMMARY

In this chapter, we have divided accounting information systems into three categories: financial accounting systems, managerial accounting systems, and more advanced systems. The latter includes decision support systems.

The characteristics and capabilities of each of the three types of systems have been discussed, and the internal controls applicable to each explained. In the next six chapters, a sample of each financial and managerial accounting function is demonstrated through a case study.

2 | Design of a System for Sales, Receivables, and Cash Collection

In the previous chapter, the nature, function, and elements of a financial accounting system were discussed. In the next three chapters we will discuss, in the form of a case study, the various applications of financial accounting with respect to individual activities. It should be borne in mind that, in the design of an integrated system, it is not appropriate to work on a single application in isolation. Therefore, in each chapter, applications developed elsewhere in the book (such as inventories) will be referred to insofar as they interact with the system under investigation.

MANAGEMENT INFORMATION REQUIREMENTS[1]

Four functional departments are essential parts of the case developed in this chapter. They are the (1) sales department, (2) credit department, (3) accounts receivable department, and (4) cash collections. Some of the objectives of these departments are closely tied to overall organizational goals. Therefore, computerization of the proposed system and timely processing of the information will assure a more efficient way of accomplishing those goals.

Sales Department

The main objective of the sales department is maintaining the profitability of the organization at a reasonable level, without compromising long-run marketing strategies. To attain this objective, four questions must be answered.

1. *Who are our customers?* Market research normally provides an approach to segmentation of the market or targeted group. Measuring the performance

---

[1] One of the primary functions of a systems analyst is to specify management's information needs. No viable system can be designed unless these needs are addressed. This step of systems design normally is done by means of a survey questionnaire, interview, or other types of fact gathering.

of the customers is extremely important. Detailed information such as total dollar value of sales to each customer and each category of customers is necessary in order to develop discount policies.

2. *What was sold?* Management is interested in knowing total sales and profitability for each product or product line. In general, performance of products must be evaluated.

3. *What is the market, or where are the customers located?* The performance of each market, the size of each sales area, total sales in each area and possibly the market share at each area are the primary concerns.

4. *What is the sales force, and who sold to the customers?* The performance of the sales representatives and supervisors will be evaluated at this level.

Some of the important reports to be prepared by the system are

- Year-to-date sales for each product in each market area and total sales for all products
- Year-to-date sales for each salesperson in each market area
- Year-to-date commission paid to each salesperson
- Total sales for each day (invoice register)
- Customers' monthly statements

Credit Department

The objectives of this department are to

- Approve credit limits for new customers
- Increase or decrease the established credit limits of current customers
- Extend the collection period
- Establish credit terms
- Evaluate the customer's payment behavior

Accounts Receivable Department

Timely and accurate processing of information in this department is crucial, due to the cost of financing receivables. Also, proper measurement of accounts receivable is required by authoritative accounting pronouncements. The specific objectives are to

- Bill the customer for the right amount
- Maintain proper records for each customer and periodically reconcile them by means of monthly statements
- Follow up on overdue accounts

The most important reports used by this department are the aging report of accounts receivable and the accounts receivable register.

Collection Department

Cash being the most volatile asset, the following objectives for this department are essential. The collection department must

- Maintain an efficient system of internal control to cover all aspects of cash collection
  - Safeguard cash
  - Maintain a cost-effective method of cash collection
  - Provide a basis for projection of cash flow
  - Maintain the record of daily cash collections

INTERNAL CONTROLS AND AUDIT IMPLICATIONS

Accounting control is divided into two categories of general controls and application controls.[2] The involvement of these controls with the case may be summarized as follows.

General Controls

Stating all the general controls existing in the organization is beyond the scope of this case. However, there are two main general controls for this particular application.

The first is a procedure for reviewing the report of master file changes. This report will be reviewed by an authorized person within the controller's department.[3]

The second is a procedure for reviewing the report on orders which are rejected because they have exceeded the credit limit. This report will be reviewed by a high-ranking individual in the credit department who can authorize increases in the credit limit.

Application Controls

These are the tests and control features that are an integral part of the computer programs which are used in this case. There are several important application controls.

- Check digit on customer's account number. This check can be performed on the basis of modulus 11 (or modulus 10), to ensure the correct transformation of the source data into machine-sensible form.

---

[2] American Institute of Certified Public Accountants, *Statement on Auditing Standards No. 3*, "The Effects of EDP on the Auditor's Study and Evaluation of Internal Control," New York, December 1974.

[3] Review by internal audit staff could be an alternative to this procedure.

- Validity check of selected transaction fields
- Hash and batch totals for checking the input data
- Record count of batched documents
- Completeness test on all fields of all the records
- Reasonableness tests for checking several selected fields

(A more detailed explanation of these tests is presented later in this case.)

CASE: Accounts Receivable, Sales, and Cash Collection

Southeastern Building Material is a medium-size company operating a building supply and material business in the southeastern part of the country. Since the major part of its activities are being handled in the states of Georgia, South Carolina, Alabama, Mississippi, and Louisiana, the company has divided its market into five areas and has assigned three sales representatives to each area.

The major customers of Southeastern are contractors who are contacted by the sales force. Sales representatives work on a commission. They place the orders in the field (customer location). Sometimes orders are phoned in to the office by a customer. The commission on the latter type of sales is usually given to the sales representative who placed the first order with the customer in the past. Both types of sales will be confirmed by a customer purchase order. The terms of the sales are 2/10, n/30 (i.e., a 2 percent discount from the invoice price is allowed if payment is made within 10 days of the invoice date; otherwise the total invoice price is due within 30 days). Before processing a customer's order, the Credit Department must evaluate and approve the creditworthiness of the customer. Monthly statements are sent to approximately 1,500 customers.

Although each sales representative has a price list for all 1,000 items of inventory, pricing is done by computer. Moreover, because of the high cost of factoring accounts receivable (approximately 16 percent), the company has established an effective follow-up system for reviewing the accounts receivable.

Before explaining how the system operates, it should be mentioned that the computerized system is capable of handling the following routines: acceptance of orders from customers with previously approved credit, acceptance of orders from new customers, rejection of orders which exceed the credit limit or have other problems.

CREDIT DEPARTMENT

As orders are obtained from new customers, they will be referred directly to the Credit Department (see Fig. 2-1). The department's job is to investigate the new customer's orders to determine whether or not credit can be granted.

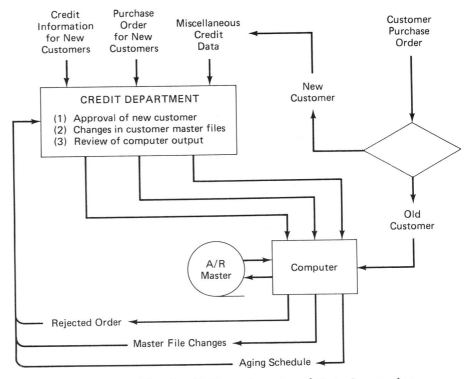

FIGURE 2-1   The Credit Department and Data Processing

If the order of the prospective customer is approved from a credit standpoint, the Credit Department must establish a credit limit for the customer and gather sufficient data for the establishment of the customer's master file (Fig. 2-2). The following information is provided to the Data Processing Department:

1. Account number (a number assigned by the Sales Department)
2. Customer's name and address
3. Customer's credit limit
4. Code number of the sales representative handling the account

The communications of the Credit Department and the Data Processing Department are not limited to new customers' information. The credit ratings of old customers have to be analyzed as well. Revised credit limits have to be forwarded to Data Processing so that the necessary changes to the master file can be initiated. Similarly, any other data related to changes in the customer master file, including deletion of a customer from the file, should be sent to

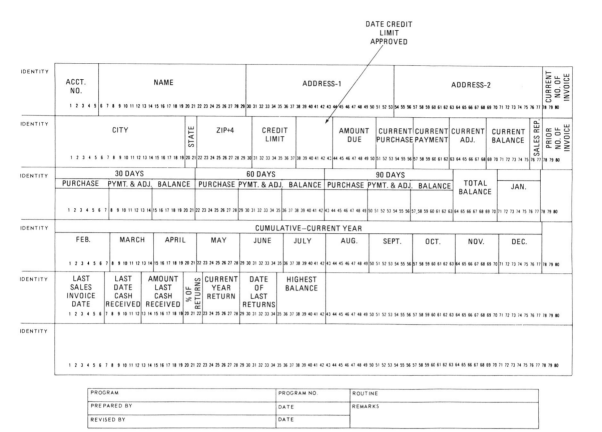

FIGURE 2-2   Layout of Customer Master File

Data Processing for necessary file maintenance activities. All data relating to changes in the master files, including addition or deletion of customers, are forwarded to Data Processing on a form labeled Data Processing File Change Record (Fig. 2-3). For control purposes, the credit manager is the only person with the authority to approve this form.

The reports, which are the output of the various computer runs concerning customer accounts, must also be sent to the Credit Department. This may provide the basis for some of the data which are initiated in this department and flow back to the Data Processing Department. An example of this situation is the aging schedule, which may serve as the basis for revision of a customer's credit limit or intensive follow-up procedure on delayed payments. Other reports sent to the Credit Department include the Master File Change Report and the Update Run Error List.

```
┌─────────────────────────────────────────────────────┐
│           DATA PROCESSING FILE CHANGE RECORD          │
├─────────────────────────────────────────────────────┤
│                                                       │
│   _____      Change No. _____     │
│      Customer No.                                     │
│                                                       │
│   _____      Date of                       │
│    Customer Address     Change _____       │
│                                                       │
│                                                       │
│   _____                                    │
│       Acct. No.                                       │
│                                                       │
│   Change initiated by _____   Date _____  │
│                                                       │
│   Approved by _____          Date _____   │
├─────────────────────────────────────────────────────┤
│   Data to be changed:                                 │
│                                                       │
│                                                       │
│                                                       │
│                                                       │
│                                                       │
├─────────────────────────────────────────────────────┤
│   New Data:                                           │
│                                                       │
│                                                       │
│                                                       │
│                                                       │
│                                                       │
└─────────────────────────────────────────────────────┘
```

FIGURE 2-3   Data Processing File Change Record Form

SALES DEPARTMENT

Sales orders are the primary source documents of the Accounts Receivable Update Run. All sales orders are forwarded to the Sales Department, where they are received by receiving clerks. The clerk checks and batches the orders on a daily basis (there are approximately 150 sales orders per day), preparing a Batch Total Control Slip for each batch (Fig. 2-4). The Batch Total Control Slip contains a hash total for both quantity and net weight. The batch number consists of two digits representing day of the month.

The Batch Total Control Slip is placed on top of the sales invoices and together they are forwarded to the sales order clerk. The clerk types each document on a terminal (see Fig. 2-5). The output of this step is the Sales Order Directive, which will be produced on the printer (Fig. 2-6). The data is also

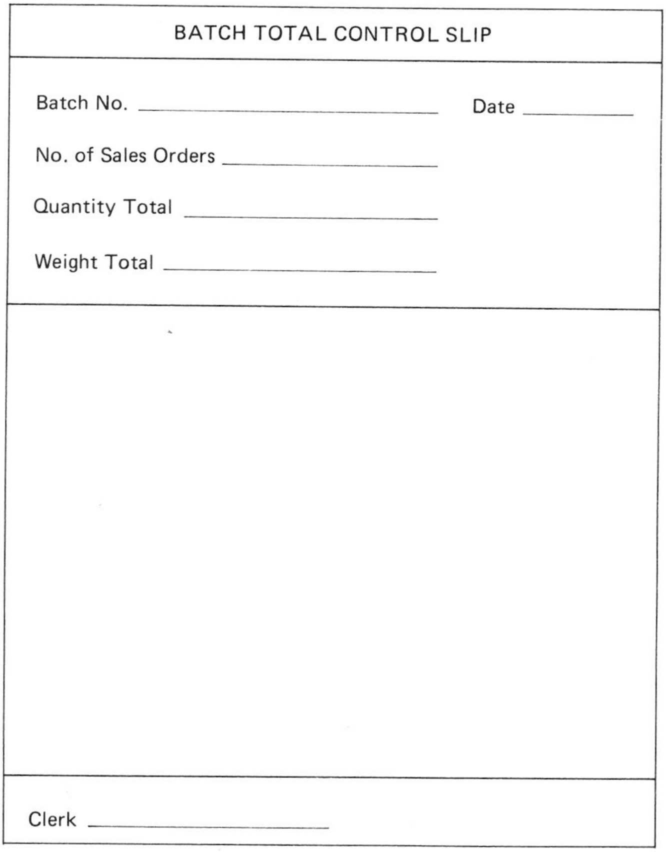

```
┌─────────────────────────────────────────────────────────────┐
│                  BATCH TOTAL CONTROL SLIP                     │
├─────────────────────────────────────────────────────────────┤
│                                                               │
│   Batch No. _____   Date _____     │
│                                                               │
│   No. of Sales Orders _____                   │
│                                                               │
│   Quantity Total _____                        │
│                                                               │
│   Weight Total _____                        │
│                                                               │
├─────────────────────────────────────────────────────────────┤
│                                                               │
│                                                               │
│                                                               │
│                                                               │
│                                                               │
│                                                               │
│                                                               │
│                                                               │
│                                                               │
│                                                               │
│   Clerk _____                                │
└─────────────────────────────────────────────────────────────┘
```

FIGURE 2-4   Batch Total Control Slip Form

captured on a magnetic tape. The system automatically furnishes certain fields, which will remain constant for each item of the sales order (the terminal in a system with this kind of capability is referred to as an *intelligent terminal*).

The fields that will be repeated for each item are

- Transaction code
- Account number
- Routing
- Sales order number
- Sales representative's code
- Batch number

The completed Sales Order Directives and Batch Total Control Slips are filed in the Sales Department for future reference. The tape resulting from this opera-

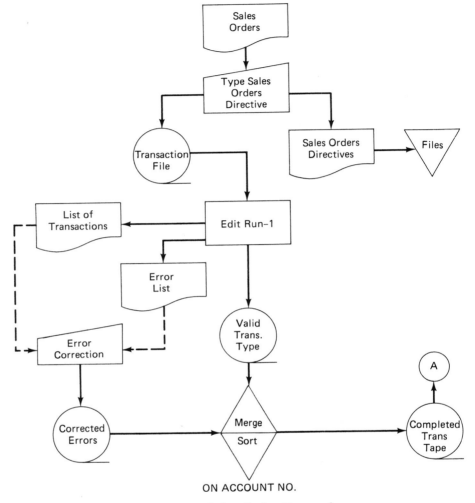

FIGURE 2-5 Sales Order Processing

tion is forwarded to the Data Processing Department, where it is properly labeled and protected by a ring protection device for future reference.

CORRECTION OF ERRORS (EDIT RUN–1)

The Data Processing Department puts the tape through computer Edit Run–1 (see Fig. 2-5). This run is very important, because unless verification for correctness is performed at the data entry stage it must be performed later, in an even more sophisticated run to detect any errors resulting from the typing operation.

Southeastern Building Material
Sales Order Directive

_____   _____
Customer Name   Order Date

_____   _____
Address   Cust. Purchase Order No.

_____
City   State   ZIP

Customer Acct. No. _____   Sales Order No. _____

Routing _____   Sales Rep _____

QTY	Description	Product Code	Net Weight	Correction Note

FIGURE 2-6 Sales Order Directive

In this run the tape's various fields are subjected to a number of tests.

Test	Item	Data Field
1. Validity	Transaction code	1
2. Check digit (modulus 11)	Account number	2–6
3. Hash total	Quantity	7–10
4. Check digit (modulus 11)	Product number	36–39
5. Hash total	Net weight	40–43
6. Completeness	All	1–72
7. Record count	By sales order number	64–68

The record layout of Batch Total Tape and each item of the sales order are presented in Fig. 2-7.

The results of Edit Run–1 are three outputs: (1) List of Transactions (including a Batch Summary Report), (2) Edit Run Error List, and (3) Valid Transaction Tape.

The List of Sales Order Transactions (Fig. 2-8) is output onto the printer and contains two main parts, (1) List of Transactions and (2) Batch Summary Report. A detailed listing of data for each sales order transition includes the following items:

1. Account number
2. Transaction code
3. Batch number
4. Quantity
5. Description
6. Product number
7. Net weight
8. Routing

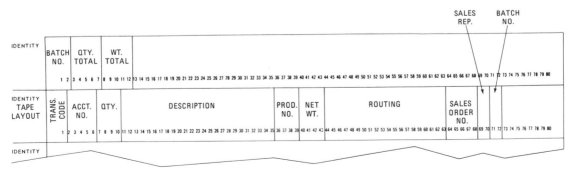

FIGURE 2-7   Layout of Batch Total Tape and Sales Order

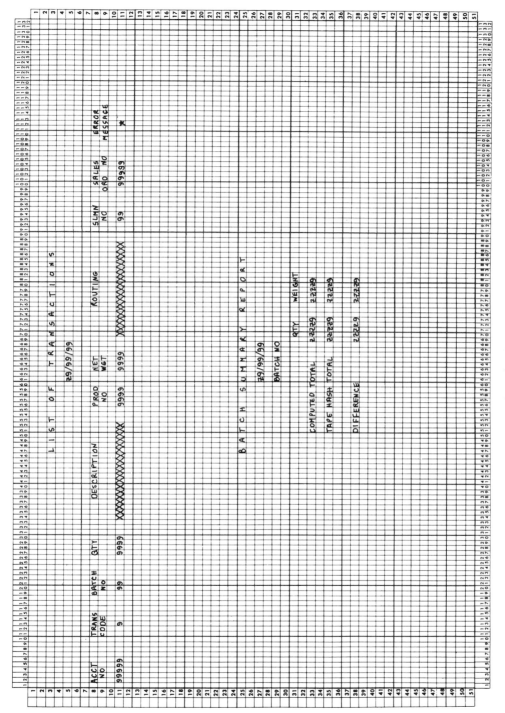

FIGURE 2-8 List of Sales Order Transactions

31

9. Sales representative's code
10. Sales order number
11. A column that indicates by an asterisk if the transaction is in error

Edit Run—1's error list (Fig. 2-9) is printed onto the console typewriter and contains error messages about the types of errors in each sales item based on sales order number. It also highlights the incorrect values that were punched into a particular field.

The list of transactions and the error list are sent to the receiving clerk, who will indicate in the Sales Order Control Book whether or not the batch totals are balanced. He or she then reviews the list of transactions noting any indication of error(s) in column 11. When an asterisk is found in column 11, the clerk locates

EDIT RUN-1 ERROR LIST			
Sales Order No.	Prod. No.	Error Message	Reference
99999	9999	INVALID — CHECK DIGIT	ACCT NO 99999
99999	9999	INVALID — TRANS CODE	9
99999	9999	INVALID — CHECK DIGIT	PROD COD 9999
99999	9999	INCOMPLETE FIELD	(NAME OF INCOMPLETE FIELD)

FIGURE 2-9   Error List of Edit Run—1

the corresponding sales order number on the list of errors. Corrections are then made by using the error list and the original Sales Order Directive and Sales Orders. After making the necessary corrections the clerk must reconcile the batch totals and forward the corrected Sales Order Directive to the Data Processing Department for key-to-tape entry and verification of the item line(s) that was(were) in error. The resulting error correction tape is then merged and sorted with the valid transactions tape on the basis of account number key.

CASH COLLECTION AND OTHER TRANSACTIONS

The Treasurer's Office batches the second copy of the Cash Remittance Advice and prepares hash totals of the net amount, discounts, and gross amount. After the clerk posts the batch number, batch totals, and serial number of Remittance Advice in the special book, the batch will be sent to the Conversion Department for keying and verification.

The Sales Department will also advise the Conversion Department about sales returns, special discounts (besides the normal discount of 2/10, n/30) and allowances. These documents also will be keyed and verified. The deck which results from these transactions will be run against Edit Run–2 (Fig. 2-10).

The process is basically similar to Edit Run–1, but the contents of the individual record vary due to the nature of the transaction. The layout of the source document is presented in Fig. 2-11. The error in this run will be corrected offline by the department responsible.

The results of these two edit runs will be merged and sorted on the basis of customer numbers assigned by the Accounts Receivable Department.

ACCOUNTS RECEIVABLE UPDATE RUN

Sorted transaction tape (Fig. 2-12) is put through an accounts receivable and inventory update run. Inputs to this run are the sorted transactions tape and the old master file tape. The Inventory Master File is on a random-access device (a disk) and will be updated.

The accounts receivable update run will result in nine different outputs.

1. Updated accounts receivable master file
2. Inventory transaction tape
3. Update run of the error list
4. Accounts receivable tape
5. Cash tape
6. Sales invoices and shipping orders
7. Sales transactions tape
8. Invoices tape
9. A tape of summary data which will be used for General Ledger Update Run (Figs. 2-12 and 2-13)

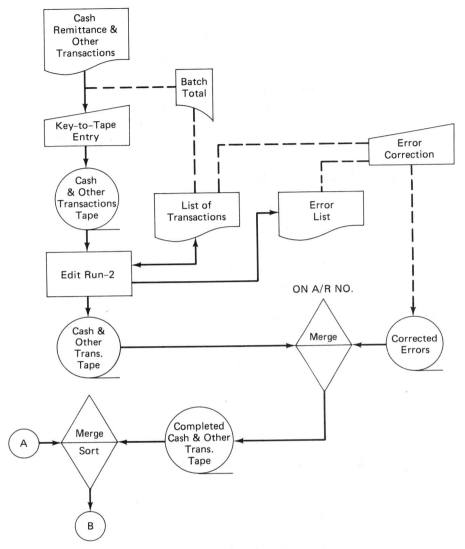

FIGURE 2-10   Cash Remittance and Other Transactions Processing

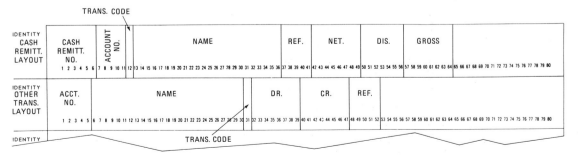

FIGURE 2-11   Layout of Cash Remittance and Other Transactions Files

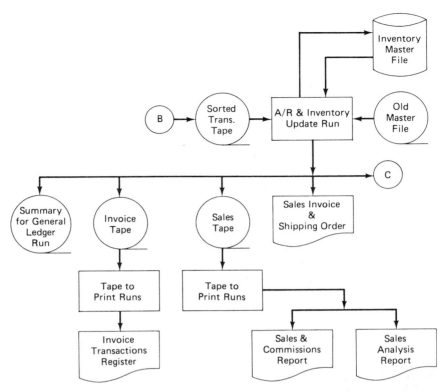

FIGURE 2-12 Accounts Receivable Update Run

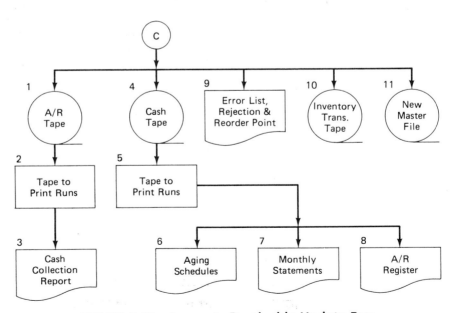

FIGURE 2-13 Accounts Receivable Update Run

The Updated Master File is correctly labeled, fitted with a file protection ring, and stored for input in the next file update run. Layout of a record from this file is presented in Fig. 2-2.

The File Update Run Error List (Fig. 2-14) is printed on the console typewriter. Four types of errors which may be printed in this report are

1. Above credit limit
2. Customer master file record does not exist
3. Item not available
4. Inventory master file record does not exist

One copy of the error message is retained in the Data Processing Department and other copies will be sent to the Credit Department, Purchasing Department, and Sales Department.

The Credit Department receives the second copy of the error list noting the message "Above credit limit." The message is the result of the computer comparing the customer's credit limit to the amount of his or her previous balance

FILE UPDATE RUN ERROR LIST							
Customer Acct. No.	Previous Balance	This Order	Total	Credit Limit	Prod. No.	Sales Order No.	Reference
99999	ZZZ9.99	ZZZ9.99	ZZZZ.99	ZZZZ9		99999	ABOVE CREDIT LIMIT
99999						99999	CUSTOMER MASTER FILE ACCOUNT DOES NOT EXIST
99999					9999		ITEM NOT AVAILABLE
99999					9999		INVENTORY MASTER FILE DOES NOT EXIST

FIGURE 2-14 Error List of File Update Run

plus the new invoice amount. The Credit Department must then notify the customer that the order was rejected and what to do before the order can be filled. The Credit Department must also handle messages concerning account numbers that do not exist in the master file.

The third copy is sent to the Purchasing Department, which is concerned with the error message "Item not available." The department uses the list to inform the customers when the merchandise will be available. They should also handle errors concerning item numbers that do not exist.

The Sales Department receives the fourth copy of the list for handling various problems that may arise due to rejection of the orders. It also will be used in assisting the other departments in making any necessary correction.

The fourth and fifth outputs of the update run are accounts receivable and cash[4] tapes. These tapes (Fig. 2-13) will be run to generate additional reports. These reports are

- *Cash collection report,* which will be used for control of cash and as a cash journal for bookkeeping purposes (Fig. 2-15)
- *Aging schedule,* the most important report for analysis of accounts receivable (Fig. 2-16)
- *Monthly statements,* which will be sent to the customer for reconciliation of accounts (Fig. 2-17)
- *Accounts receivable register,* which will be used mainly as a receivables journal, and for control purposes (Fig. 2-18)

Sales invoices and shipping orders (Fig. 2-19) are printed using a preprinted four-copy form. The first copy is sent to the customer, the second copy to the Sales Department, and the third copy is stored in the general invoice file for reference purposes. The fourth copy is used as the shipping order and is sent to the Shipping Department. The price per unit and total amount columns of this form are blanked. Omission of these figures is accomplished by not carbonizing the back of the third copy over the price per unit and total amount columns.

Two more outputs of the update run are invoices and sales tapes, which contain all pertinent data needed for sales analysis, calculation of commissions, and the Invoice Transaction Register (Fig. 2-12), and the printing of the aforementioned reports. The Sales Analysis Report simply provides management with specific information about various categories of the product. In order to achieve this goal, the inventory processing system has to classify products into different categories. In Southeastern Building Material, the products have been classified into fifty categories based on recommendations of the Trade Association (Fig. 2-20).

The sales tape includes total sales of each sales representative, total commissions of each, and total sales in each area. It is also used to produce the Sales Commissions Report (Fig. 2-21).

---

[4] The layouts of these two tapes are not provided. The contents of these files are generated by extracting data from other files involved in the accounts receivable and inventory update run.

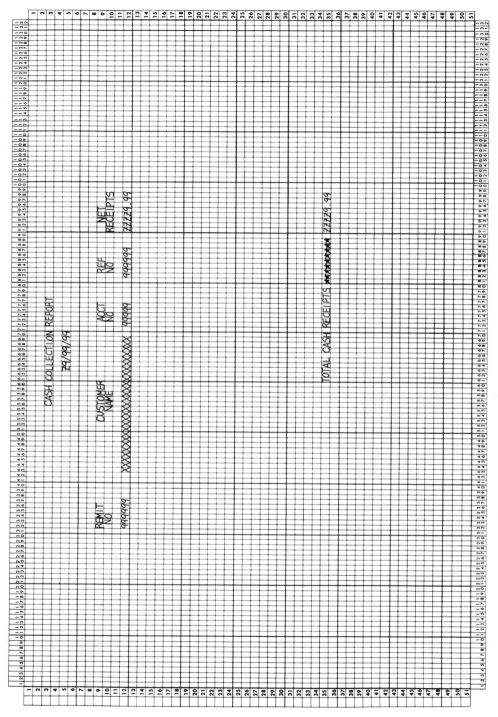

FIGURE 2-15 Cash Collection Report

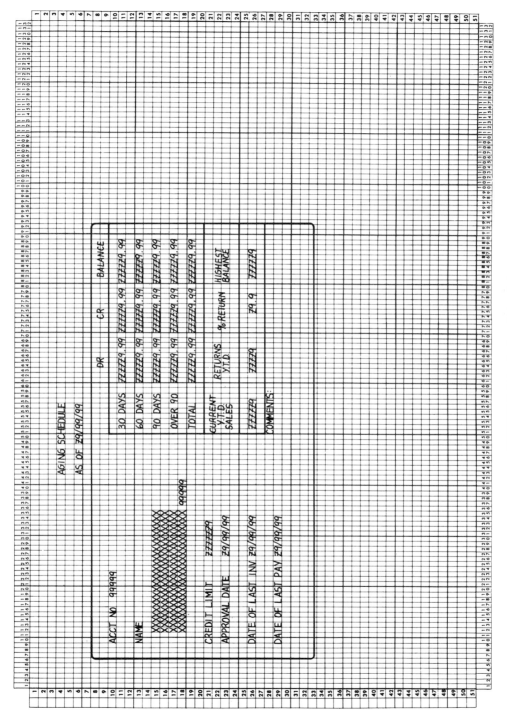

FIGURE 2-16 Aging Schedule

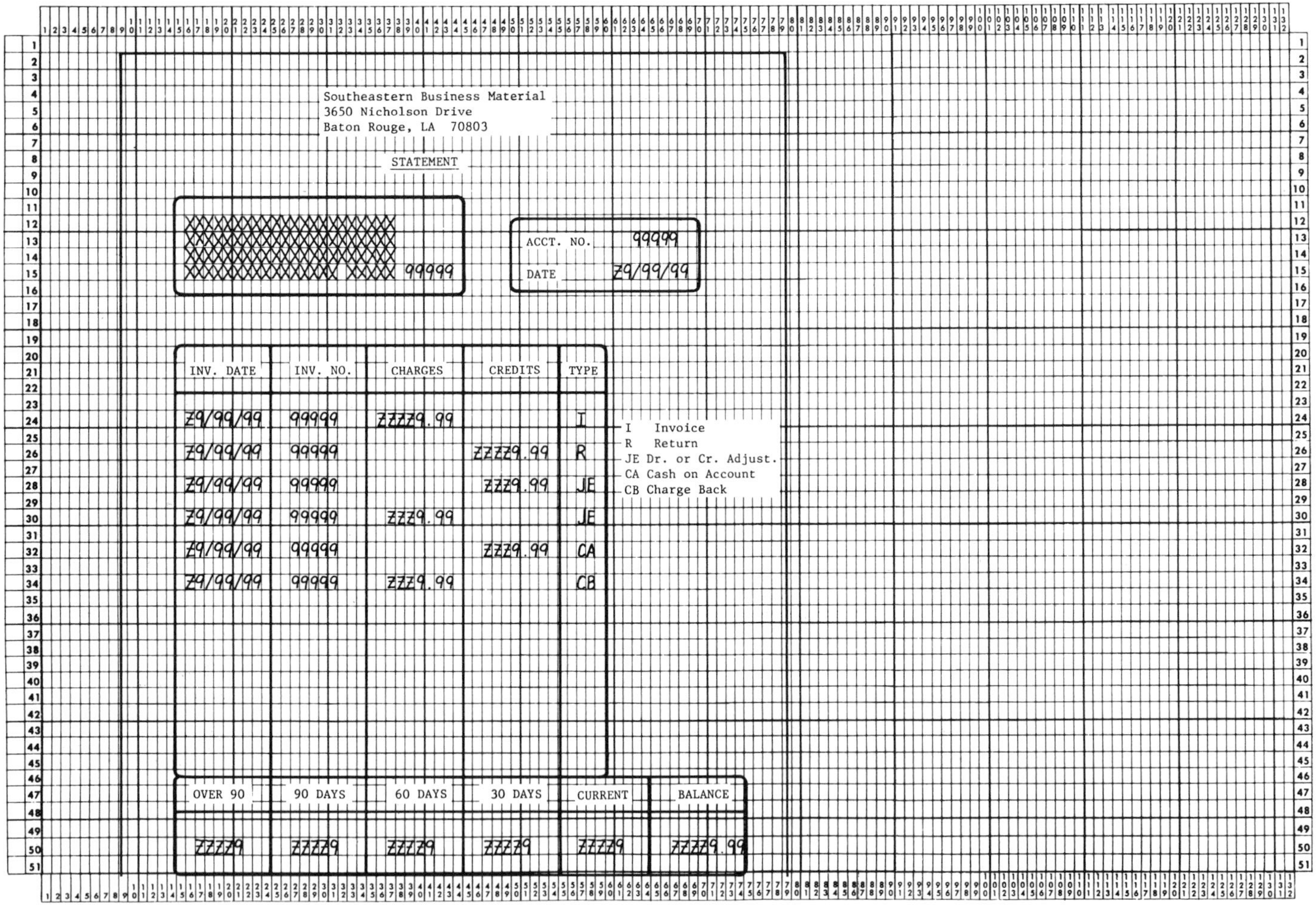

Southeastern Business Material
3650 Nicholson Drive
Baton Rouge, LA 70803

STATEMENT

99999

ACCT. NO. 99999

DATE Z9/99/99

INV. DATE	INV. NO.	CHARGES	CREDITS	TYPE
Z9/99/99	99999	ZZZZ9.99		I
Z9/99/99	99999		ZZZZ9.99	R
Z9/99/99	99999	ZZZ9.99	ZZZ9.99	JE
Z9/99/99	99999		ZZZ9.99	JE
Z9/99/99	99999		ZZZ9.99	CA
Z9/99/99	99999	ZZZ9.99		CB

I   Invoice
R   Return
JE Dr. or Cr. Adjust.
CA Cash on Account
CB Charge Back

OVER 90	90 DAYS	60 DAYS	30 DAYS	CURRENT	BALANCE
ZZZZ9	ZZZZ9	ZZZZ9	ZZZZ9	ZZZZ9	ZZZZ9.99

FIGURE 2-17 Monthly Statement

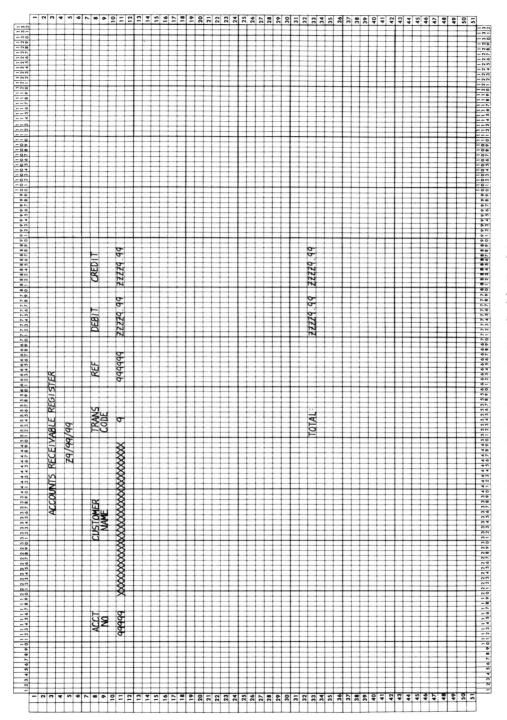

FIGURE 2-18 Accounts Receivable Register

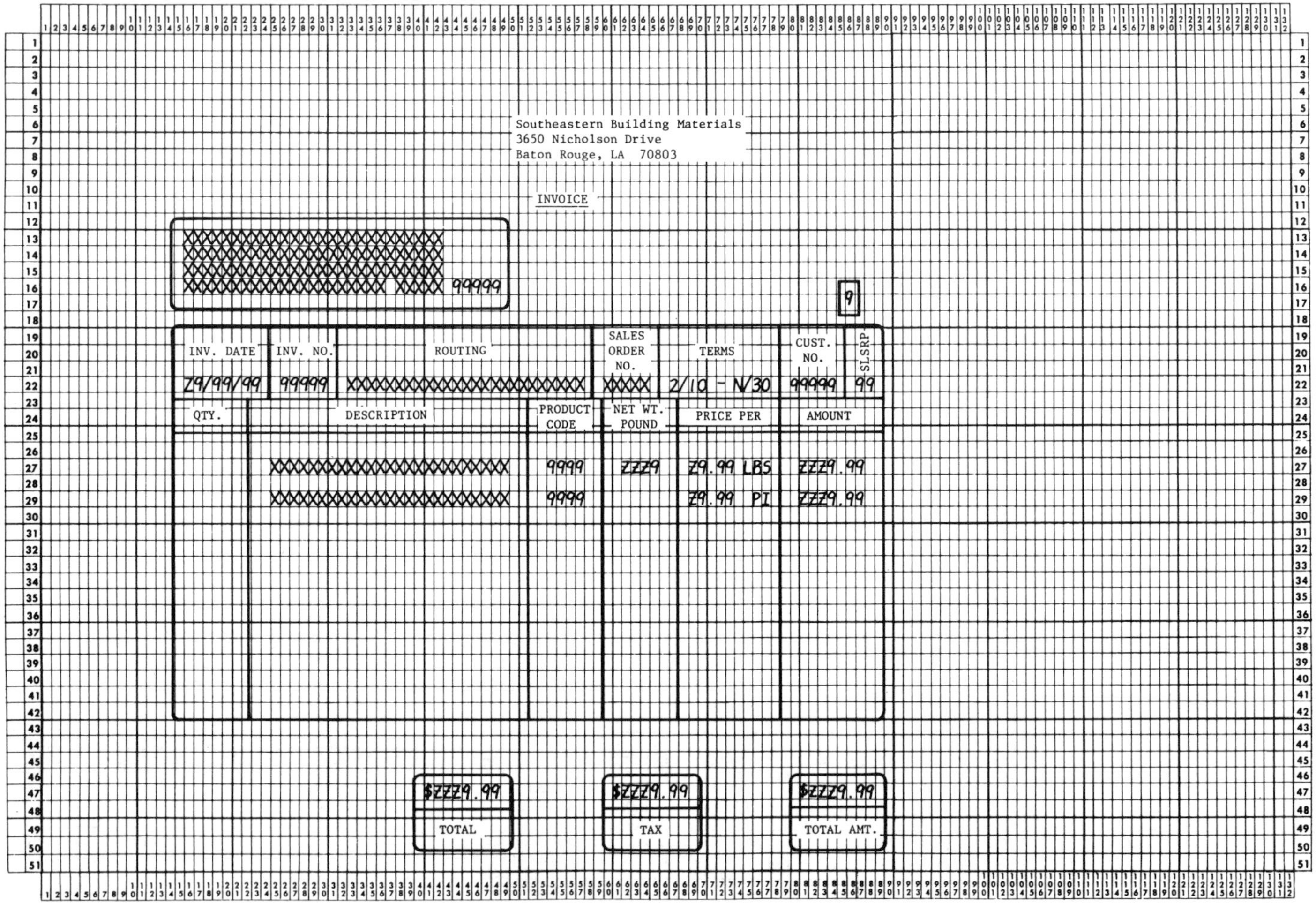
Southeastern Building Materials
3650 Nicholson Drive
Baton Rouge, LA 70803
INVOICE
XXXXXXXXXXXXXXXXXXXXXXXXX
XXXXXXXXXXXXXXXXXXXXXXXXX
XXXXXXXXXXXXXXXXXXXXXXXXX
XXXXXXXXXXXXXXXXXXX XXXXX 99999
9
INV. DATE
INV. NO.
ROUTING
SALES ORDER NO.
TERMS
CUST. NO.
SLSRP
Z9/99/99
99999
XXXXXXXXXXXXXXXXXXXXXXXXX
XXXXX
2/10 - N/30
99999
99
QTY.
DESCRIPTION
PRODUCT CODE
NET WT. POUND
PRICE PER
AMOUNT
XXXXXXXXXXXXXXXXXXXXXXXXX
9999
ZZZ9
Z9.99 LBS
ZZZ9.99
XXXXXXXXXXXXXXXXXXXXXXXXX
9999
Z9.99 PI
ZZZ9.99
$ZZZ9.99
TOTAL
$ZZZ9.99
TAX
$ZZZ9.99
TOTAL AMT.

FIGURE 2-19 Invoice Form

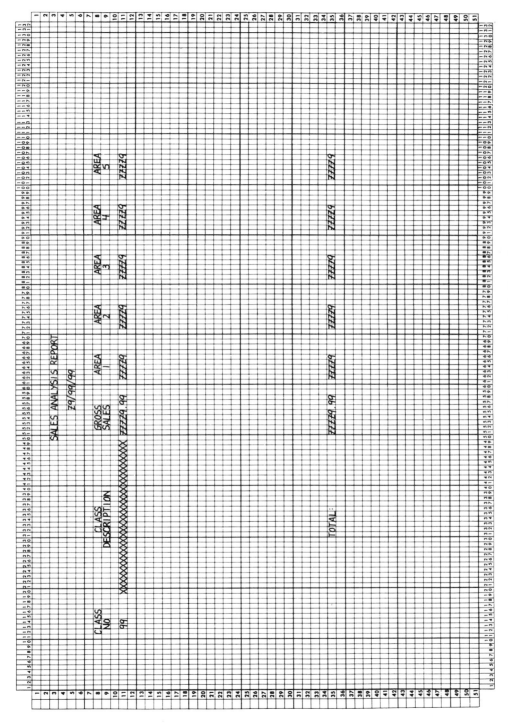

FIGURE 2-20 Sales Analysis Report

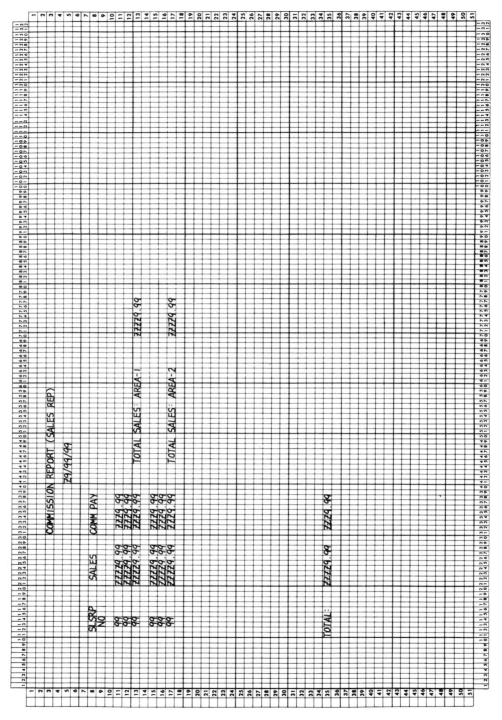

FIGURE 2-21 Commission Report (Sales Rep)

The Invoice Transactions Register is merely a list of all invoices which are issued in each run. This report will be used as a sales journal. Moreover, there are some advantages in using this report for internal control purposes and maintaining an audit trail (Fig. 2-22).

Figure 2-13 also shows an Inventory Transaction Tape which will be used in inventory recordkeeping, producing a journal, and other related data.

The final output of the update run is a tape of summary data, which includes total figures for accounts receivable transactions, cash collections, and sales to be used later in the general ledger update run. The process is fully explained later in the text when the general ledger system case is discussed.

ASSESSMENT OF NEEDED STORAGE

The following are approximations of the storage needed to accommodate the various files of the above system. (See the chapter appendix for details.)

Accounts Receivable Master File

This file has fixed-length records. From the file layout and by adding the number of bytes required, the size of the record is 261 bytes.[5] One record is established for each of the 1,500 customers; therefore, the file requires 1,500 × 261 = 391,500 bytes.

Transaction File

This is a fixed-length record file. Each record is 65 bytes in length. Assuming 150 transactions per day, this results in 150 × 65 = 9,750 bytes of storage being required per day. The transaction file is used to update the master file on a daily basis; therefore, data is not accumulated from day to day.

Cash Payment Transaction File

This file has fixed-length records. Each record is 51 bytes in length. Assume, on the average, that there is one cash payment per customer per day, thus 1,500 × 51 = 76,500 bytes are needed for the file.

Other Transactions File

This file has fixed-length records, 43 bytes each. Assume 10 other transactions per day results in 430 bytes for the file.

---

[5] The number of bytes required will seldom agree with the number of bytes or characters shown in a file layout. Why? Because *numeric* fields employ the "packed decimal" format, where two digits can often (but not always) be "packed" into one byte.

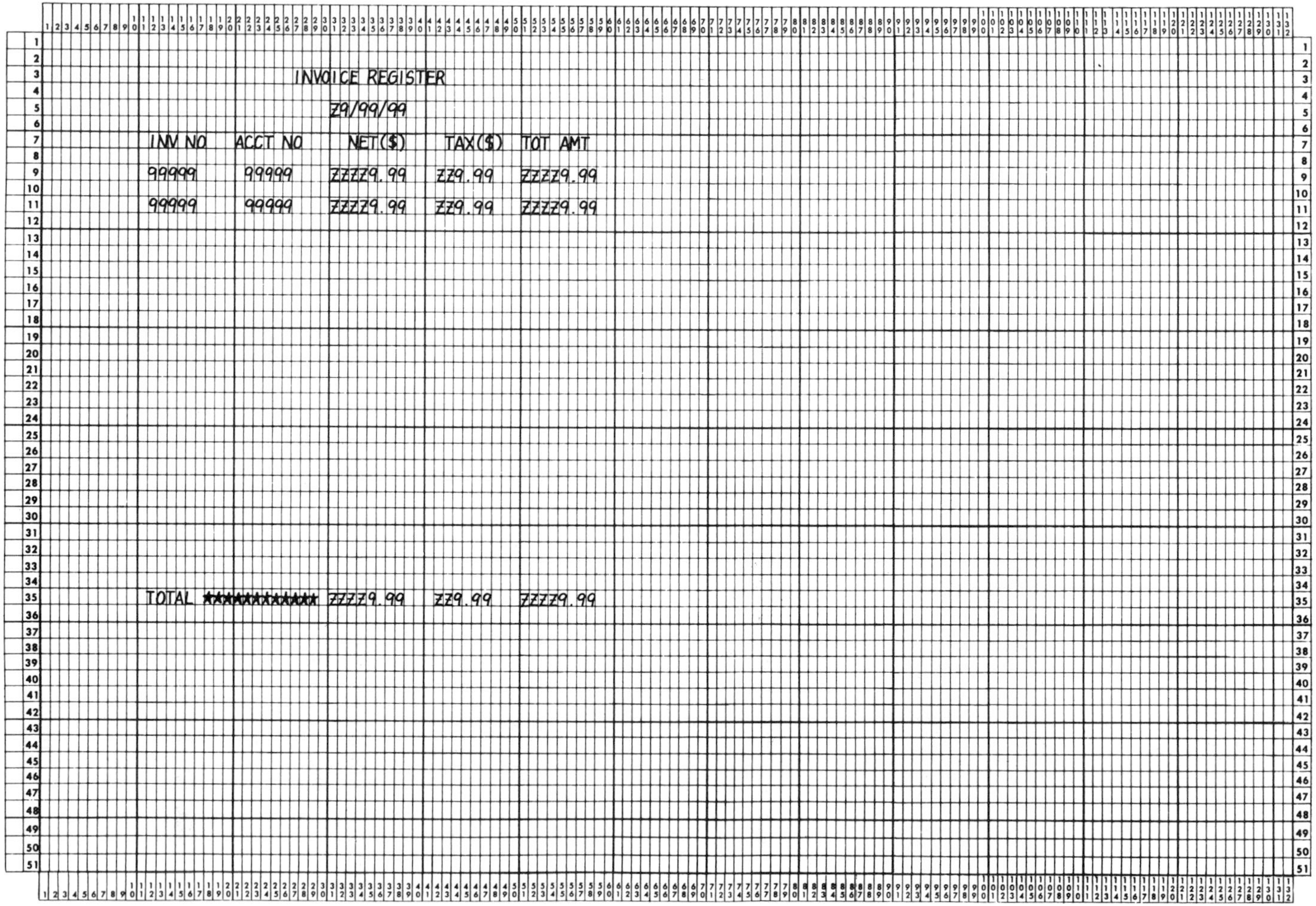

FIGURE 2-22 Invoice Register

In summary, the file requirements are as follows:

Accounts Receivable Master File	391,500 bytes
Transaction File	9,750 bytes
Cash Payment Transaction File	76,500 bytes
Other Transactions File	430 bytes
Total	478,180 bytes

SUMMARY

Management information needs with respect to sales, accounts receivable, and cash collection have been explained. The list of information needs is merely representative and could very well be expanded according to the nature of business activities, the industry's practice, and the size of the organization.

A case employing these applications was developed. Although the degree of sophistication of hardware and software may vary according to design of the system, the basic steps are those explained.

A housekeeping run of accounts receivable is important, but it is not explained because it is beyond the scope of this discussion. Efficient organizational and processing controls should be employed in the design of the housekeeping run. One of the main features of the system is the process of authorization of any change of accounts receivable, aside from what is caused by normal business transactions. The report of this type of maintenance run usually should be reviewed by a responsible person in the accounting hierarchy (usually the controller or assistant controller).

PROBLEMS

1. If Southeastern Building Material decided to utilize random-access devices to capture the input data both for sales orders and cash remittance advice, how would your flowchart change?

2. Assuming the same facts stated in the case, except that the Inventory Master File is stored on a magnetic tape: how would you change your flowchart in order to compensate for this situation?

3. Prepare the layout of an Inventory Master Record based on the information provided in the case.

4. How will your Edit Run–1 change if both the list of transactions and error list are to be printed on the line printer? (In the flowchart presented, the list of error(s) is prepared on a console typewriter.)

5. Redesign the system developed in the case study to use the minimum number of hardware units. Draw a flowchart of the entire system according to the chronological sequence of all the runs.

6. In the case it was assumed that *quantity* discounts will be granted at the end of year to each customer. (Do not confuse this with the 2/10, n/30 terms.) If the company wished to offer quantity discounts as each order arrived, how would you change the system to accommodate this requirement?

7. Design the layout of a Sales Analysis Report which highlights sales per area and sales per sales representative within each area.

8. If the company wishes to tie the commissions earned on each product to the gross margin of each product, redesign the Sales Commission Report to accommodate this need.

9. Redesign all the sales related reports discussed in the case by including year-to-date information.

APPENDIX

Accounts Receivable Master File Layout

Data Element	Format	Number of Bytes	Notes
Account Number	9(5)	3	
Name	X(24)	24	
Address—1	X(24)	24	
Address—2	X(24)	24	
Current No. of Invoice	9(3)	2	
City	X(19)	19	
State	X(2)	2	
ZIP Code	X(9)	9	
Credit Limit	9(7)	4	
Date Cr. Limit Approved	X(6)	6	
Amount Due	9(7)	4	
Current Purchase	9(6)	4	
Current Payment	9(6)	4	
Current Adjustment	9(6)	4	
Current Balance	9(7)	4	
Sales Rep.	99	2	
Prior Number of Invoices	999	2	
Purchase	9(7)	4	30 days
Payment and Adjustment	9(7)	4	
Balance	9(7)	4	
Purchase	9(7)	4	60 days
Payment Adjustment	9(7)	4	
Balance	9(7)	4	
Purchase	9(7)	4	90 days
Payment Adjustment	9(7)	4	
Balance	9(7)	4	
Total Balance	9(7)	4	
January Sales	9(7)	4	Cumulative year-to-date sales
.	.	.	
.	.	.	
.	.	.	
December Sales	9(7)	4	
Last Sales Invoice Date	X(6)	6	
Date Last Cash Received	X(6)	6	
Amount Last Cash Received	9(7)	4	
% Return	999	2	
Current Return	9(6)	4	
Date of Last Return	X(6)	6	
Highest Balance	9(7)	4	
		261 bytes	

Transaction File Layout

Data Element	Format	Number of Bytes	Notes
Transaction Code	9	1	
Account Number	9(5)	3	
Quantity	9(4)	3	Item quantity
Description	X(25)	25	
Product Number	9(4)	3	
Net Weight	9(4)	3	
Routing	X(20)	20	
Sales Order Number	9(5)	3	
Sales Rep.	99	2	
Batch Number	99	2	
		65 bytes	

Cash Payment Transaction File Layout

Data Element	Format	Number of Bytes	Notes
Cash Remittance Number	9(6)	4	
Account Number	9(5)	3	
Transaction Code	9	1	
Name	X(24)	24	
Reference	X(5)	5	
Net Amount	9(8)	5	
Discount	9(7)	4	
Gross	9(8)	5	
		51 bytes	

Other Transactions File Layout

Data Element	Format	Number of Bytes	Notes
Account Number	9(5)	3	
Name	X(24)	24	
Transaction Code	9	1	
Debit Amount	9(8)	5	
Credit Amount	9(8)	5	
Reference	X(5)	5	
		43 bytes	

3 | Design of a System for Purchases, Accounts Payable, and Cash Disbursements

In this chapter, the nature, function, and design of a system for purchasing, accounts payable, and cash disbursements are discussed. The degree of sophistication a firm requires in this system is closely correlated with the organization's goal, its management philosophy, and its political environment. Applications such as preparing and processing requisitions, order processing and updating, vendor rating and selection, economic order quantity (EOQ) computation, preparation of checks, and providing for on-line query are among those applications that have been designed and implemented in many business organizations.

As in the previous case, some applications (such as inventory) will be discussed only to the extent that they interact with this system.

MANAGEMENT INFORMATION REQUIREMENTS

The functional departments which are major parts of this system are (1) the requesting department, (2) purchasing department, (3) accounts payable department, and (4) cash disbursement department.

The relationships of these departments with each other and with outside vendors, as well as the sequence of events in this system, are depicted in Fig. 3-1. These events are chronologically numbered from 1 through 6. The time interval from event 1 through event 6 is roughly 60 days.

The objectives of each of the departments and their specific informational needs are listed in the following sections. However, some overlapping between the information needs of these departments occurs.

Requesting Department

Since this department is the user of the purchased products and services, it should be mainly concerned with the timely delivery and the quality of the goods or services acquired. In some organizations, the requesting department is kept informed of the status of the order in the system. Therefore, it would be possible for the department to react to unexpected developments.

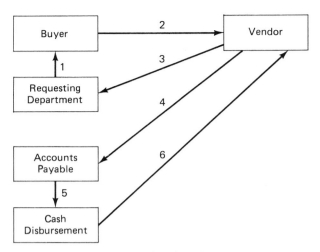

**FIGURE 3-1   The Relationships Among Functional Areas of a
Purchasing System**

Purchasing Department

Purchasing involves recognizing the need for goods or services, selecting a source (supplier), negotiating price, and ensuring the delivery of goods or services to an organization. In other words, it means procuring materials and services required for operating and maintaining a business. One of the major concerns of a business is the effective operation of its purchasing department, because one-half of the money generated by sales is spent through this department purchasing goods and services.

The size of the purchasing department varies according to the size of the organization. One individual with limited clerical experience may be able to carry out this operation for a small business. However, in large organizations, a separate department which employs a number of people handles the purchasing function. Regardless of the size, acquiring goods or services at a competitive market price is the main objective of any purchasing organization.

The information needs of management in this area can be recurring or nonrecurring. Information about types of materials which may be used in more advantageous ways, market trends of material, services prices, and new products or services that are available, are of the nonrecurring type that will be useful to the management. However, most of the information that will be used is of a recurring nature:

- Quantity and types of items used (by group and subgroup)
- Sales volume of the finished products

- Unit price of purchased items
- Vendors (source of supplies)
- Variety and types of services demanded within organizations
- Placement of the order at the right time
- Status of open orders
- Products or services that have been received
- Whether delivery date is consistent with vendor's promise
- Completed orders
- Status of exceptions such as past due shipments and rejected orders
- Purchasing agents' performances

In large organizations, the purchasing department might be interested in total dollars spent with each vendor, and the parent company of the vendor. The latter might provide an opportunity for package dealing, when the buyer deals with several subsidiaries of a single parent.

Accounts Payable Department

A liability created as a result of purchase of materials and services must eventually be paid. The accounts payable department is basically charged with the responsibility for prompt payment of invoices by taking advantage of maximum amount of cash discounts. This department must make sure that they only pay for the orders that were properly requested and received.

The informational needs of this department are

- List of daily activities of the department (such as daily payment list)
- List of open liability items and unfilled purchase orders
- List of lost cash discounts
- Total volume of purchase from each vendor
- Ranking of suppliers in terms of volume
- Vendors with largest volume of returns and exceptions
- Projected cash budget, in order to maximize anticipated discounts

Cash Disbursement Department

Disbursements refer to the payment of invoices for goods or services acquired by a company. Acquisition of goods or services creates liabilities and these liabilities must be paid. The main objective of the disbursement department is to make sure that the correct amount is disbursed to the proper vendor. Moreover, an accurate and detailed record of transactions provides management with useful information, allowing management to make many policy decisions which affect the business positively.

The information required at this stage is data on (1) daily, weekly, and monthly cash requirements and (2) a check register.

INTERNAL CONTROLS AND AUDIT IMPLICATIONS

The internal controls related to this application may be summarized as follows.

General Controls

The main general controls are

- Procedure for reviewing the report of open purchase order file change(s). This report will be reviewed by an authorized person within the purchasing department or by internal audit staff.
- Procedure for reviewing the report of change(s) in the master file of vendors. This report will be reviewed by an authorized person within the controller's department or by internal audit staff.
- Procedure for maintaining the transaction files for a certain period of time for audit trail and backtracking.

Application Controls

These controls are normally integrated into the computer programs which are to be designed for the different stages of this case. The following is a list of these controls.

- Check digit on vendor's account number, performed on the basis of modulus 11 (or modulus 10), to ensure the correct transcription of the source data into the computer terminal
- Validity check on the various types of transaction fields
- Sequence check on purchase order number
- Record count of all the input documents
- Record count of different computer runs
- Completeness test on all fields of all the records
- Reasonableness test for checking the validity of several selected fields

A more detailed explanation of these tests is provided later in this case.

CASE: Purchases, Accounts Payable, and Cash Disbursements

Scott Discount Stores is a relatively large discount store chain which operates in Nebraska. The chain consists of 10 stores throughout the state, with the headquarters located in Lincoln. Scott has approximately 3,500 suppliers scattered across the country from the East Coast to the West Coast. All the merchandise and supplies are delivered to Scott's central warehouse at Lincoln and then distributed among the stores upon request. The daily number of invoices which Scott receives is approximately 250. Based on past information, 95 percent of the suppliers allow Scott "prompt payment" cash discounts.

Currently Scott's accounting system is totally manual. Because of several problems that have been encountered such as loss of cash discounts, inventory overstock, and loss of cash, the management has decided to hire an outside consultant to look into these problems. The consulting firm submitted its preliminary report after four weeks. The report concluded that management is currently suffering from the lack of relevant and timely information. Therefore, computerization of the purchasing, accounts payable, and cash disbursement system was recommended with the highest degree of priority.

Scott's management decided to go ahead with the consultant's recommendation. The following system is the result of the consultant's work.

The recommended computerized system is capable of handling the following routines:

- Acceptance of requisitions from the requesting department
- Acceptance and modification or correction of prior orders
- Rejection of orders that are inaccurately filled
- Processing of orders where merchandise and invoices have been received
- Preparation of checks
- Preparation of various reports for managerial use

REQUESTING DEPARTMENT

When needs for goods or services arise, the requesting department will send an approved copy of the requisition form to the Purchasing Department. The requisition forms are serially numbered. The important data on this form are quantity, part number (or material code), description, date material needed, and the signature of the authorized person who requested the item(s). The layout of this form could vary depending on the nature and type of the organization.

PURCHASING DEPARTMENT

The Purchasing Department prepares a purchase order based on the data found on the requisition form and other data which is available within the department. Examples of "other data" are supplier's number and name, shipping route, and unit price. This data may be found in different directories (such as directory of suppliers) within the Purchasing Department. The purchase order form is shown in Fig. 3-2.

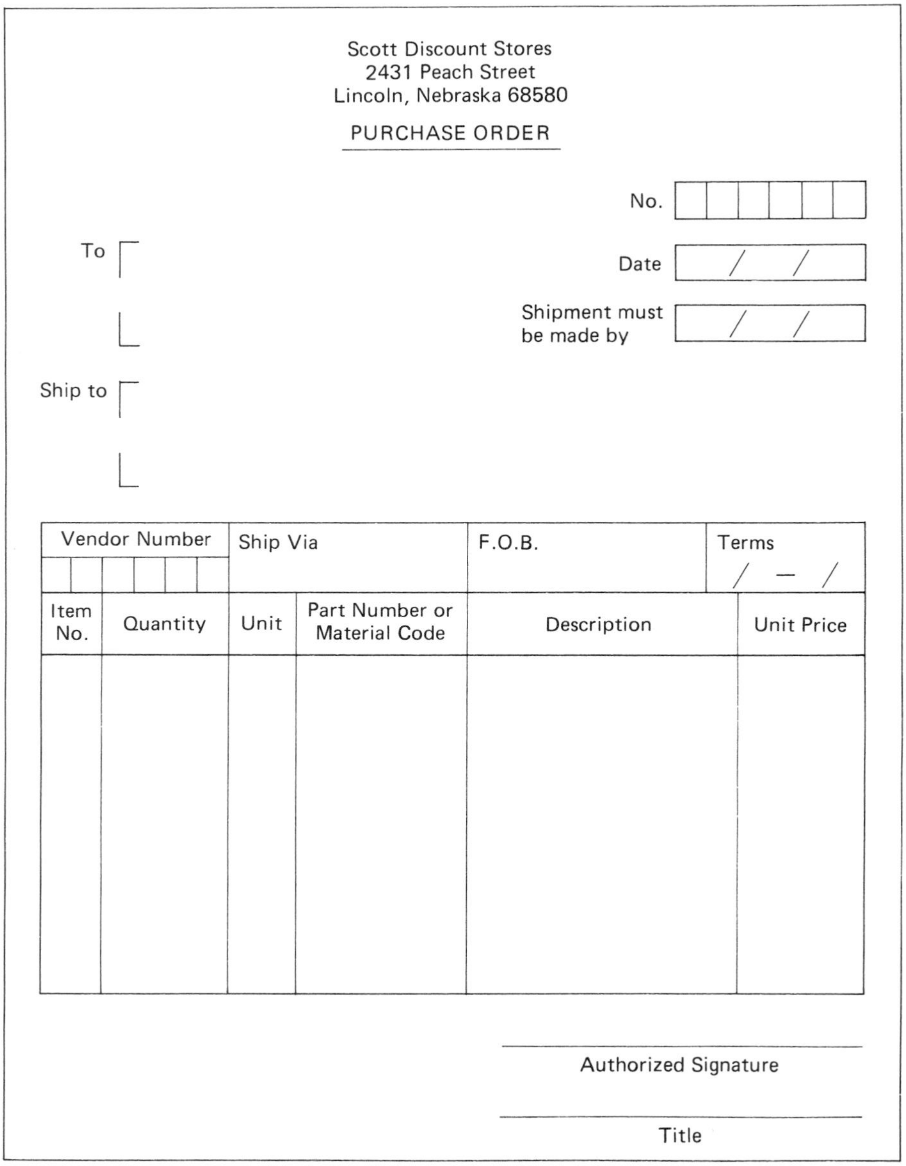
Scott Discount Stores
2431 Peach Street
Lincoln, Nebraska 68580

PURCHASE ORDER

No.

To

Date / /

Shipment must be made by / /

Ship to

Vendor Number	Ship Via	F.O.B.	Terms / — /

Item No.	Quantity	Unit	Part Number or Material Code	Description	Unit Price

Authorized Signature

Title

FIGURE 3-2 Purchase Order Form

This form is prepared in multiple copies. The first two copies, which are treated as a legal offer, are sent to the supplier. The supplier acknowledges the approval of the order by signing and returning the second copy to the Purchasing Department. The third and fourth copies are sent to the Accounts Payable and Receiving Departments. One copy is sent to the requesting department so that they know that their order has been processed; and the last copy is used as a reference file in the Purchasing Department. It should be noted that the quantity and unit price columns are left blank on the Receiving Department copy (fourth copy).

The Purchasing Department will prepare a daily batch from all these purchase orders and modification (or correction) and cancellation notices and will send it to the Information Processing Department. The modification (or correction) and cancellation notices pertain to purchase orders which have previously been sent to the Information Processing Department. An example of a correction is a change in unit price of a given item, as a result of a counteroffer by a supplier.

A Batch Control Slip (Fig. 3-3) is prepared and the number of documents in the batch is used as a control figure. Since the purchase orders are serially numbered, the starting and ending numbers are recorded on the Batch Control Slip.

BATCH CONTROL SLIP

Batch No. _____   Date _____

    Last Number on Purchase Order   _____

    First Number on Purchase Order   _____

       Total Purchase Orders   _____

    Number of Correction Slips   _____

    Number of Cancellation Slips   _____

    Total Number of Documents
      in the Batch   _____

Clerk _____

FIGURE 3-3   Batch Control Slip

DATA ENTRY

The batch of documents, as shown in Fig. 3-4, will be keyed into the system through an intelligent terminal. The data will be edited while being entered into the computer system. Since the purchase order entry routine is menu driven, the editing process is somewhat simple. The first two screen layouts of the menu are shown in Figs. 3-5 and 3-6, respectively. The key operator specifies the option number (Fig. 3-5) and then enters the data according to the selected option. Fig. 3-6 shows the layout screen for the order-entering routine. Any error committed as a result of entering any of the data fields is highlighted at the lower portion of the screen through an appropriate error message.

The screen layout for modification (or correction) and cancellation of previous purchase orders is similar to the screen layout of a new order. However, the operator must key in the purchase order number first, in order to access the record for modification or deletion. After the record is accessed, the key operator modifies the value of any desired field or fields and saves the modified record. In order to protect the system against unwarranted deletion of a purchase order record, a reinforcement message is programmed into the system. That is, in order to delete a particular record, the operator would have to strike the "Y" key twice, in response to the question "Delete Record?"

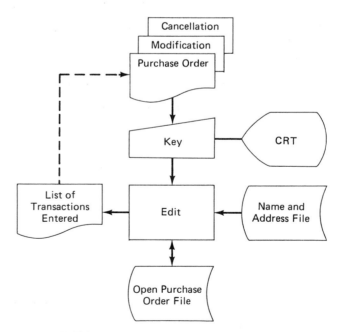

FIGURE 3-4   Data Entry Procedures

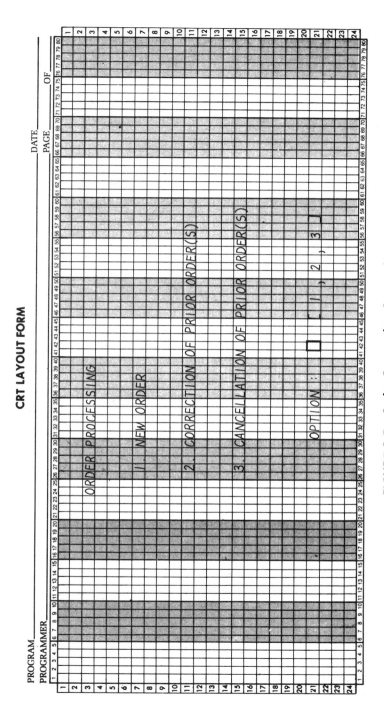

CRT LAYOUT FORM

PROGRAM
PROGRAMMER
DATE
PAGE ___ OF ___

ORDER PROCESSING

1. NEW ORDER

2. CORRECTION OF PRIOR ORDER(S)

3. CANCELLATION OF PRIOR ORDER(S)

OPTION: ☐ [1 , 2 , 3]

FIGURE 3-5 Order Processing Screen Layout

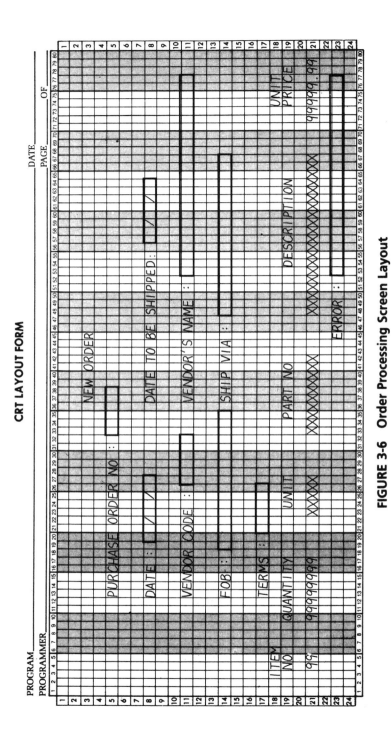

FIGURE 3-6 Order Processing Screen Layout

EDIT PROCESS

The edit process at this stage is based on the "front-end" method. That is, an error is detected immediately after the data is keyed into the system.

The tests designed for the various fields are as follows:

Test	Item
1. Sequence check	Purchase order number
2. Validity	All data fields
3. Check digit (modulus 11)	Vendor's code
4. Validity	Terms
5. Consistency (matching)	Vendor's code to vendor's name
6. Completeness	All fields
7. Record count	By purchase order number

Test 5 is performed by referring to the file of vendors' names and addresses. The primary key of this file is vendor's code. The layout of this file is shown in Fig. 3-7.

The outputs of the edit process are (1) a list of transactions (including a batch summary report) and (2) an open purchase order file.

The list of transactions (Fig. 3-8) is output by the printer and contains two parts. A detailed listing of data on each purchase order form consists of the following items:

1. Purchase order number
2. Date of purchase order
3. Date to be shipped
4. Vendor's code
5. Vendor's name
6. Ship via

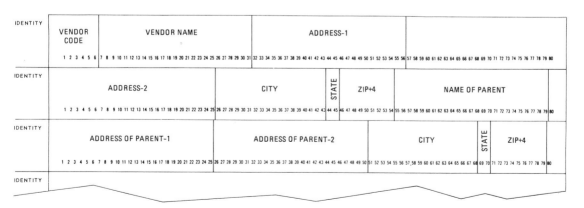

FIGURE 3-7   Layout of Vendors Name and Address File

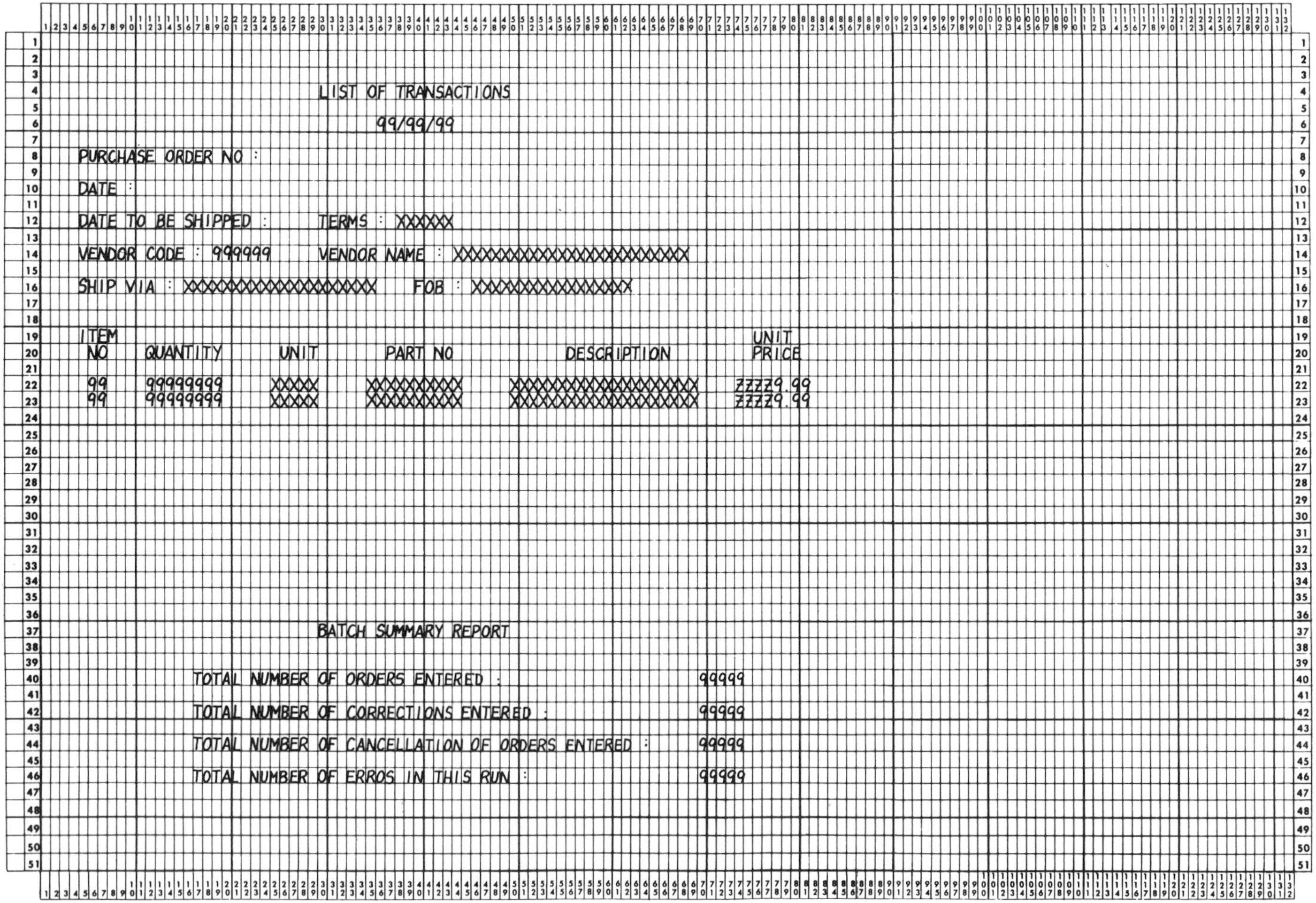

LIST OF TRANSACTIONS
99/99/99

PURCHASE ORDER NO :
DATE ::
DATE TO BE SHIPPED :   TERMS : XXXXX
VENDOR CODE : 999999   VENDOR NAME : XXXXXXXXXXXXXXXXXXXXXX
SHIP VIA : XXXXXXXXXXXXXXXXXX   FOB : XXXXXXXXXXXXX

ITEM NO	QUANTITY	UNIT	PART NO	DESCRIPTION	UNIT PRICE
99	9999999	XXXXX	XXXXXXX	XXXXXXXXXXXXX	ZZZZ9.99
99	9999999	XXXXX	XXXXXXX	XXXXXXXXXXXXX	ZZZZ9.99

BATCH SUMMARY REPORT

TOTAL NUMBER OF ORDERS ENTERED : 99999
TOTAL NUMBER OF CORRECTIONS ENTERED : 99999
TOTAL NUMBER OF CANCELLATION OF ORDERS ENTERED : 99999
TOTAL NUMBER OF ERRORS IN THIS RUN : 99999

FIGURE 3-8 List of Transactions

7. F.O.B.
8. Terms
9. For each item
    a. Item number
    b. Quantity
    c. Unit
    d. Part number
    e. Description
    f. Unit price

The listing of the modified and deleted records is slightly different. In the case of a modified (corrected) record, both the pre- and postvalue of the field being changed must be shown. The entire contents of any deleted record(s) must be printed on this listing.

The batch summary report portion of the transactions report contains the number of records of each type that have been passed through the edit process (bottom portion of Fig. 3-8).

The list of transactions is used for audit trail purposes and correction of errors which have not been detected at the data entry level. It also provides a breakdown of the number of records of the various types that have been processed into the system. It must be emphasized that the report of the changes made on any record or the deletion of any record must be reviewed by a member of the internal audit staff or another authorized person.

The other output of the edit run is the file of open purchase orders. This file is organized on a disk using a variable-length record format. Each record consists of a fixed-length and a variable-length section. The fixed-length section denotes the general information about each purchase order such as purchase order number and date. The variable-length portion (trailer part) relates to the number of items being ordered on every purchase order. Figure 3-9 shows the

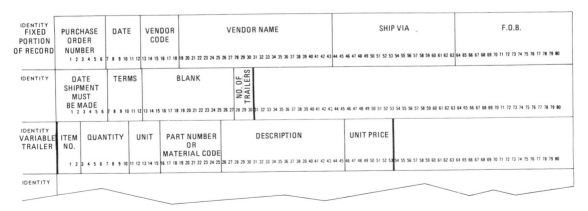

FIGURE 3-9 Layout of the Purchase Order Records

layout of this record. The last field in the fixed portion of the record contains the number of trailer parts in each purchase order record (that is, the number of items listed in each purchase order form). The primary key for each record is the purchase order number field.

ACCOUNTS PAYABLE DEPARTMENT

The Accounts Payable Department has already been notified about the order by receiving the third copy of the purchase order. All these copies are kept in an open purchase order file organized alphabetically according to vendor's name.

As soon as the vendor's invoice arrives, it should be matched with the related purchase order and receiving report. These documents will be examined and authorized for payment.

CREATION OF THE INVOICE FILE

The invoices authorized for payment must be entered in the Invoice File. The Invoice File is created by the Accounts Payable Department. Therefore, all the information is keyed into the system in almost the same way as purchase orders (Fig. 3-10). The information also is being edited by use of a "front-end" editing program.

The output of this run consists of the invoice file and a list of purchase invoices. The invoice file has a variable-length record format and is organized on disk. The primary key of this file is the purchase order number. The layout of each invoice record is shown in Fig. 3-11.

A field called Discount Code shows two codes. Code 1 is used when the company decides to take advantage of cash discounts. In this case, computation of net amount payable is based on the terms of the purchase. Code 2 identifies the situation when taking the cash discount is not economically justifiable, or there is no early payment incentive.

The Purchase Invoices Report (Fig. 3-12) is used for the purpose of audit trail and correction of errors caused by keying data into the system. Data included in this report are

- Purchase order number
- Vendor code
- Vendor name
- Invoice number
- Gross amount of invoice
- Tax
- Freight

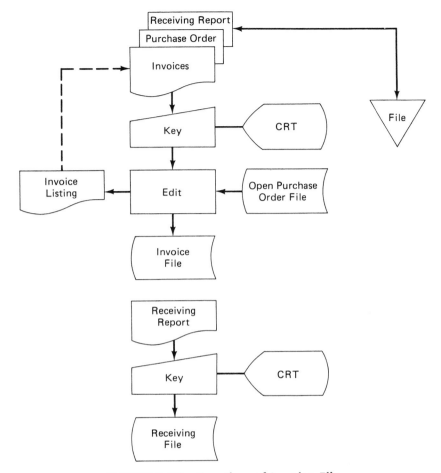

FIGURE 3-10 Creation of Invoice File

IDENTITY										
FIXED PORTION OF RECORD	PURCHASE ORDER NUMBER	VENDOR CODE	VENDOR NAME		INVOICE NUMBER	INVOICE DATE	GROSS AMOUNT	TAX	FREIGHT	STATE TAX RATE
	1 2 3 4 5 6	7 8 9 10 11 12	13 14 15 16 17 18 19 20 21 22 23 24 25 26 27 28 29 30 31 32 33 34 35 36 37		38 39 40 41 42 43 44 45	46 47 48 49 50 51	52 53 54 55 56 57 58 59 60 61	62 63 64 65 66 67	68 69 70 71 72 73 74 75	76 77 78 79 80

IDENTITY	DISCOUNT CODE	DEBIT ACCT. NUMBER	BLANK	NO. OF TRAILERS	
	1	2 3 4 5 6 7 8 9 10 11	12 13 14 15 16 17 18 19 20 21 22 23 24 25 26 27 28 29	30 31 32 33 34 35 36 37 38 39 40 41 42 43 44 45 46 47 48 49 50 51 52 53 54 55 56 57 58 59 60 61 62 63 64 65 66 67 68 69 70 71 72 73 74 75 76 77 78 79 80	

IDENTITY VARIABLE TRAILER	ITEM NO.	QUANTITY	UNIT	PART NUMBER	DESCRIPTION	UNIT PRICE	
	1 2 3	4 5 6 7 8 9 10	11 12 13 14 15	16 17 18 19 20 21 22 23 24 25	26 27 28 29 30 31 32 33 34 35 36 37 38 39 40 41 42 43 44 45	46 47 48 49 50 51 52 53	54 55 56 57 58 59 60 61 62 63 64 65 66 67 68 69 70 71 72 73 74 75 76 77 78 79 80

IDENTITY

FIGURE 3-11 Layout of Invoice File

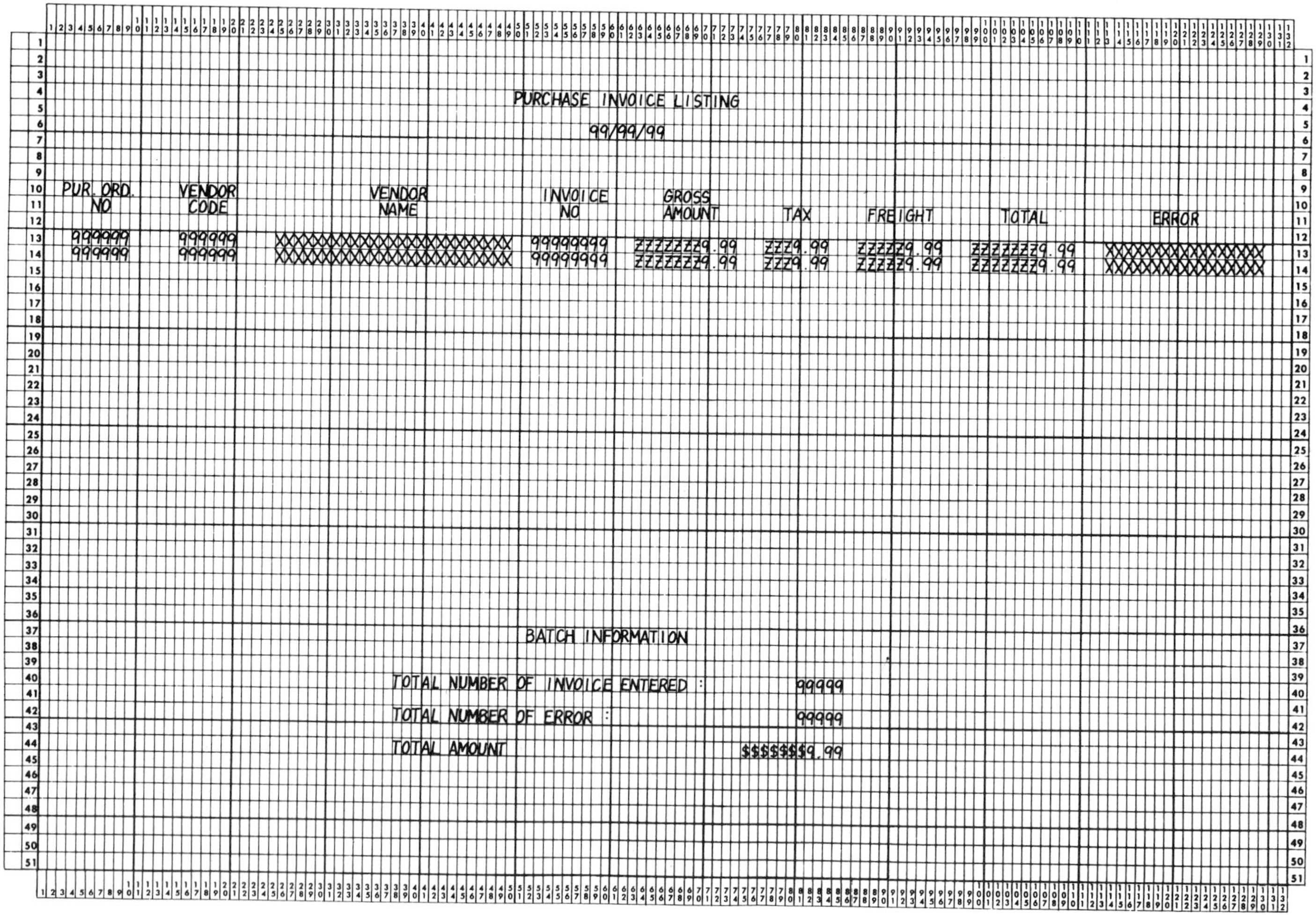

PURCHASE INVOICE LISTING

99/99/99

PUR. ORD. NO	VENDOR CODE	VENDOR NAME	INVOICE NO	GROSS AMOUNT	TAX	FREIGHT	TOTAL	ERROR
999999	999999	XXXXXXXXXXX	99999999	ZZZZZZ9.99	ZZZ9.99	ZZZZZ9.99	ZZZZZZ9.99	XXXX
999999	999999		99999999	ZZZZZZ9.99	ZZZ9.99	ZZZZZ9.99	ZZZZZZ9.99	XXXX

BATCH INFORMATION

TOTAL NUMBER OF INVOICE ENTERED : 99999

TOTAL NUMBER OF ERROR : 99999

TOTAL AMOUNT $$$$$$9.99

FIGURE 3-12 Purchase Invoice Listing

- Total amount payable
- Error message

The computer program computes the amounts payable based on the facts entered into the system and compares it with the amount demanded by the vendor. Any discrepancy between details of the transaction and aggregate amount is noted in the appropriate column of the Purchase Invoices Report (last column).

After keying all the data into the system, invoices, purchase orders, and receiving reports are collated and kept in a separate file for future audit by an external auditor or the internal audit staff. Furthermore, the Accounts Payable Department may request a report on future cash requirements. This report can be generated by reading the contents of Open Purchase Orders File and computing the estimated cash requirement based on the date of shipment.

RECEIVING DEPARTMENT

After the merchandise is received on the receiving dock, the receiving clerk pulls the fourth copy of the purchase order from the temporary file. The merchandise is counted and the fourth copy of the purchase order is initialed and sent to the Accounts Payable Department.

The receiving clerk also creates a record of the received merchandise on the Receiving File through the use of an on-line terminal provided for the Receiving Department (bottom section of Fig. 3-10). The file has a variable-length record format with purchase order number field being the primary key of the records. Layout of the receiving record is shown in Fig. 3-13.

As an internal control feature, the quantity and unit price columns of the fourth copy of the purchase order are left blank. This feature guarantees the counting of the items received.

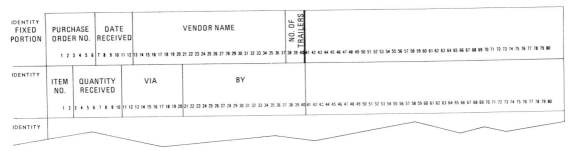

FIGURE 3-13 Layout of Receiving Items

ACCOUNTS PAYABLE UPDATE RUN

This run is the most important run of the system (Fig. 3-14). The inputs to this run are

- Open Purchase Order File
- Invoice File
- Receiving File
- Vendors Master File (Accounts Payable Master File)

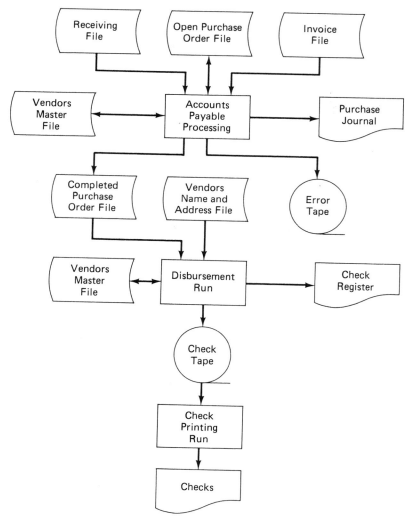

FIGURE 3-14   Accounts Payable Update Run

The outputs of this file are

- Updated Open Purchase Order File
- Updated Vendors Master File
- Completed Purchase Order File
- Purchase Journal
- File of Errors

The primary keys of the first three input files (the purchase order number) are matched and the vendors master record is extracted. Vendor's code is the primary key of the Vendors Master File. The layout of this file is shown in Fig. 3-15. This file is a variable-length record. It also contains four types of trailers for different types of transactions. The four types of transactions are

- Purchase transaction (invoice)
- Disbursement transaction (payment of check)
- Debit adjustment (such as purchase return or lost cash discount)
- Credit adjustment (transportation or other charges)

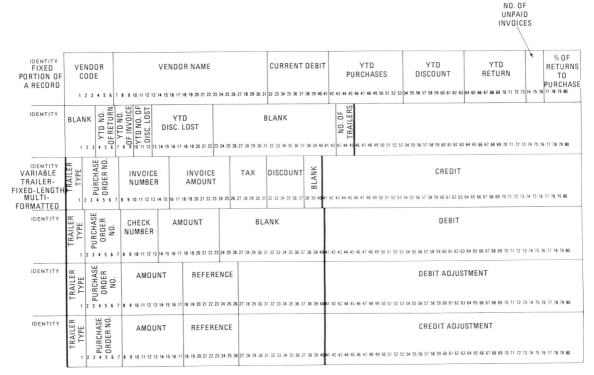

FIGURE 3-15 Layout of the Vendors Master File

It should be noted that all the trailers have a fixed length, but they are multiformatted, and each type is identified by the trailer type field.

The program in this run compares quantity received with the quantity ordered, quantity invoiced, and other related fields with each other. As a result, it creates the following:

- Updated Vendor Record, written on Vendors Master File
- Completed Purchase Order Record, indicating that the order has been filled and will be used in future runs as an input to the check processing run
- Purchase Journal, to be printed.
- Error Tape, a record of each error that was encountered during the process

The layout of the Vendors Master File has already been shown in Fig. 3-15.

The layout of the Completed Purchase Order Record is shown in Fig. 3-16. Creating this record is an indication that the order has been properly filled and payment must be made. This file is used in future runs for the preparation of checks and for reporting on completed orders.

The Updated Open Purchase Order File contains only the unfilled orders. That is, the file contains no record for those orders that pass through the Accounts Payable Update Run without any inconsistency.

The Purchase Journal created in this run is the basis for the audit trail and is shown in Fig. 3-17. Data included in this report are

- Account number—debit account
- Vendor's name
- Invoice number
- Invoice date
- Gross amount

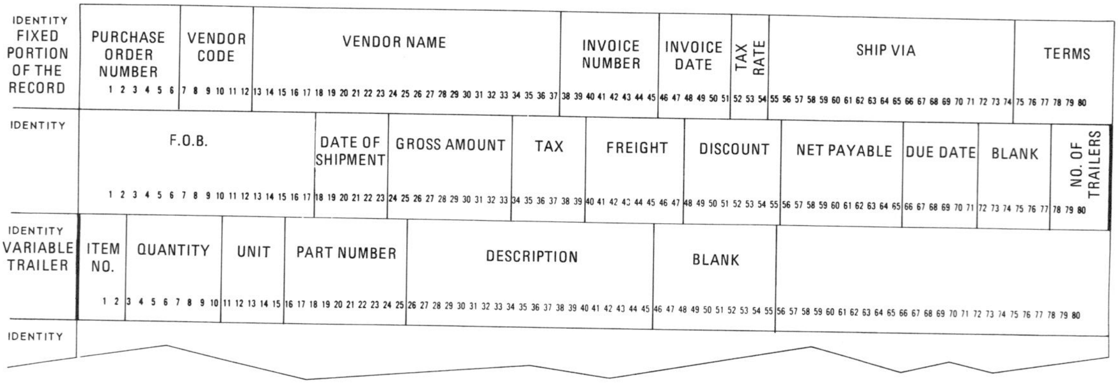

FIGURE 3-16 Layout of Completed Purchase Order Record

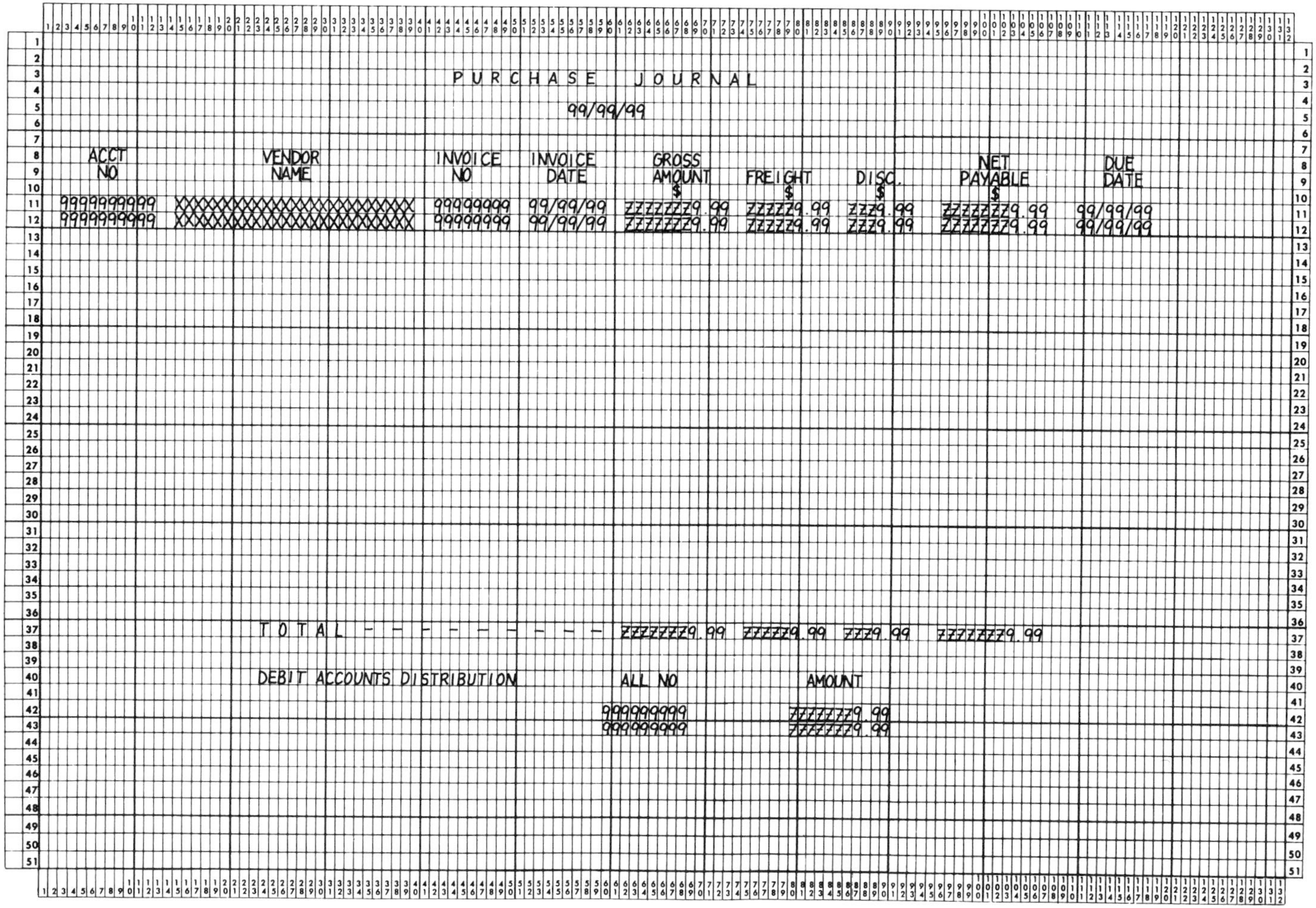

PURCHASE JOURNAL

99/99/99

ACCT NO	VENDOR NAME	INVOICE NO	INVOICE DATE	GROSS AMOUNT $	FREIGHT $	DISC. $	NET PAYABLE $	DUE DATE
999999999	XXXXXXXXX	99999999	99/99/99	ZZZZZZZ9.99	ZZZZZ9.99	ZZZ9.99	ZZZZZZZ9.99	99/99/99
999999999	XXXXXXXXX	99999999	99/99/99	ZZZZZZZ9.99	ZZZZZ9.99	ZZZ9.99	ZZZZZZZ9.99	99/99/99

TOTAL | | - - - | - - - | ZZZZZZZ9.99 | ZZZZZ9.99 | ZZZ9.99 | ZZZZZZZ9.99

DEBIT ACCOUNTS DISTRIBUTION

ALL NO	AMOUNT
99999999	ZZZZZZ9.99
99999999	ZZZZZZ9.99

FIGURE 3-17 Purchase Journal

71

- Freight charges
- Discount taken
- Net amount payable
- Due date of the invoice

The bottom portion of this report shows a debit accounts distribution for the total purchases of the day. The record of errors detected in this run is saved on a magnetic tape. This tape is used in the next run to create the error list for the Accounts Payable Update Run. Possible errors in this run are of three kinds.

- Vendors master file record is not found. For instance, when the corporation deals with a new vendor, the master record may not have been created yet. This situation can be settled through a maintenance or housekeeping run.
- Invalid field in any of the four input records.
- Inconsistency between the fields of the records of the merchandise ordered (Open Purchase Record), merchandise received (Receiving Record), and merchandise billed (Invoice Record).

All errors, identified by purchase order number or vendor's code, are printed in a report. This report is used by the staff of the control group or internal auditing for follow-up. Examples of these situations are price and terms discrepancies.

DISBURSEMENT RUN

The inputs to this run as shown in Fig. 3-14 are

- Completed Purchase Order File
- Vendors Master File
- Vendors Name and Address File

The Vendors Name and Address File is used primarily for the creation of address labels. The name and address of the parent company (if any) is also available in this file (Fig. 3-7). The main reason for including this data is that some firm might be able to request higher amounts of discount by bulk purchasing from the parent company rather than dealing with the individual subsidiaries.

The outputs of this run are the Check Register Report and the Check Tape.

The Check Register Report is prepared daily and basically used as an audit trail (Fig. 3-18). The contents of this report are as follows:

1. Heading, including the bank account number from which the checks are drawn

2. Check number

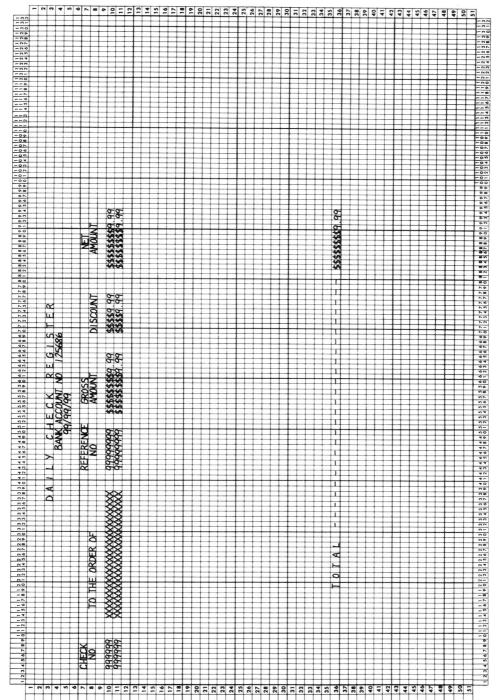

FIGURE 3-18 Daily Check Register

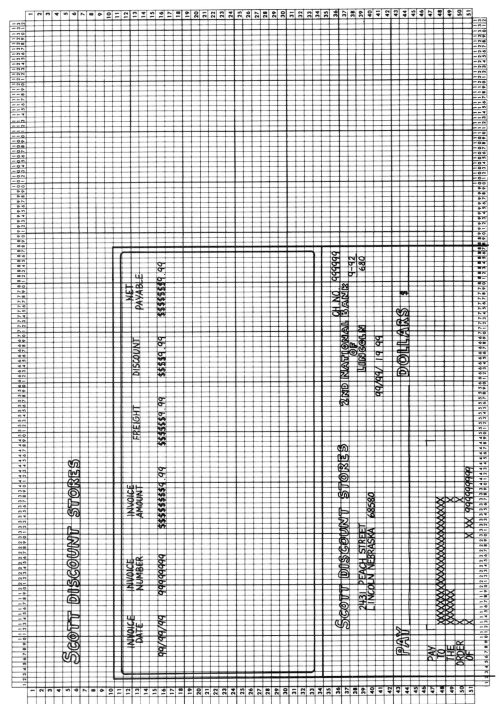

FIGURE 3-19 Checks and Remittance Advice

3. Payee of the check
4. Reference number (In this case, invoice number)
5. Gross amount of invoice
6. Cash discounts taken
7. Net amount of a check
8. Total amount of checks drawn

The Check Tape is used for two purposes. The first is preparation of the checks and remittance advice as shown in Fig. 3-19. Second, it will be used by the system as an input to the Bank Reconciliation Run. The layout of this tape is shown in Fig. 3-20.

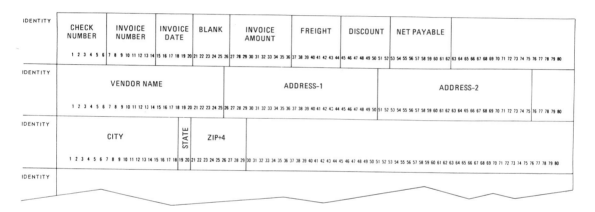

FIGURE 3-20   Layout of Check Tape Files

OTHER RUNS

The following runs, which are shown in Fig. 3-21, constitute an important part of this system:

• Accounts Payable Analysis. A variety of reports are prepared by analyzing the Vendors Master File. (One possible form is shown in Fig. 3-22.)
• Status Report of the Orders. The contents of the Open Purchase Order File are analyzed periodically and the appropriate report is sent to the Purchasing Department.
• Inventory Update. The Receiving File is used to update the Inventory Master File.
• Report on Completed Orders. This report is prepared at the end of every day and sent to the Purchasing Department.

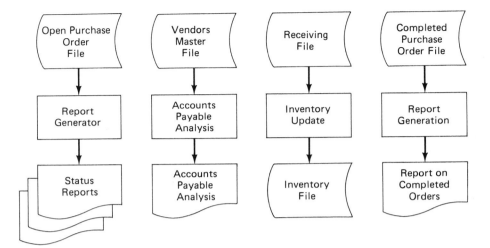

FIGURE 3-21   Various Report Generating Runs

ASSESSMENT OF NEEDED STORAGE

The following are approximations of the storage needed to accommodate the various files of the system described in this case. (See the chapter appendix for details.)

Vendors Name and Address File

This file has fixed-length records. From the file layout and by adding the number of bytes required, we find that the size of the record is 214 bytes.[1] One record is established for each supplier. Scott Discount Stores has 3,500 suppliers; therefore, the file requires 3,500 × 214 = 749,000 bytes.

Purchase Order File

This file has variable-length records. Each record is composed of a fixed-length part, 87 bytes, and a variable-length part. The variable-length part is the result of including a fixed number of bytes (the data about each item which is 47 bytes) and a variable number of times (indicated by the value of the data element "No. of Trailers"). Suppose that, on the average, there are three items per purchase order. This results in records of size 3 × 47 + 87 = 141 + 87 =

---

[1] The number of bytes required seldom agrees with the number of bytes or characters shown in a file layout: *numeric* fields employ the "packed decimal" format, where two digits can often (but not always) be "packed" into one byte.

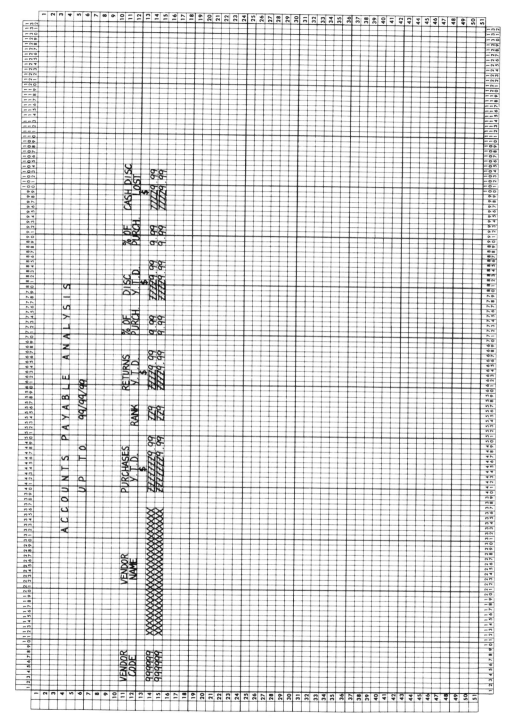

FIGURE 3-22 Accounts Payable Analysis

228 bytes, on the average. Furthermore, suppose that Scott produces 250 purchase orders/day on the average. Hence, $250 \times 228 = 57,000$ bytes/day are required to accommodate this file. The size of the file grows and shrinks from day to day following the addition of new purchase orders and the deletion of old purchase orders which have been invoiced, paid for, and analyzed. Let us assume that Scott needs to keep 30 days worth of purchase order records on file. This assumption yields a file size of $30 \times 57,000 = 1,710,000$ bytes. In order to keep the file from overflowing, the file should be purged and reorganized on a regular basis. More accurate estimates and better assumptions can be formulated when performance data are available.

Invoice File

This file has variable-length records. Each record consists of two parts: a fixed-length part which is 87 bytes long and a variable-length part composed of 47 bytes which appears in the record a variable number of times. The value of the repetition factor is given by the data element No. of Trailers.

The Purchase Order File and Invoice File complement each other; that is, a purchase order generates an invoice and a paid invoice results in the deletion of the corresponding purchase order. Therefore, the same estimates and assumptions may be used to estimate the storage requirements of both files. And hence, the estimated record's size of the Invoice File is $3 \times 47 + 87 = 228$ bytes, and the estimated storage need per day is $250 \times 228 = 57,000$ bytes/day. Finally, the estimated size of the file is $30 \times 57,000 = 1,710,000$ bytes.

This file needs to be purged and reorganized in a similar fashion to the Purchase Order File and with the same frequency.

Receiving Items File

This file has the same structure as the previous two. Its fixed-size component is 37 bytes long; and the length of its repeated part is also 37 bytes. Using the same estimates we have used before—3 items per shipment, 250 shipments per day, and 30 days worth of records—the estimated size of the Receiving Items file is $30 \times (250 \times (3 \times 37 + 37)) = 1,110,000$ bytes.

This file also needs to be purged and reorganized as frequently as the previous two files.

Vendors Master File

The fixed-size part of this record is 98 bytes long. However, the variable-size part has a multiple of 29 bytes component. Assume that, on the average, there are 8 components per record. Therefore, the estimated size of the file is $8 \times 29 + 98 = 330$ bytes; and the estimated size of the file is $3,500 \times 330 = 1,155,000$ bytes. Maintenance operations should be performed on this file regularly so that its size can be kept within bounds.

Completed Purchase Order File

The fixed-size part of this record is 140 bytes long. Suppose that, on the average, there are 3 items per purchase order. This results in a variable-size part of 3 × 52 = 156 bytes long. Therefore, the estimated size of a record is 140 + 156 = 296 bytes. Considering 250 completed purchase orders per day, and 30 days' worth of completed purchase order records, the estimated size of the file is 30 × 250 × 296 = 2,220,000 bytes. It is necessary that this file receive the required purging and reorganization on a regular basis.

Check Tape File

This is a fixed-length record file. Each record is 152 bytes long. One reel of tape is sufficient to hold the file. The file is purged and reorganized on a regular basis such that enough space is maintained for new transactions.

In summary the file storage requirements for this system are as follows:

1. One reel of tape
2. 749,000 + 1,710,000 + 1,710,000 + 1,110,000 + 1,155,000 + 2,220,000 = 8,654,000 bytes or about 8,500 K bytes disk storage

SUMMARY

Management information needs with respect to purchases, accounts receivable, and cash collection have been explained. The list of information suggested is not comprehensive and varies from company to company.

The case developed based on the above applications is somewhat sophisticated. The system has utilized variable-length-format files, thus saving substantially on storage.

Some details of the system, such as screen layout of input, have purposely not been exposed. This will provide ample opportunity for assignment of those parts as a class assignment.

PROBLEMS

1. If Scott Discount Stores decided to computerize the preparation of purchase orders, how would your flowchart change assuming that the initial input to the system is the Requisition Request only?

2. Refer to Fig. 3-8 (Layout of Transactions List Report) and design the layout of the report for the modification (or corrections) of a record.

3. Refer to Fig. 3-8 again and design the layout for the report for the deletion of a record.

4. Design the CRT screen layout for keying invoices into the Invoice File.

5. Discuss and explain the tests that are being used to edit the creation of the Invoice File. (Be specific.)

6. Design the output layout of the Cash Requirement Report that is requested by the Treasurer's Office.

7. Prepare the Status Report Analysis from the Open Purchase Orders File.

8. How would the contents of the Vendors Master File change if the file was on a magnetic tape? (Give a tentative layout of a Vendors Master Record.)

APPENDIX

Vendors Name and Address File Layout

Data Element	Format	Number of Bytes	Notes
Vendor Code	X(6)	6	Numeric code may be used
Vendor Name	X(25)	25	
Address–1	X(25)	25	First address
Address–2	X(25)	25	Second address
City	X(18)	18	
State	X(2)	2	
ZIP+4	X(9)	9	Accommodate new ZIP Code possibility
Name of Parent	X(25)	25	Parent company
Address–1	X(25)	25	
Address–2	X(25)	25	Address of parent company
City	X(18)	18	
State	X(2)	2	
ZIP+4	X(9)	9	
		214 bytes	

Purchase Order File Layout

Data Element	Format	Number of Bytes	Notes
Purchase Order Number	9(6)	4	
Date	X(6)	6	
Vendor Code	X(6)	6	Numeric code may be used
Vendor Name	X(25)	25	
Ship via	X(20)		
F.O.B.	X(17)	17	
Date Shipment Must Be Made	X(6)	6	
Terms	X(6)	6	Discount terms
Blank	X(15)	15	Filler
No. of Trailers	9(3)	2	Number of variable-size parts of the record to follow
		87 bytes	Fixed-length part
Item No.	9(2)	2	
Quantity	9(8)	5	
Unit	X(5)	5	This is the layout for one part of the variable-size trailer
Part Number or material code	X(10)	10	
Description	X(20)	20	
Unit Price	9(8)	5	
		47 bytes	Each trailer

Invoice File Layout

Data Element	Format	Number of Bytes	Notes
Purchase Order Number	9(6)	4	
Vendor Code	X(6)	6	
Vendor Name	X(25)	25	
Invoice Number	X(8)	8	
Invoice Date	X(6)	6	
Gross Amount	9(10)	4	
Tax	9(6)	4	
Freight	9(8)	4	
State Tax Rate	9(3)	4	
Discount Code	X(1)	1	
Debit Amount Number	9(10)	4	
Blank	X(15)	15	Filler
No. of Trailers	9(3)	2	
		87 bytes	Fixed-length part
Item Number	9(2)	2	
Quantity	9(8)	5	
Unit	X(5)	5	This is the layout for one part
Part Number	X(10)	10	of the variable-size trailer
Description	X(20)	20	
Unit Price	9(8)	5	
		47 bytes	Each trailer

Receiving Items File Layout

Data Element	Format	Number of Bytes	Notes
Purchase Order Number	9(6)	4	
Data Received	X(6)	6	
Vendor Name	X(25)	25	
No. of Trailers	9(3)	2	
		37 bytes	Fixed-length part
Item Number	9(2)	2	This is the layout for one
Quantity Received	9(8)	5	part of the variable-size
Via	X(10)	10	trailer
By	X(20)	20	
		37 bytes	Each trailer

Vendors Master File Layout

Data Element	Format	Number of Bytes	Notes
Vendor Code	X(6)	6	
Vendor Name	X(25)	25	
Current Debit	9(10)	6	
YTD Purchases	9(12)	7	
YTD Discounts	9(10)	6	
YTD Return	9(10)	6	
Number of Unpaid Invoices	9(3)	2	
% of Return to Purchase	9(4)	3	
Blank	X(3)	3	Filler
YTD Number of Return	9(3)	2	
YTD Number of Invoice	9(3)	2	
YTD Number of Discount Lost	9(3)	2	
YTD Discount Lost	9(10)	6	
Blank	X(10)	20	Filler
No. of Trailers	9(3)	2	
		98 bytes	Fixed-length part
Trailer Type	X(1)	1 ⎫	This is the layout of the first
Purchase Order Number	9(6)	4 ⎪	of several record types
Invoice Number	X(8)	8 ⎪	found as trailer records.
Invoice Amount	9(8)	5 ⎬	This type is for a purchase
Tax	9(6)	4 ⎪	transaction.
Discount	9(6)	4 ⎪	
Blank	X(3)	3 ⎭	Filler
		29 bytes	Trailer part
Trailer Type	X(1)	1 ⎫	This is the layout of the
Purchase Order Number	9(6)	4 ⎪	second type of trailer.
Check Number	9(6)	4 ⎬	This type is for disburse-
Amount	9(8)	5 ⎪	ment transaction.
Blank	X(15)	15 ⎭	
Trailer Type	X(1)	1 ⎫	This is the layout of the
Purchase Order Number	9(6)	4 ⎪	third type, the debit
Amount	9(8)	5 ⎬	adjustment.
Reference	X(9)	9 ⎪	
Blank	X(10)	10 ⎭	Filler
Trailer Type	X(1)	1 ⎫	This is the layout of the
Purchase Order Number	9(6)	4 ⎪	fourth type, the credit
Amount	9(8)	5 ⎬	adjustment.
Reference	X(9)	9 ⎪	
Blank	X(10)	10 ⎭	Filler

Completed Purchase Order File Layout

Data Element	Format	Number of Bytes	Notes
Purchase Order Number	9(6)	4	
Vendor Code	X(6)	6	
Vendor Name	X(25)	25	
Invoice Number	X(8)	8	
Invoice Date	X(6)	6	
Tax Rate	9(3)	2	
Ship Via	X(20)	20	
Terms	X(6)	6	Discount terms
F.O.B.	X(17)	17	
Date of Shipment	X(6)	6	
Gross Amount	9(10)	6	
Tax	9(6)	4	
Freight	9(8)	5	
Discount	9(8)	5	
Net Payable	9(10)	6	
Due Date	X(6)	6	
Blank	X(6)	6	Filler
No. of Trailers	9(3)	2	
		140 bytes	Fixed-length part
Item Number	9(2)	2	
Quantity	9(8)	5	This is the layout for one
Unit	X(5)	5	part of the variable-size
Part Number	X(10)	10	trailer
Description	X(20)	20	
Blank	X(10)	10	
		52 bytes	

Check Tape File Layout

Data Element	Format	Number of Bytes	Notes
Check Number	X(6)	6	
Invoice Number	X(8)	8	
Invoice Date	X(6)	6	
Blank	X(6)	6	Filler
Invoice Amount	9(10)	6	
Freight	9(8)	5	
Discount	9(8)	5	
Net Payable	9(10)	6	
Vendor Name	X(25)	25	
Address—1	X(25)	25	
Address—2	X(25)	25	
City	X(18)	18	
State	X(2)	2	
ZIP+4	X(9)	9	
		152 bytes	

4 | Design of a System for Inventories

Inventory is one of the most important assets on every balance sheet. Inventory planning and controls are critical activities for merchandising and manufacturing firms. Inventory information systems can be designed with different degrees of sophistication. In systems design, the level of services to be expected from the system must first be established. This level of service may be targeted to the desired satisfaction level of customers. If so, the organization determines the impact of a particular service level on costs. A system can be designed to provide only status reports. Or it may be built to satisfy the information needs of more sophisticated users, by providing system users with advanced modeling techniques.

MANAGEMENT INFORMATION REQUIREMENTS

The management information needs regarding inventory are closely correlated with the firm's philosophy regarding inventory planning and controls. In some firms, the inventory system is a part of a larger system: a logistic system. In other firms, it is considered as a stand-alone system, capable of interacting with other subsystems such as a production subsystem and a purchasing subsystem. Yet, in major companies in Japan that have adapted "just-in-time" inventory systems, no inventory records are maintained. Such systems assume that materials and parts should be received as they are about to be used.[1]

In this chapter the inventory system is considered as a stand-alone system. In this context, the objective of an inventory system is to maintain an adequate supply of items on hand, so as to satisfy the needs of sales and production departments. To implement this objective, a service level of satisfaction must be adopted for a firm. Firms try to avoid overstocking inventory in order to avoid carrying costs; they also must avoid understocking so as not to lose sales. In

---

[1] *Automotive News,* September 6, 1982, p. 36.

short, a firm tries (with an eye on customer service) to minimize the cost of carrying as well as ordering inventories.

The other major subsystems that interact with the inventory subsystems are purchasing and sales. These relationships are established either through physical transfer of goods or through exchange of information between interested departments. Figure 4-1 depicts these relationships.

The task of defining the informational requirements of each of the functional departments involved with inventory systems is difficult. Designing inventory planning and control systems entails many decisions, each of which has a different impact on the organization. At one extreme, inventory decisions have strategic implications. Examples of strategic decisions are those about the types of inventory to be carried and the level of customer service desired. At the other extreme are decisions with operational impact, such as the number of units to be received and issued from a warehouse.

Depending on the nature of decisions to be made in this area, it should be possible, through adequate research, to program some of the decisions. For instance, reordering, economic order quantity, and even vendor selection can easily be programmed into a computerized inventory system.

Generally, the information generated by the inventory system is classified into two major categories: status reports and planning and control reports.

Status Reports

As their name suggests, status reports deal with the state of different aspects of the inventory system. An inventory status report may be any of the following:

• List for each class of inventory, for each vendor, or for any other salient characteristics

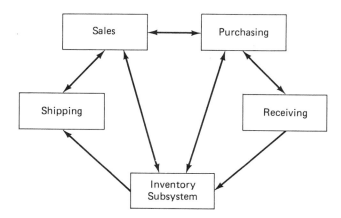

FIGURE 4-1 Relationships of Inventory Subsystem with Other Subsystems

- List of items on order
- List of vendors and value of purchases for each vendor
- Cost list of inventory for use by accounting department
- List of items by spoilage amounts and dates

Planning and Control Reports

The form of planning and control reports differs from one organization to another. Some examples are

- A usage report that provides a basis for determination or modification of economic order quantity of each item
- Ad hoc reports to satisfy the needs of internal auditing
- Various statistical analyses of different items in inventory
- List of overdue orders or items
- List of high-value and low-value items for application of an ABC inventory control system
- List of high-turnover and low-turnover items in inventory, to establish a safe stock policy

Both status reports and planning and control reports are useful to many functional and staff departments within a given organization. For instance, the list of inventory items classified according to the spoilage date is useful to the sales departments. Purchasing departments could use the list of high-turnover or low-turnover items to establish their purchasing strategies.

INTERNAL CONTROLS AND AUDIT IMPLICATIONS

The internal controls are divided into the two categories of general controls and applications controls.

General Controls

The following general controls are considered to be the most important in the area of inventory processing.

- Management authorization of inventory transactions
- Recording of authorized transactions so that financial statements are prepared according to the Generally Accepted Accounting Principles
- Limitation of access to inventories except by authorization of management[2]

---

[2] For further discussion of this control feature refer to AICPA, *Audit Approaches for a Computerized Inventory System* (New York: American Institute of Certified Public Accountants, 1980).

- Establishment of procedures for authorization and review of the master file change report
- Establishment of a policy for backup in case of catastrophe
- Establishment of procedures for reviewing overdue orders
- Establishment of procedures for large purchases from a given vendor

Application Controls

The bulk of inputs to this system is initiated in sales and purchasing subsystems (see Chapters 2 and 3 for a complete list of application controls). The following application controls are the most important controls to be integrated into this system.

- Self-checking digit test for item number, a check performed using modulus 11
- Validity check for all transaction codes
- Completeness tests to check the validity of several selected fields
- Record count of one run when moving on to another run

CASE: Inventory Planning and Control

Lambert Dental Products (LDP) is a medium-size distributor of dental products in Chicago. It receives merchandise from 75 suppliers, mostly manufacturers of the products. Lambert's sells and distributes these products to its customers. Since customers are always interested in the most efficient supplier from price and delivery standpoints, the number of customers who rely on Lambert fluctuates. However, a history of the past five years suggests that LDP serves nearly 500 steady customers. These customers are mainly laboratories and dentists. The total number of orders from all types of customers is nearly 250 in each business day.

The suppliers of Lambert are scattered throughout the United States. The total number of purchase orders is about 50 per day. Merchandise from suppliers is normally shipped to Lambert by the manufacturers' own transportation systems or by nationally recognized parcel companies such as United Parcel Service (UPS).

The number of products carried in the inventory is about 1,000. These products range from the expensive x-ray equipment that is used in dentists' offices to the tools and supplies for daily operations of laboratories and dentists. Many sizes, styles, and colors of teeth account for a large portion of Lambert customer orders.

One of Lambert's problems is the large amount of working capital tied up in inventory. As a result, the company incurs substantial interest expense. A clear need to establish an effective inventory control system for the high-volume, slow-moving dental products is felt throughout the organization.

The company has hired a management consulting firm to help solve the problem. As part of his report, the consultant suggested the establishment of an "800" telephone number for order taking. He also recommended that LDP use UPS to serve remote customers.

From the outset, the consultant realized that the dental field requires prompt order processing and delivery of goods. An effective inventory control system, therefore, must not only smooth out inventories and reduce them to less costly levels, but also allow the company to satisfy its customers' needs more promptly.

The system proposed by the consultant is discussed in three parts: issue of inventories, adding to inventories, and inventory file maintenance procedures.

ISSUE OF INVENTORIES

Order Taking

Customers' orders arrive three different ways: by telephone, by sales representative, and by mail (customers' purchase orders). At the onset, the orders are classified into two groups; old customers' orders and new customers' orders. When a new customer order is not prepaid or C.O.D., it is automatically sent to the Credit Department. Flow of the order entry process is shown in Fig. 4-2.

The Credit Department makes a routine credit check on each prospective new customer. If the credit risk is acceptable, the order enters the system and a new account number is generated. Otherwise, the customer is notified of the Credit Department's decision immediately.

As they arrive, the orders are entered into the system through an intelligent terminal. The data entry is menu driven. The proper menu for this run is called and the following data are entered.

1. Customer name
2. Date
3. Customer number
4. Customer purchase order number (if applicable)
5. Item number
6. Description of the item ordered
7. Number of units ordered
8. Transaction code (if applicable)
9. Sales representative's code
10. Shipping cost
11. Order code (method of ordering; see next subsection)

Layout of the screen for this menu is shown in Fig. 4-3. In case the item number is not included in a customer's order, the data entry clerk must look at

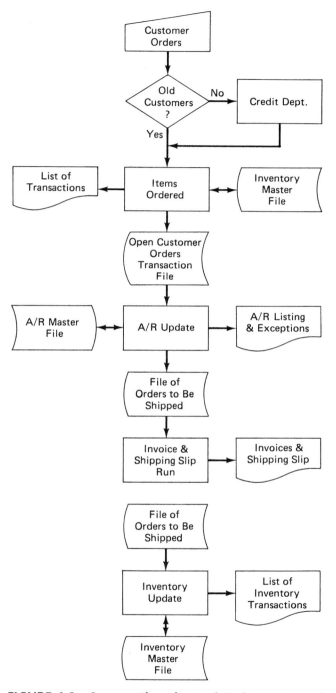

FIGURE 4-2 System Flowchart of Order Entry and Inventory Update Run

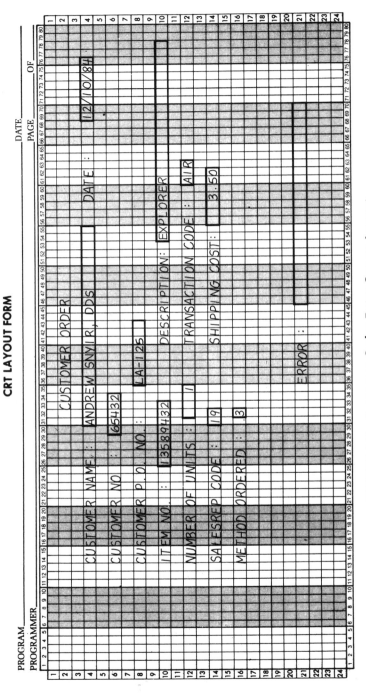

FIGURE 4-3 Customer Order Entry Screen Layout

Lambert's Directory of Products to find the appropriate code. The code is extremely important, because the Inventory Master File uses this field as the primary key.

Moreover, Lambert has developed a standard shipping cost list for different classes of the products. By referring to this list, the operator figures the shipping cost for each order and enters it into the system.

The inventory system is interactive. That is, prior to creating any transaction record, the data entry program searches the Inventory Master File to see if the products ordered are available. If an item is available, the number of units ordered are added to the "quantity on hold" field. The transaction record is created and the order is processed further through the system. Layout of the Inventory Master File is shown in Fig. 4-4. This file is fixed-length and is indexed sequentially.

In case an item is not available, the customer is asked about the possibility of back-ordering. The operator will also create a record for this type of order if the customer agrees to back-order. Therefore, for every order entered a record is created. The file for these records is referred to as the Open Customer Order Transaction File.

In order to create a record in the Open Customer Order Transaction File, part of the data must be entered by the order entry clerk, and part of the data are copied from the Inventory Master File. The field that is copied from the Inventory Master File is "Unit Price," the unit sale price of each item. This field is included to facilitate billing. Layout of the Open Customer Order Transaction File is shown in Fig. 4-5.

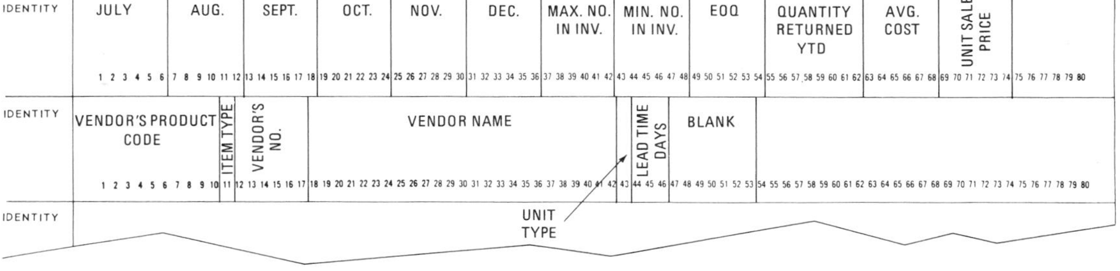

IDENTITY	ITEM NO.	DESCRIPTION	AVAIL.	QUANTITY ON HAND	QUANTITY ON HOLD	QUANTITY ON ORDER	JAN.	FEB.	MAR.	APR.	MAY

IDENTITY	JUNE	JULY	AUG.	SEPT.	OCT.	NOV.	DEC.	QUANTITY SOLD JAN.	FEB.	MAR.	APR.	MAY	JUNE

IDENTITY	JULY	AUG.	SEPT.	OCT.	NOV.	DEC.	MAX. NO. IN INV.	MIN. NO. IN INV.	EOQ	QUANTITY RETURNED YTD	AVG. COST	UNIT SALE PRICE

IDENTITY	VENDOR'S PRODUCT CODE	ITEM TYPE	VENDOR'S NO.	VENDOR NAME	LEAD TIME DAYS	BLANK

IDENTITY				UNIT TYPE

FIGURE 4-4 Layout of Inventory Master File

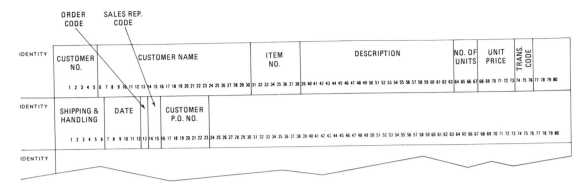

FIGURE 4-5 Layout of Open Customer Order Transaction File

Edit Process

The edit process is <u>front end</u>. That is, any error is detected immediately, while the data are being entered. Tests performed by the computer on various fields of each record are as follows:

Test	Field
1. Self-checking digit	Customer number
2. Self-checking digit	Item number
3. Limit test	Number of units (ordered)
4. Validity	Transaction code
5. Validity	Sales representative's code
6. <u>Consistency</u>	All data fields
7. Completeness	All records
8. Validity	Order code
	Code 1 = Telephone order
	Code 2 = Customer purchase order
	Code 3 = Sales representative

One of the important features of this system is utilization of a transaction code. This code consists of three characters. The first and third characters are alphabetic. The second character is numeric. The following is a list of the options available:

Code A = Customer order (first character)
    1 = In stock (second character)
      R = On account (receivable) (third character)
      C = C.O.D. (cash on delivery) (third)
    2 = Back-order (second)
      R = On account
      C = C.O.D.

$$
\begin{array}{lll}
\text{Code B} = \text{Customer returns} & \text{(first)} \\
\text{O} = \text{(not used)} & \text{(second)} \\
\text{R} = \text{On account} & \text{(third)} \\
\text{C} = \text{C.O.D.}
\end{array}
$$

In this coding scheme, Code "A1C" indicates the state of a "customer order": that the item ordered is available (in stock) and it is on a cash basis. Because of the importance of this code to future runs, the validity checks of this field are a major feature of the front-end editing during data entry. Any type of error is reflected on the screen immediately. The data entry clerk can thus correct errors promptly.

The outputs of the edit process are the List of Transactions and the Open Customer Order Transaction File.

The List of Sales Entry Transactions, which also serves as audit trail, is output to the printer. This list, shown in Fig. 4-6, has the following fields.

1. Customer number
2. Customer name
3. Customer purchase order number
4. Item number
5. Description of an item
6. Number of units
7. Unit price
8. Transaction code
9. Shipping cost
10. Sales representative's code
11. Method of payment
12. Order code (method of ordering)

The Open Customer Transaction File (Fig. 4-5), the other output of the data entry process, is run against the Inventory Master File at the end of each day. The purpose of this run is to find out about availability of goods on back-order.[3] As soon as goods on back-order become available, the appropriate status (transaction) code is changed for the "Transaction Code" field. That is, the second character in this field is changed from Code "2" to Code "1."

Accounts Receivable Update

The next step in the inventory update process (see Fig. 4-2) is updating accounts receivable. The inputs to this run are the Open Customer Order Transaction File and the Accounts Receivable Master File.

---

[3] Additions to the Inventory Master File are possible through other computer runs to be discussed later in this chapter. Merchandise not available yesterday may be available today as a result of such additions.

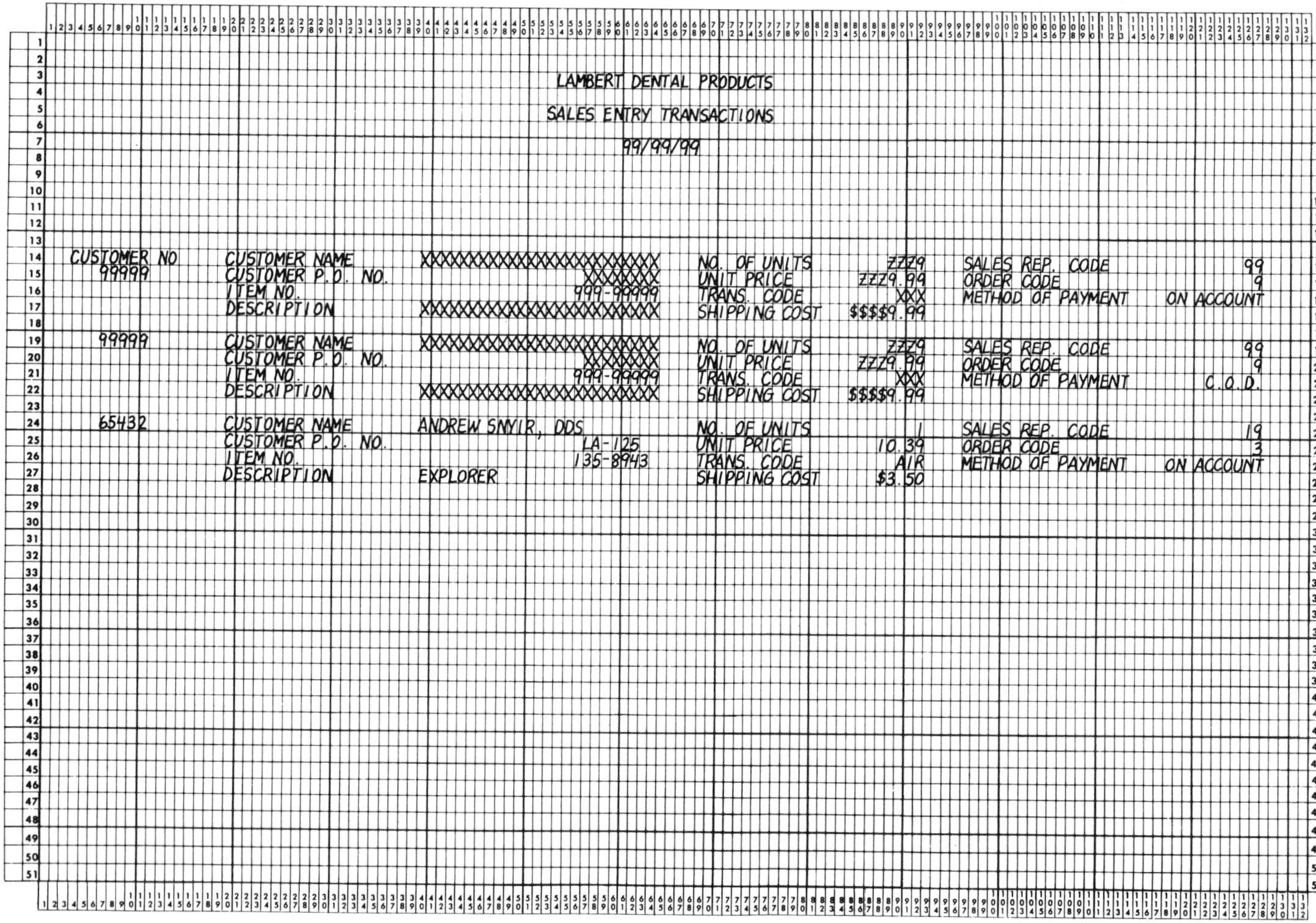
LAMBERT DENTAL PRODUCTS
SALES ENTRY TRANSACTIONS
99/99/99
CUSTOMER NO
99999
CUSTOMER NAME XXXXXXXXXXXXXXXXXXXXXXXXX NO. OF UNITS ZZZ9 SALES REP. CODE 99
CUSTOMER P.O. NO. XXXXXXX UNIT PRICE ZZZ9.99 ORDER CODE 9
ITEM NO. 999-99999 TRANS. CODE XXX METHOD OF PAYMENT ON ACCOUNT
DESCRIPTION XXXXXXXXXXXXXXXXXXXXXXXXX SHIPPING COST $$$$9.99
99999
CUSTOMER NAME XXXXXXXXXXXXXXXXXXXXXXXXX NO. OF UNITS ZZZ9 SALES REP. CODE 99
CUSTOMER P.O. NO. XXXXXXX UNIT PRICE ZZZ9.99 ORDER CODE 9
ITEM NO. 999-99999 TRANS. CODE XXX METHOD OF PAYMENT C.O.D.
DESCRIPTION XXXXXXXXXXXXXXXXXXXXXXXXX SHIPPING COST $$$$9.99
65432
CUSTOMER NAME ANDREW SNYIR, DDS NO. OF UNITS 1 SALES REP. CODE 19
CUSTOMER P.O. NO. LA-125 UNIT PRICE 10.39 ORDER CODE 3
ITEM NO. 135-8943 TRANS. CODE AIR METHOD OF PAYMENT ON ACCOUNT
DESCRIPTION EXPLORER SHIPPING COST $3.50

FIGURE 4-6 Sales Entry Transactions

For those orders where a proper code is found in the Transaction Code field, the accounts receivable master records are called in and are updated. The proper code in this case is "A1R," which identifies customer orders for which merchandise is available and which are "on account."

The Accounts Receivable Master File is a variable-length file with fixed-length trailers. For each type of transaction involving Accounts Receivable, one trailer is produced. Thus each record may have four types of trailers—that is, purchases on account, payments, debit adjustments, and credit adjustments. The format of this file is shown in Figs. 4-7 and 4-8.

The outputs of this run are the Updated Accounts Receivable Master File, the Accounts Receivable Listing and Exceptions, and the File of Orders to be Shipped. The Updated Accounts Receivable Master File is used to create the aging schedule and other related reports.

The Accounts Receivable Listing serves as a sales journal and at the same time is used for audit trail purposes. This type of report is useful in recovery of destroyed (crashed) files in catastrophic situations.

The layout of this report is shown in Fig. 4-9. This report consists of two parts. The first part is the list of accounts receivable that have been updated.

It is possible for an erroneous transaction to pass the Edit Run without being detected. In this case, one or more of the fields in the Open Customer Order Transaction File or Accounts Receivable Master File might be in error. An error at this stage is reflected in an inconsistency between the two files. This situation is shown in the Remarks column of this report and suggests that, for example, a master file record was not located for a given record.

The second part of the report consists of the list of all C.O.D. transactions. This

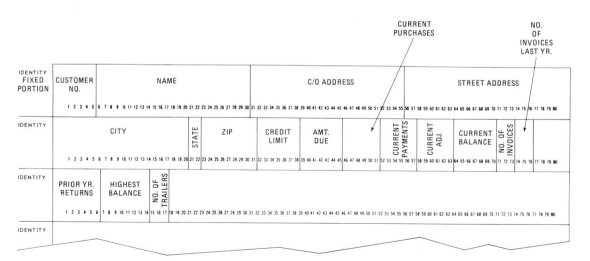

**FIGURE 4-7 Layout of Accounts Receivable Master File—
Fixed Portion**

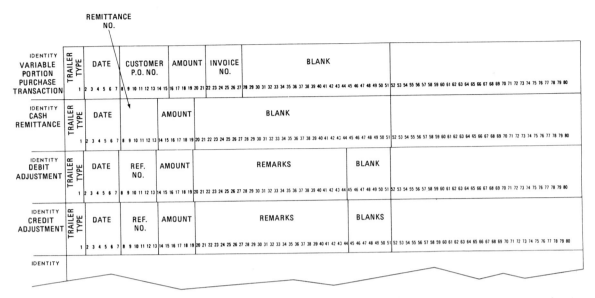

FIGURE 4-8 **Layout of Accounts Receivable Master File—
Variable Portion (Trailers)**

list is used as a control tool to verify the collection of cash. The contents of this report are

1. Customer number
2. Customer name
3. Customer purchase order number
4. Sales representative's code
5. Debit amount
6. Credit amount
7. Remarks
8. List of C.O.D. transactions
   a. Customer number
   b. Customer name and address
   c. C.O.D. amount

The last output of this run is a file of transactions that are to be processed further (see Fig. 4-2). This File of Orders to Be Shipped is used in future runs to print invoices and shipping orders. It is also used to update the Inventory Master File. Therefore, its contents are those data which are needed to update the master file and print invoices and shipping orders.

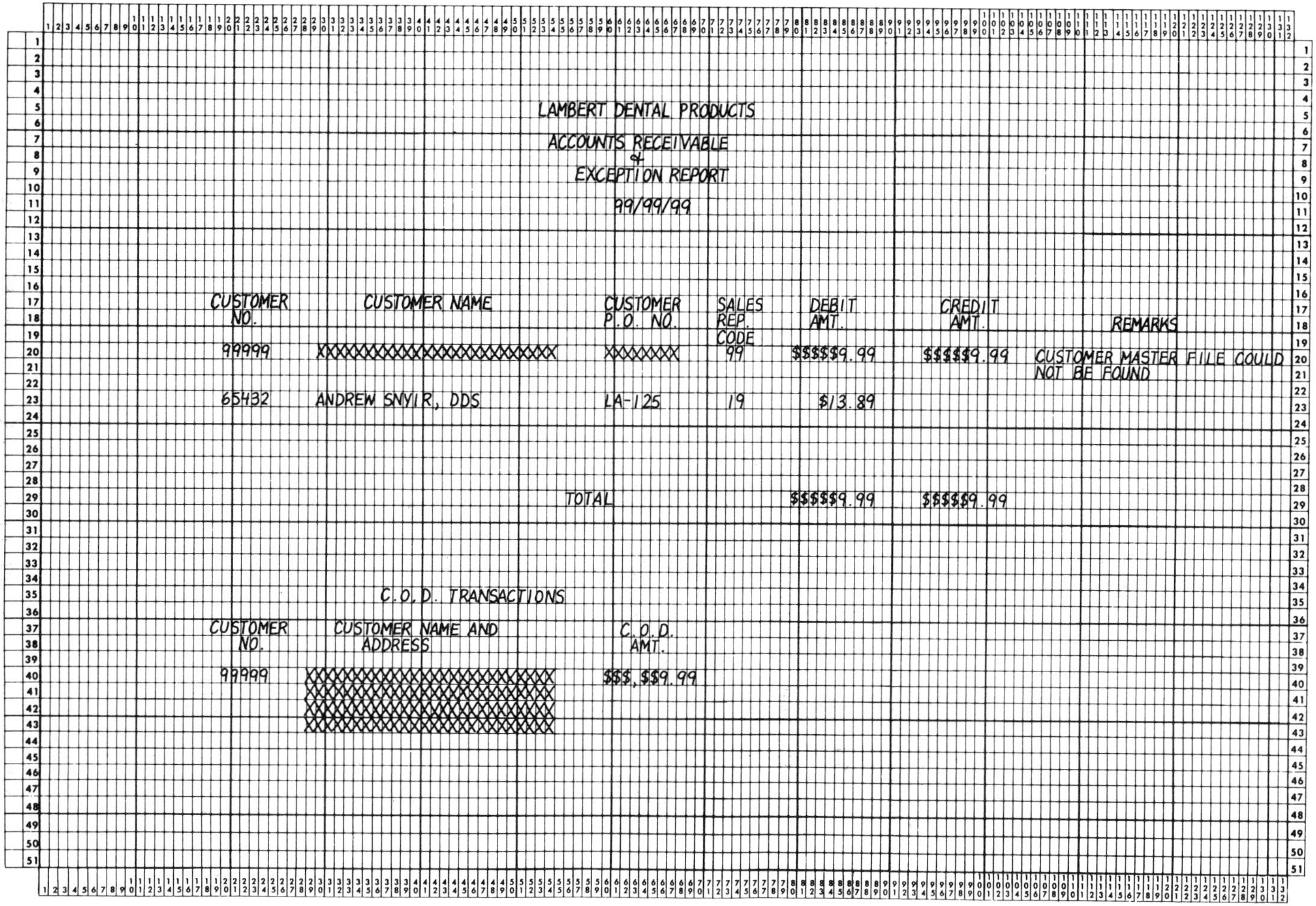

LAMBERT DENTAL PRODUCTS

ACCOUNTS RECEIVABLE
&
EXCEPTION REPORT

99/99/99

CUSTOMER NO.	CUSTOMER NAME	CUSTOMER P.O. NO.	SALES REP. CODE	DEBIT AMT.	CREDIT AMT.	REMARKS
99999	XXXXXXXXXXXXXXXXXXXX	XXXXXXX	99	$$$$$9.99	$$$$$9.99	CUSTOMER MASTER FILE COULD NOT BE FOUND
65432	ANDREW SWIR, DDS	LA-125	19	$13.89		
TOTAL				$$$$$9.99	$$$$$9.99	

C.O.D. TRANSACTIONS

CUSTOMER NO.	CUSTOMER NAME AND ADDRESS	C.O.D. AMT.
99999		$$$,$$9.99

FIGURE 4-9 Output Layout of Accounts Receivable and Exception Report

This file is fixed-length and organized on disk. Its format is shown in Fig. 4-10 and its contents are

1. Item number
2. Description
3. Number of units
4. Customer number
5. Customer name
6. Customer address
7. Transaction code
8. Unit price
9. Amount
10. Tax
11. Subtotal
12. Shipping cost
13. Total
14. Invoice date
15. Routing
16. Customer purchase order number
17. Sales representative's code
18. Order code (method of ordering)

As you can observe, each record in this file is created by combining the selected data fields of the Open Customer Order Transactions File and Accounts Receivable Master File. For instance, the fields "Number of Units Ordered" and "Cus-

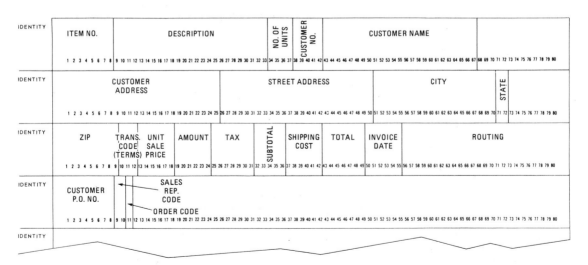

FIGURE 4-10   Layout of File of Orders to Be Shipped

tomer Number'' are copied from the first file, while the customer address fields are copied from the Accounts Receivable Master File.

This newly created file is added to the cumulative file of the transactions. There are three cumulative transaction files, weekly, monthly, and yearly, from which different cumulative reports are prepared. This phase of the process is not shown in the flowchart (Fig. 4-2). The cumulative files play an important role in maintaining an effective audit trail. These files are used to recreate files that might have been destroyed by accident. Therefore, they are part of a backup procedure for this segment of the process.

Invoices and Shipping Slips Run

The File of Orders to be Shipped includes all the necessary information to print the invoices and shipping slips. The invoices are printed on preprinted and prenumbered forms. Prenumbering is done to satisfy one of the main internal controls criteria regarding protection of documents from unauthorized use. The layout of the invoice is shown in Fig. 4-11. This form is multicopy. The last copy of this form is used as a shipping slip. The layout of the latter is shown in Fig. 4-12. It should be noted that the columns used for unit price or total prices are blanked. This is another internal control feature that should be observed.

Furthermore, some statistical analysis of the number of records processed and printed is provided in the form of ''record count'' test. This, in turn, is another internal control feature of the system; it provides assurance that all the records in the file have been printed.

Inventory Update Run

This run concludes the process shown in the bottom part of Fig. 4-2. The inputs to this run are the File of Orders to Be Shipped and the Inventory Master File. The outputs of this run are the Updated Inventory Master File and the Inventory Issue Report.

The Inventory Master File, whose layout was shown in Fig. 4-4, is indexed-sequential and organized on disk. The primary key for this file is the ''Item Number'' field. It also uses ''Availability,'' ''Item Type,'' ''Vendor Number,'' and ''Vendor Name'' fields as secondary keys.

The primary key consists of eight digits. The first three digits are used to show the location of an item in the stock room. The first digit indicates the aisle number, the second digit is used for shelf number, and the third digit represents the bin number.

The other five digits are used for coding of the goods according to prespecified guidelines. In all printed outputs, the ''Item Number'' field is broken down into a three-digit and a five-digit code, for example, 423-85943.

The Availability code is used for flagging the items that may be unavailable either currently or permanently. The importance of this field is noticed at the ordering step; if a given item is not available, it is pointless to send the orders

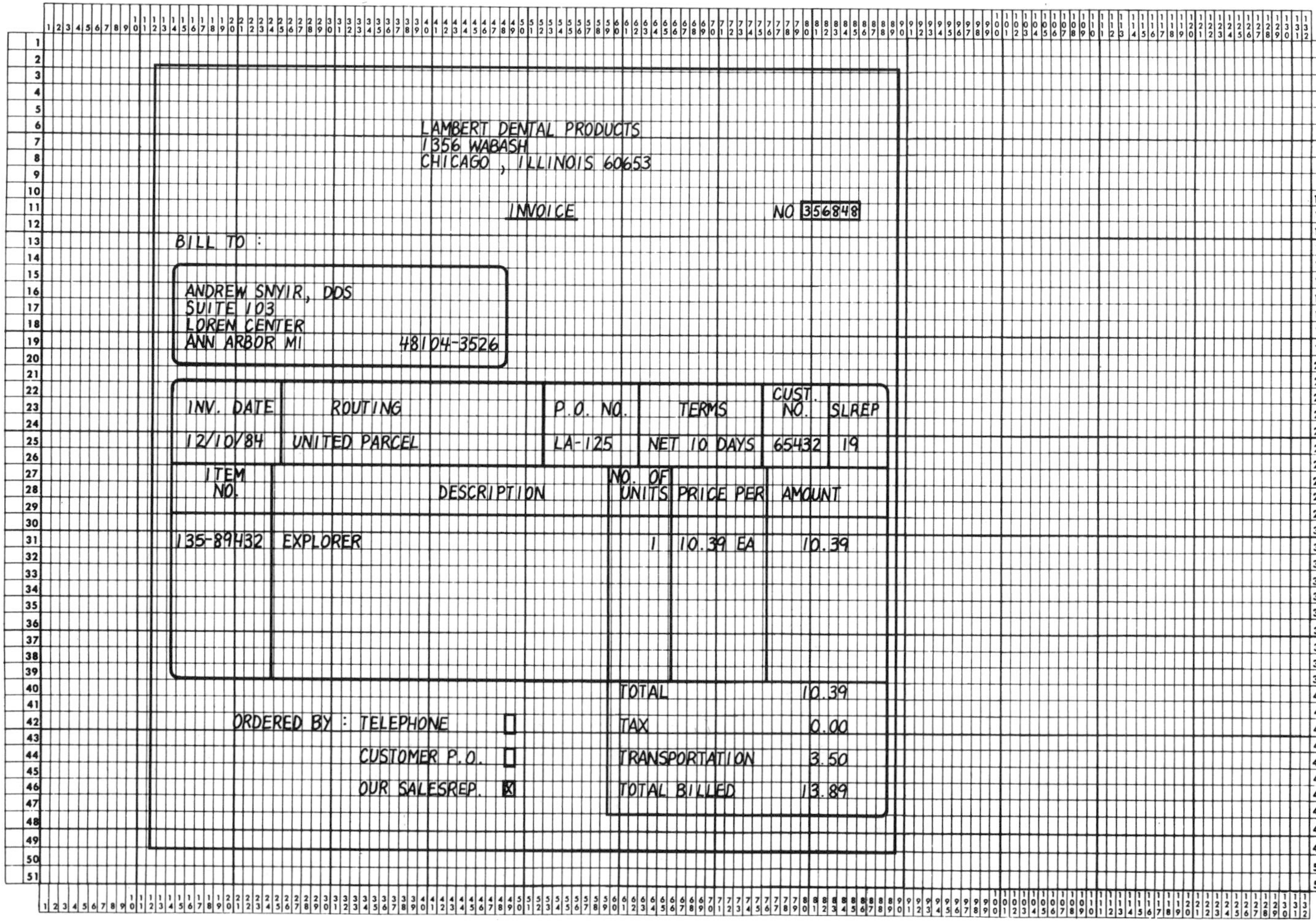

FIGURE 4-11 Output Layout of Invoice

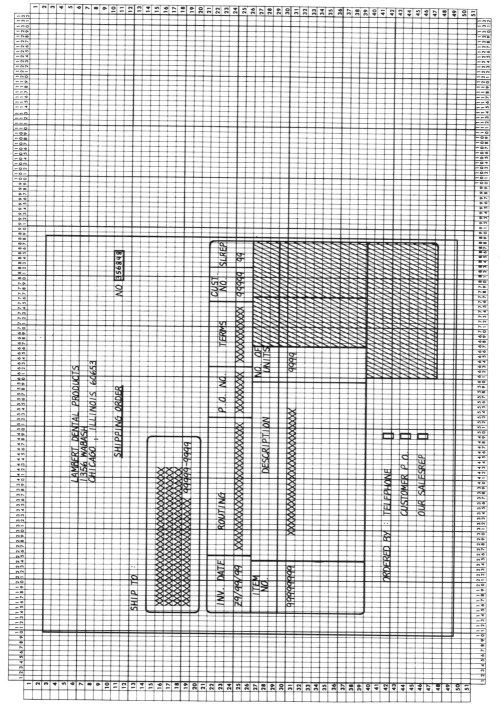

FIGURE 4-12 Output Layout of Shipping Order

for that particular item into the system. In this case, the customers may want to use an alternative product that might be available.

The Item Type field represents different classes of goods in the inventories. Lambert has divided all of its inventories into the three classes of Dental Products, Supplies, and Equipment. Therefore, the appropriate valid codes for this field are "D", "S", and "E". The field "Unit Type" is used for measurement of the goods. In this field, Code "1" refers to the goods sold by weight (lb.) and Code "2" refers to items sold by unit.

In order to provide accurate information about the ordering and sales, a field is used to record the number of units sold or ordered in each of the twelve months (refer to Fig. 4-4). This type of file organization allows the preparation of year-to-date type of reports.

The inventory costing method utilized by Lambert is weighted average costing. That is a unit average cost calculated anytime a new shipment is added to the inventory. This point is discussed further in this chapter.

Other fields that are important for strategic decisions are

- Quantity on hand
- Quantity on hold
- Maximum number allowed
- Minimum number to be carried
- Economic order quantity (EOQ)
- Vendor product code
- Lead time
- Vendor name

It was mentioned earlier in this chapter that as soon as a customer order is processed, the quantity is added to the field "Quantity on Hold." In the update run, since the order has already been filled, a "hold" must be removed. Therefore, the "Number of Units" field in the customer order is added to the "Quantity Sold" field, and subtracted from "Quantity on Hold" and "Quantity on Hand" fields.

The ordering process of the goods to replenish the inventory is based on economic order quantity. The EOQ for each item is calculated and stored in the master file, when a master record has been created for the first time in the Inventory Master File.

The other output of this run is the Inventory Issue Report. The following data items are reflected on this report.

1. Item number
2. Item description
3. Number of items issued
4. Cost per pound or unit
5. Total

The layout of this report is shown in Fig. 4-13. This report is used as a journal for all the items issued from the inventory. The "total" figure in this report is used to record the credit entry of the inventory account in the general ledger.

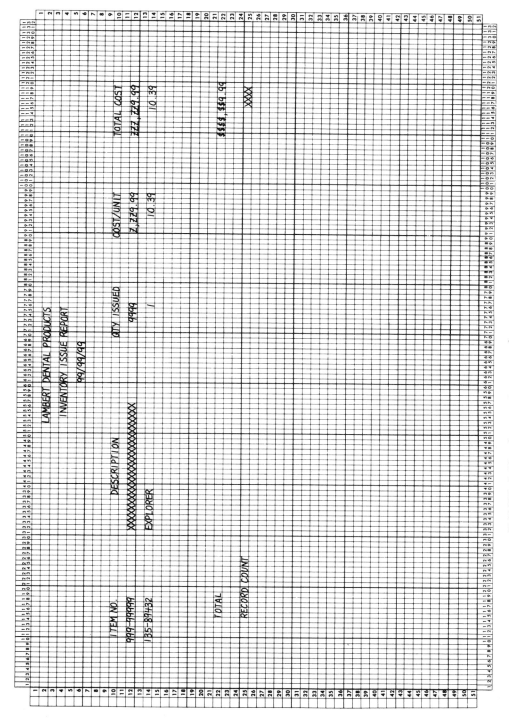

FIGURE 4-13 Output Layout of Inventory Issue Report

It is possible for some of the errors committed at the data entry stage to go this far into the system. In this case, an appropriate message is created to highlight such errors. These types of messages could be recorded on an auxiliary disk unit, and be printed later when the printer unit becomes available.

Moreover, the record count of the inventory records updated is provided, so that inconsistencies between the number of records processed from the transaction file and the number of records updated in the Inventory Master File are highlighted.

ADDING TO THE INVENTORIES

This part of the system handles the addition to the inventory file as a result of purchase of goods or customer returns.

Creating the Transaction File

All goods, including customer returns, must pass through the receiving dock. The goods must be inspected first. The objective of inspection is twofold. First, the quality and condition of the new products are controlled. Second, the reason for merchandise returns is determined. After inspection, the receiving clerk enters the appropriate information into the computer terminal.

To enter the data, the clerk normally uses three sources: (1) the directory of the products which includes all the product codes (Item Number), (2) a copy of the Lambert Purchase Order Form sent earlier, and (3) the packing slip of the seller. Based on these three sources, the clerk is able to enter the appropriate information into the system.

The data entry process is similar to the process discussed earlier in this chapter. After the proper menu is called by the clerk, the data are entered according to the screen format. This phase of the process is also front-end edited; that is, the clerk corrects the erroneous data as soon as they are discovered. The tests designed for this step are as follows:

Test	Field
1. Self-checking digit	Item number
2. Validity	Transaction code
	Code 1 = Purchase
	Code 2 = Customer return
3. Consistency	All data fields
4. Completeness	All records

The outputs of this run as they are indicated in the flowchart (Fig. 4-14) are the Goods Received Transactions File and Receiving Reports.

The Transaction File of Goods Received is organized on disk and has a fixed-length format. The primary key of this indexed-sequential file is the Item Num-

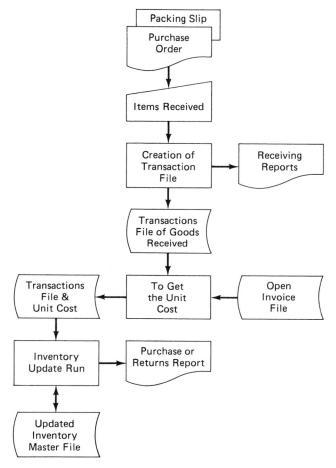

FIGURE 4-14   Flowchart of Receiving of Goods

ber field. The Date and the Transaction Code fields could be used as secondary access keys. The layout of this file is shown in Fig. 4-15. The fields included in each record are

1. Item number
2. Description of item
3. Name of supplier
4. Purchase order number
5. Number of units received
6. Number of units damaged or unacceptable
7. Date
8. Transaction code
9. Reason for returning the merchandise

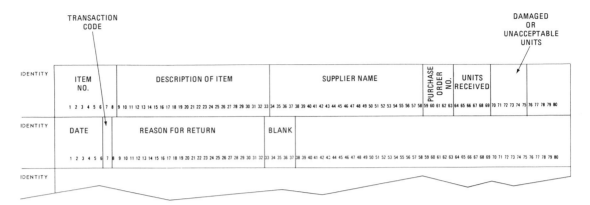

FIGURE 4-15   Layout of Receiving Transaction File

In some instances, all or part of a batch of goods might be damaged. In this situation, the appropriate field in the record (Damaged or Unacceptable Units) should be created. For example, if two units in a batch of 10 units are damaged, the number "10" is entered in the "Units Received" field and number "2" is recorded in the field Damaged or Unacceptable Units.

Furthermore, since the receiving clerk records the reason for returned merchandise, the information collected at this stage could have an impact on future supplier selection.

The other output of this run is the Receiving Report. The form used at this stage is preprinted and prenumbered. The form is a multicopy form and usually must be signed by a receiving clerk or the supervisor of the receiving dock. The signed copies are distributed to various departments such as Accounts Payable and Purchasing. The output layout of this form is shown in Fig. 4-16.

Completing the Transaction File

To update the Inventory Master File, the transactions file created in the previous run must be run against the master file. However, Fig. 4-15 indicates the unit cost is not recorded as part of the receiving process. Therefore, to add the unit cost figure to this file, the file of goods received must be run against the Open Invoice File.

The Open Invoice File is a file created from all invoices received from the suppliers. This file is an integral part of the accounts payable system. A suggested format for this file is illustrated in Chapter 3.

The inputs to this run are the Transaction File of Goods Received and the Open Invoice File. The output of this run is the Transaction File with unit costs added to it. In order to cover the shipping and handling costs, the unit cost figure is retrieved from the Open Invoice File and after being increased by 10 percent of the unit cost, the resulting figure is stored on the newly created transaction file. The format of the new Transaction File is shown in Fig. 4-17.

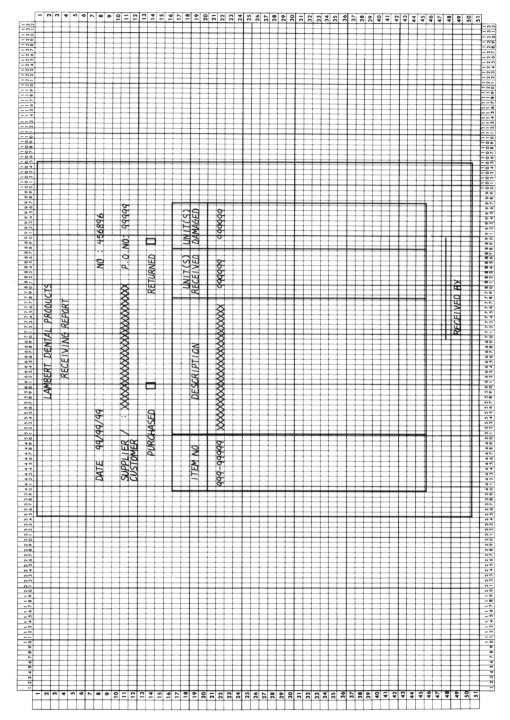

FIGURE 4-16 Output Layout of Receiving Report

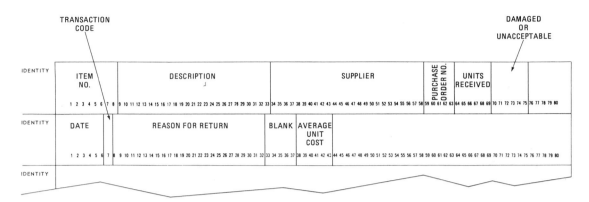

FIGURE 4-17   Layout of Receiving Transaction File after Adding Unit Cost

It should be mentioned that the new transaction file for items received, in addition to the Open Invoice File, is used to update the accounts payable master file. Details are discussed in Chapter 3.

Inventory Update Run

The inputs to this run are the Transaction File from receiving activities and the Inventory Master File. The layout of the Inventory Master File is shown in Fig. 4-4. The outputs of this update run are an Updated Inventory File and a Purchases/Returns Report.

The computer program of this run calculates a new average unit cost anytime a new item is purchased. The new unit average cost replaces the old unit average cost in the Inventory Master Record. For records indicating a customer return, no unit cost is found in the records; therefore, as the new average need not be calculated, the old unit cost field in the master file remains unchanged. The number of units in each transaction record is simultaneously added to the "Quantity on Hand" field and subtracted from the "Quantity on Order" field.

The other output of this run is the Purchases/Returns Report. This report serves the purpose of a journal. The fields in the report are

1. Item number
2. Description of item
3. Supplier name
4. Purchase order number
5. Number of units received
6. Number of units damaged
7. Remarks[4]

The output layout of this report is shown in Fig. 4-18.

---

[4] This field indicates the customer's reason for returning merchandise.

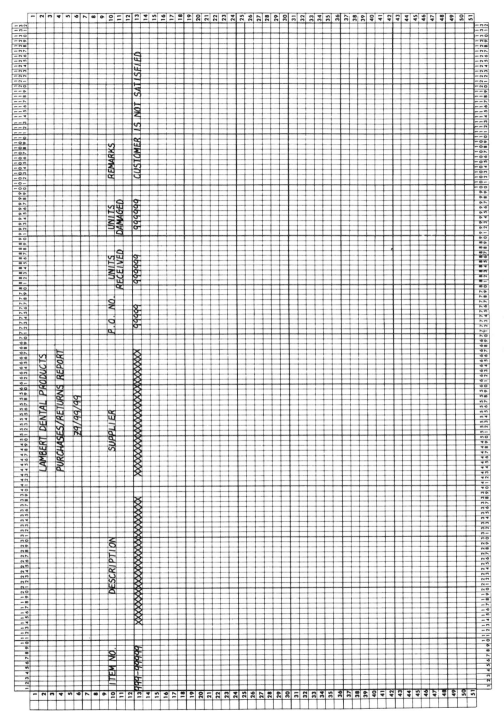

FIGURE 4-18 Output Layout of Purchases/Returns Report

After completion of the update run, the weekly, monthly, and yearly cumulative transaction files are created and the transaction file is saved for at least one week for backup purposes. This is an essential procedure for recovery of a destroyed file.

Purchase Order Run

The purchase order run is one of the routines that is handled at the end of each day. The flowchart of this run is shown in Fig. 4-19.

The inputs to this run are the Inventory Master File and the Vendor Name and Address File. Based on the data on each master record, the reorder point is determined. The program of this run compares "Quantity on Hand," "Quantity on Order," "Quantity on Hold," "Maximum Number in Inventory," "Minimum Number in Inventory," and "Economic Order Quantity" fields, and calculates the quantity that should be ordered. Since the vendor's code is part of the Inventory Master File, the vendor's address is retrieved from the Vendor Name and Address File. The format of this file is illustrated in Fig. 3-7 in Chapter 3.

The outputs of this run are the Open Purchase Order File and purchase orders.

The Open Purchase Order File is used to update the accounts payable file. A suggested format for this file is shown in Fig. 3-7 in Chapter 3.

The purchase order form is preprinted, prenumbered, and is prepared in multicopy. The layout of this form is shown in Fig. 4-20. It should be emphasized that this form must be signed by an authorized individual before being mailed to the vendor. In some computer facilities, a stamp of the authorized signature is mounted on the printer and the process of authorization is done automatically. However, protection of the signature stamp is another internal control matter that ought to be noticed.

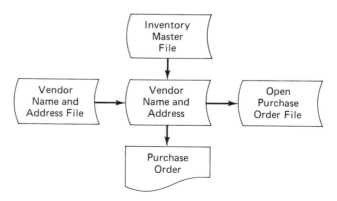

FIGURE 4-19   Flowchart of Purchase Order Run

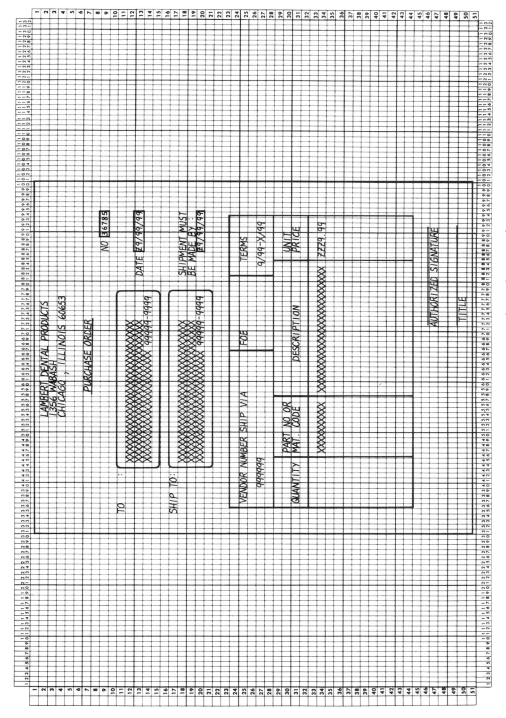

FIGURE 4-20 Output Layout of Purchase Order

113

INVENTORY FILE MAINTENANCE PROCEDURES

This run, an important part of the system, is done in Lambert at the end of each week. The flowchart of this run is shown in Fig. 4-21.

Similar to any other maintenance run, the authorization of the changes is the most important initial step. A special form (Request for Inventory Master File Change) is used (Fig. 4-22). The data that are included in this form are

1. Item number (primary key of the Inventory Master File)
2. Transaction code
3. Old value of the field
4. New value of the field

This form must be signed and dated by both requesting party and authorization party. Then, as illustrated in the flowchart, they are entered into the system.

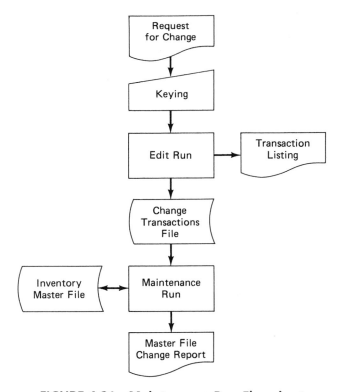

FIGURE 4-21   Maintenance Run Flowchart

Request for Inventory Master File Change

Item Number | 2 | 3 | 5 | – | 8 | 6 | 2 | 3 | 5 |

Transaction Code | 0 | 3 |

Field Old Value   X – R A Y   F I L M

Field New Value   X – R A Y   L I Q U I D

John Hall   12/01/84
Requested by/Date

Mark Morsfield   12/01/84
Authorized by/Date

FIGURE 4-22 Request for Inventory Master File Change Report

The editing during data entry automatically performs the following tests on each field:

Type of Test	Field
1. Self-check digit	Item number
2. Validity	Transaction code
3. Consistency	Old and new value of the field based on the transaction code

The reports of the transactions listing for the edit run on the Master File Change Report must be reviewed by an authorized individual[5] and any deviation from the authorized changes must be investigated. The output layout for transaction listing is not shown. If you are interested in the layout, look at similar designs in other chapters of this text.

The layout of the Maintenance Transaction File is shown in Fig. 4-23. This file is indexed-sequential and has a fixed-length format.

FIGURE 4-23   Layout of Maintenance Transaction File

The outputs of this run are the Updated Inventory Master File and the Master File Change Report.

The layout of the Master File Change Report is shown in Fig. 4-24. Note that, from lines 16 through 28, the entire contents of a record are to be dumped on the printer. If preferred, only the value of the field before and after the change is printed, as shown for the second item in lines 31 and 32.

ASSESSMENT OF NEEDED STORAGE

In this section the storage needed to accommodate each of the files is computed. These computations are at best approximations to the actual storage needed when a real system is implemented. However, this discussion provides a method that can be used or modified for assessing needed storage of similar systems. (See the chapter appendix for details.)

Inventory Master File

This file has fixed-length records. From the file layout and by adding the number of bytes required, we find that the size of the record is 134 bytes. One record is established for each item in inventory. Lambert Dental Products keeps 1,000 items in its inventory; therefore, this file requires 1,000 × 134 = 134,000 bytes.

---

[5] An alternative in some firms is an internal auditing staff.

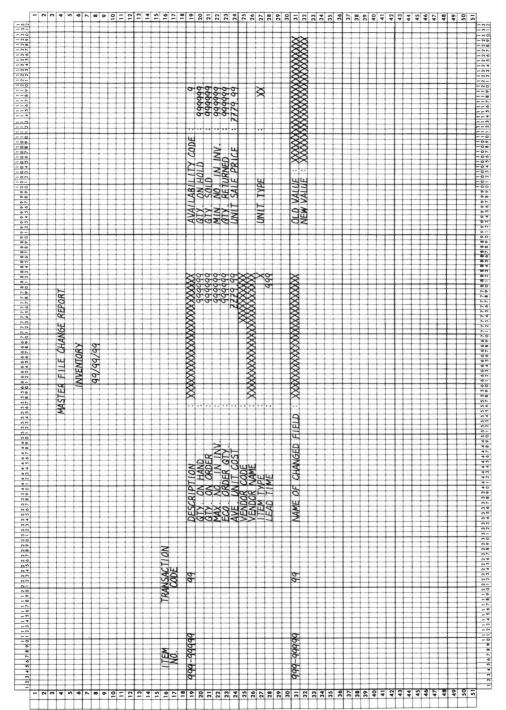

FIGURE 4-24 Output Layout of Master File Change Report

117

Open Customer Order Transaction File

This file has fixed-length records. Each customer transaction requires one record. On the average there are 250 orders per day. From the file layout and by adding the number of bytes required to store the various data elements, we find that the size of each record is 89 bytes. Therefore, the estimated size of this file is $250 \times 89 = 22,250$ bytes.

Accounts Receivable Master File

This file has variable-length records. Each record is composed of a fixed-length part, 144 bytes; and a variable-length part. The variable-length part is the result of including a fixed number of bytes (the data about the various types of transactions) which is 47 bytes in length, a variable number of times (indicated by the value of the data element "No. of Trailers"). Every record may use all four different types of transactions while it is kept in the system. Suppose that, on the average, every type of transaction is used three times. This results in records of size $3 \times 4 \times 47 + 144 = 708$ bytes. However, there are 250 orders per day, on the average. Therefore, $250 \times 708 = 177,000$ bytes per day are needed to accommodate this file. The size of the file grows and shrinks from day to day, following the addition of new invoices and the deletion of old invoices (which have been paid for and analyzed). Let us assume that Lambert Dental Products needs to keep 60 days of invoices on file. This assumption yields a file size of $60 \times 177,000 = 10,620,000$ bytes. In order to keep the file from overflowing, the file should be purged and reorganized on a regular basis. More accurate estimates and better assumptions can be formulated when performance data are available.

Orders to Be Shipped File

This file has fixed-length records. From the file layout and by adding the number of bytes required to store the data elements, we find that the size of each record is 207 bytes. One record is established for each transaction. On the average Lambert handles 250 orders per day; therefore, the size of the file is $250 \times 207 = 51,750$ bytes. This file is reusable for next day processing.

Receiving Transaction File

This file has a fixed record format. From the file layout and by adding the number of bytes needed, we find that the size of each record is 105 bytes. Lambert Dental Product issues, on the average, 50 purchase orders per day. Assume that, on the average, every purchase order has two different inventory products. This results in about 100 different products being ordered per day. Now let us assume that Lambert receives the same number of products that it orders per day. Hence, we have 100 products arriving at the receiving dock per day. Furthermore, assume that about 1 percent of the items that are shipped to customers are returned. This results in about 2.5 orders per day (1 percent of 250). Suppose that, on the average, each customer order has 10 different items; hence, 25 items are returned per day. In total, 125 items are received at the dock per day. Therefore, the size of the file is $125 \times 105 = 13,125$ bytes. Because we have an on-line inventory system, the Inventory Master File is updated daily. Therefore, this transaction file is reusable for next day processing.

Receiving Transaction File after Adding Unit Cost

After adding unit cost, this file is produced from the previous file by appending a unit cost item to each record. The size of the unit cost data element is 4 bytes. Therefore, the size of this file is $125 \times 109 = 13,625$ bytes.

Maintenance Transaction File

This file has fixed-length records. From the file layout and by adding the number of required bytes, we find that the size of each record is 57 bytes. Suppose that 100 changes are to be accommodated before the file is reusable again. Therefore, the size of the file is $100 \times 57 = 5,700$ bytes.

In summary, the file storage requirements for this inventory system are $134,000 + 22,250 + 10,620,000 + 51,750 + 13,125 + 13,625 + 5,700 = 10,860,450$ bytes or about 10,000 K bytes of disk storage.

PROBLEMS

1. Redesign this system by integrating the cash collection procedures for C.O.D. items into this system.

2. Design the output layout of the Accounts Receivable Master File for this case.

3. Design the Accounts Receivable Journal for this case. Also include in the report the exceptions of the accounts receivable run.

4. The system as it is designed handles only one transaction per invoice. Redesign the system so that multitransactions per invoice could be processed.

5. Redesign the system introduced in this chapter by including returns to the supplier.

6. Design an output layout for the transaction listing of the maintenance run.

7. What is the best method of handling the adjustment for other debits or credits to the inventory file?

8. Design the output layout of four reports that can be generated from different files used in the case, to be used mainly for planning and control decisions.

9. Identify the types of decisions that are made based on each of the reports designed in problem 8.

10. If you decided to remove undesirable inventories from the warehouse as soon as possible, how do you have to redesign the system and what type of report do you have to generate in order to satisfy this requirement?

APPENDIX

Inventory Master File Layout

Data Element	Format	Number of Bytes	Notes
Item Number	9(8)	5	
Description	X(25)	25	
Availability	X(1)	1	
Quantity on Hand	9(6)	4	
Quantity on Hold	9(6)	4	
Quantity on Order Jan.	9(6)	4	"Quantity on Order" field for every month
.	.	.	
.	.	.	
.	.	.	
Quantity on Order Dec.	9(6)	4	
Quantity Sold Jan.	9(6)	4	"Quantity Sold" field for every month
.	.	.	
.	.	.	
.	.	.	
Quantity Sold Dec.	9(6)	4	
Maximum No. in Inventory	9(6)	4	Maximum level
Minimum No. in Inventory	9(6)	4	Minimum level of inventory
EOQ	9(6)	4	
Quantity Returned YTD	9(8)	5	
Average Cost	9(6)	4	
Unit Sale Price	9(6)	4	
Vendor's Product Code	9(10)	6	
Item Type	X(1)	1	
Vendor Number	9(6)	4	
Vendor Name	X(25)	25	
Unit Type	X(1)	1	
Lead Time Days	9(3)	2	
Blank	X(7)	7	Filler
		134 bytes	

Open Customer Order Transaction File Layout

Data Element	Format	Number of Bytes	Notes
Customer Number	9(5)	3	
Customer Name	X(25)	25	
Item Number	9(8)	5	
Description	X(25)	25	
No. of Units	9(4)	3	
Unit Price	9(6)	4	
Transaction Code	X(3)	3	
Shipping & Handling	9(6)	4	
Date	X(6)	6	
Order Code	9(1)	1	
Sales Rep. Code	X(2)	2	
Customer P.O. Number	X(8)	8	
		89 bytes	

Accounts Receivable Master File Layout

Data Element	Format	Number of Bytes	Notes
Customer Number	9(5)	3	
Name	X(25)	25	
C/O Address	X(25)	25	
Street Address	X(25)	25	
City	X(20)	20	
State	X(2)	2	
ZIP	X(9)	9	
Credit Limit	9(7)	4	
Amount Due	9(7)	4	
Current Payment	9(6)	4	
Current Adjustment	9(6)	4	
Current Balance	9(7)	4	
No. of Invoices	9(3)	2	
No. of Invoices Last Year	9(3)	2	
Prior Year Returns	9(6)	4	
Highest Balance	9(8)	5	
No. of Trailers	9(3)	2	
		144 bytes	Fixed-length part

continued

Data Element	Format	Number of Bytes	Notes
Trailer Type	9(1)	1	This is the variable-part layout
Date	X(6)	6	for a purchase transaction.
Customer P.O. Number	X(8)	8	
Amount	9(6)	4	
Invoice Number	9(6)	4	
Blank	X(24)	24	Filler
		47 bytes	Variable-length part
Trailer Type	9(1)	1	This is the variable-part layout
Date	X(6)	6	for a cash remittance.
Remittance Number	9(6)	4	
Amount	9(6)	4	
Blank	X(32)	32	Filler
		47 bytes	Variable-length part
Trailer Type	9(1)	1	This is the variable-part layout
Date	X(6)	6	for a debit adjustment.
Reference Number	9(6)	4	
Amount	9(6)	4	
Remarks	X(25)	25	
Blank	X(7)	7	Filler
		47 bytes	Variable-length part
Trailer Type	9(1)	1	This is the variable-part layout
Date	X(6)	6	for a credit adjustment.
Reference Number	9(6)	4	
Amount	9(6)	4	
Remarks	X(25)	25	
Blank	X(7)	7	
		47 bytes	Variable-length part

Orders to Be Shipped File Layout

Data Element	Format	Number of Bytes	Notes
Item Number	9(8)	5	
Description	X(25)	25	
No. of Units	9(4)	3	
Customer Number	9(5)	3	
Customer Name	X(25)	25	
C/O Address	X(25)	25	
Street Address	X(25)	25	
City	X(20)	20	
State	X(2)	2	
ZIP	X(9)	9	
Transaction Code	X(3)	3	
Unit Sale Price	9(6)	4	
Amount	9(6)	4	
Tax	9(6)	4	
Subtotal	9(6)	4	
Shipping Cost	9(6)	4	
Invoice Date	X(6)	6	
Routing	X(25)	25	
P.O. Number	X(8)	8	
Sales Rep. Code	X(2)	2	
Order Code	9(1)	1	
		207 bytes	

Receiving Transaction File Layout

Data Element	Format	Number of Bytes	Notes
Item Number	9(8)	5	
Description	X(25)	25	
Supplier Name	X(25)	25	
Purchase Order No.	X(5)	5	
Units Received	9(6)	4	
Damaged or Unacceptable	9(6)	4	
Date	X(6)	6	
Transaction Code	X(1)	1	
Reason for Return	X(25)	25	
Blank	X(5)	5	Filler
		105 bytes	

Receiving Transaction File after Adding Unit Cost

Data Element	Format	Number of Bytes	Notes
Item Number	9(8)	5	
Description	X(25)	25	
Supplier	X(25)	25	
Purchase Order No.	X(5)	5	
Units Received	9(6)	4	
Damaged or Unacceptable	9(6)	4	
Date	X(6)	6	
Transaction Code	X(1)	1	
Reason for Return	X(25)	25	
Blank	X(5)	4	Filler
Average Unit Cost	9(6)	4	
		109 bytes	

Maintenance Transaction File Layout

Data Element	Format	Number of Bytes	Notes
Item Number	9(8)	5	
Transaction Code	X(2)	2	
Old Value	X(25)	25	
New Value	X(25)	25	
		57 bytes	

5 | Design of a System for Payroll

The objective of this chapter is to design a system for payroll. Payroll systems traditionally were considered independent of production and accounting. However, as the manufacturing processes have become more complex, this system has come to be more closely tied to production information systems and cost accounting systems. In the case described in this chapter, the design of the system is based on the first approach. That is, the system is treated as a stand-alone system having minimum interaction with other systems. A more interactive version of a payroll system is introduced in Chapter 7.

MANAGEMENT INFORMATION REQUIREMENTS

Two functional departments provide most of the interaction with this system. These departments are the payroll department and the personnel department. Other departments also use the information generated by this system. However, the extent of their usage depends upon the nature of the activities performed within the organization and the organizational structure. For instance, in a manufacturing setting, the payroll department is closely tied to the production cycle. Therefore, most of the input to the systems is generated at the production (operations) line. The relationships of the departments that are involved with this payroll system are depicted in Fig. 5-1.

Operations

Operations is used here to mean production of goods or services. The main objective of any operations department is to produce quality goods or services in a most efficient manner while incurring the least possible cost. In order to accomplish this objective, two types of information are necessary: information to help in planning the operations and information to help in controlling the operations.

The exact form of the information required and the extent that management uses this information vary between organizations. However, in the planning

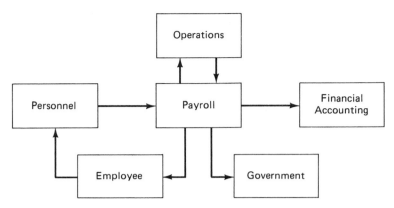

**FIGURE 5-1 Relationships Between Functional Areas and
the Payroll System**

area, management uses payroll-generated information to forecast cash requirements for payments of wages and salaries. Furthermore, the system could
generate most of the raw data needed for the budgeting system.

Management normally requires the following information for more effective
control of operations.

- The number of hours worked by each employee on each job or department
- The labor turnover in each department
- The average hourly earnings by job
- The total number of hours worked on each job or in each department
- The total cost of labor for each job or in each department
- The absentee ratio by department
- The average incentive and overtime earnings per employee
- The total direct and indirect costs of labor and comparison of the cost with
the budget

The operating departments provide the payroll system with the necessary
input: the results of the occurrence of certain events in those departments.
These events are employees' (1) reporting to work, (2) starting on a new job, (3)
stopping work on a job, (4) working overtime or on holidays, and so on. These
events are reported to the payroll system by means of a work ticket, time card,
work requisition form, or some other device.

Financial Accounting Department

The objective of this department is to prepare a set of financial statements that
fairly presents the financial position and the results of the operations. Most of
the information needed from the payroll system to satisfy this objective is of a

monetary nature. This information is used for two purposes. The first, to express the financial position, is satisfied by two kinds of information. One is the labor cost for each production department that becomes part of the inventory cost. The other is total employee deductions that would be considered as liabilities. The second purpose is to present the results of operations. This information includes total wage and salary expenses that form the selling and administrative expenses, and other employee-related expenses, such as medical insurance expenses, which are reported in the Income Statement.

Government Agencies

The main objective of government agencies such as the Internal Revenue Service or the Social Security Administration is to collect the fair share of the taxes specified in law or regulation. In order to satisfy their needs, certain types of standardized reporting must be integrated with the payroll system. Examples of the information that must be generated to fulfill governmental requirements are the W-2 Form (the annual reporting of an employee's earnings) and the 941-A Form (quarterly reporting of earnings).

Employees

Employees want to be able to substantiate the payment of the taxes or other types of deductions such as retirement and credit union. Providing each employee with an earnings statement at the end of each period and yearly earnings statement generally satisfies their needs.

Payroll

Since the payroll department is a service department, it might not need the type of information which is used by an operating department. However, they are the main providers of managerial reports for other decision-making areas.

INTERNAL CONTROLS AND AUDIT IMPLICATIONS

Because of governmental requirements, the control features built into this system must be effective. The controls that are discussed in this case may be summarized as follows:

General Controls

The main general controls of this application are

- Procedure for maintenance of the payroll master file and review of the report of the master file changes

- Procedure for review of the report of exceptions such as "overtime above limit" or "excessive payrate"
- Separation of duties among persons dealing with time cards and computerized payroll systems (such as the systems analyst, programmer, and computer operator)
- Separation of functions of payroll processing and hiring
- Procedure for maintaining an audit trail

Application Controls

These are the tests and control features that are built into the computer programs written for the payroll application. These controls are

- Self-checking digit for employee number, a check is performed on the basis of modulus 11, ensuring proper transformation of the source data into machine readable form.
- Batch and hash totals for checking the input data
- Validity check for transaction code
- Self-checking digit on location code
- Completeness tests for checking the validity of several selected fields

More detailed explanations of these tests are provided later in the case study.

CASE: Payroll System

Capital Parking Incorporated (CPI) is a company which operates parking lots in the Washington, D.C. metropolitan area. It provides parking services in more than 100 locations in the city, and in the Maryland and Virginia suburbs. The locations of the parking lots and garages are leased.

Each location has a manager, several parking attendants, and a cashier. A supervisor is assigned to each group of locations to coordinate the activities and maintain a consistent level of operation.

The company has approximately 430 employees, of whom 400 are classified as operations personnel—that is, supervisors, managers, attendants and cashiers. The other 30 employees are administrative staff. Operations staff, except the supervisors, receive overtime for the number of hours worked beyond 40 hours in each week. However, the administrative staff are on straight salary and are entitled to no overtime. Furthermore, the operations personnel (except supervisors) receive one paycheck every Thursday, while the administrative staff and the supervisors are paid bi-weekly.

In response to employee complaints about not receiving their paychecks on time, as well as a squeeze in the firm's operating margin, CPI has decided to install a more effective payroll processing system. A team of consultants was hired and the following system is the result of their effort.

PAYROLL PROCESSING

The designed payroll system has the following capabilities:

- Calculates pay for each period
- Supports hourly as well as salaried personnel
- Supports weekly and bi-weekly payments
- Prints checks
- Prints various reports such as the Payroll Register, Labor Distribution, and Monthly Summary
- Calculates the pay based on three types of tax structures (those of Washington, D.C., as well as Maryland and Virginia)
- Prints Form 941-A (at the end of each quarter) and Form W-2 (at the end of the year)
- Maintains the Payroll Master File

PREPARATION OF TIME CARDS

The Payroll Department is responsible for the preparation of time cards. Time cards are prepared for operations staff except the supervisors. The cards are prepared by use of the information available on the Personnel Information List. The data recorded on each time card are

1. Name of the employee
2. Employee number
3. Position
4. Location code
5. Social security number
6. Last day of the week (for this time card)

The time cards are sent to the various parking lots one week before the start of each week. The format of the time card is shown in Fig. 5-2.

COMPLETION OF TIME CARDS

Unused time cards are kept in the custody of the lot manager. After cards are distributed, the employees record their time-in and time-out by "punching" a time clock. The manager of each location collects the cards at the end of the shift on Wednesdays. The managers must sign the time cards after verifying

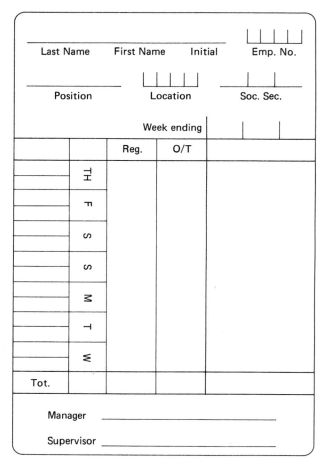

FIGURE 5-2   Time Card

their validity. Then, after supervisor's approval of all the cards (including the managers' own cards), the cards are sent to the Payroll Department.

PREPARATION OF THE SOURCE DOCUMENTS

A clerk in the Payroll Department calculates total hours worked by subtracting time-in from time-out for each approved card. Then he or she prepares four batches of 100 (or fewer) time cards for all nonsupervisory operations personnel. An adding machine tape of total number of hours worked for all the cards in each batch is prepared and attached to each batch.

Similar information is recorded on the batch listings for supervisory and ad-

```
┌─────────────────────────────────────────────┐
│              Batch Control Slip               │
├─────────────────────────────────────────────┤
│                                               │
│   Batch No. _____    Date _____   │
│                                               │
│                                               │
│   Total Number of Time Cards                  │
│      in This Batch          _____    │
│                                               │
│                                               │
│   Total Number of Hours Worked _____   │
│                                               │
│                                               │
│   Total Number of Salaried                    │
│      Employees              _____    │
│                                               │
├─────────────────────────────────────────────┤
│                                               │
│                                               │
│                                               │
│                                               │
│                                               │
│                                               │
│                                               │
├─────────────────────────────────────────────┤
│   Clerk _____        │
└─────────────────────────────────────────────┘
```

FIGURE 5-3   Batch Control Slip

ministrative personnel although no time cards are used for these employees. Since the administrative staff and supervisors are paid bi-weekly, the payroll clerk only prepares a list of these employees every two weeks. A Batch Control Slip is attached to each batch. Fig. 5-3 is a sample of a Batch Control Slip. After this step, all batches are sent to the Data Processing Department.

DATA ENTRY

The data entry system is menu-driven. The operator calls the appropriate program after being identified through a password. Then he or she keys the Batch Control Slip into the system through an intelligent terminal. The process of keying and the related system flowchart are shown in Fig. 5-4.

Calling the appropriate screen for keying the time cards is the next step. The screen layout for keying time cards is shown in Fig. 5-5.

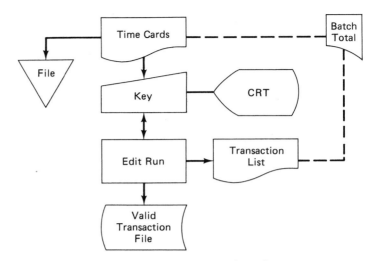

FIGURE 5-4   Edit Run Flowchart

Various types of tests are included in the Edit Run (Fig. 5-4). Each error committed in the data entry stage is highlighted at the lower portion of the screen (Fig. 5-5) through an appropriate error message.

EDIT PROCESS

The edit process is a front-end method. Each error is detected immediately, while the data are being entered into the system. The tests designed for the various fields are as follows:

Test	Item
1. Validity	Employment
2. Validity	Position code
	Code 1 = Attendant
	2 = Cashier
	3 = Manager
	4 = Supervisor
	5 = Staff
	6 = Executive
3. Completeness	All fields
4. Self-checking digit	Employee number
5. Consistency	All data fields
6. Validity	Location code
7. Self-checking digit	Social security number
8. Limit test	Number of hours worked
9. Logical check	Number of hours worked versus position code

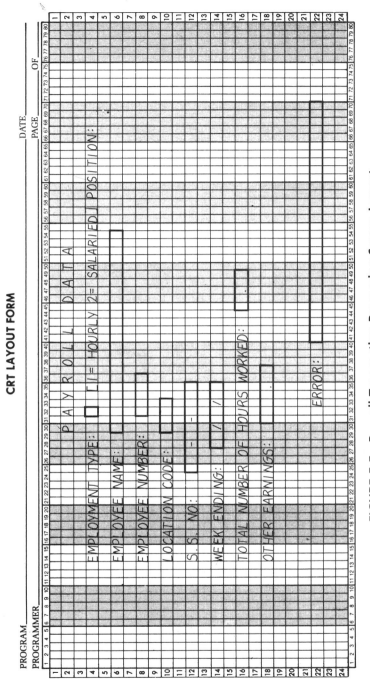

FIGURE 5-5 Payroll Transaction Processing Screen Layout

133

Test number 9, logical check, is an essential test in this application. The edit process checks the logical relationships between the fields for position code and number of hours worked. The payroll program does not require an hours figure to calculate the pay for salaried employees. Moreover, omission of the "Number of Hours" field from the record of the hourly employees is easily detected.

The outputs of the edit process are the List of Transactions (including Batch Summary Report) and the Payroll Valid Transaction File. The list of transactions (Fig. 5-6) is output on the printer and contains two parts:

A. A detailed listing of data on each time card which contains the following items:
1. Employee number
2. Position code
3. Employee name
4. Social security number
5. Location code
6. Hours worked
7. Other earnings
8. Remarks

B. Batch Summary Report (bottom of Fig. 5-6)
1. Batch number
2. Total number of hours for all records entered
3. Hash total of number of hours from the Batch Control Slip
4. Difference between item 2 and item 3
5. Total number of records entered
6. Total number of records from the Batch Control Slip
7. Difference between items 5 and 6

The List of Transactions is used for an audit trail and (possibly) for those errors not being detected during the data entry process.

The Payroll Valid Transaction File is the other output of this run. This file is organized on a disk using a fixed-length format. Fig. 5-7 shows the layout of this file. The primary key for Payroll Valid Transaction record is the "Employee Number" field. Furthermore, the transaction code field is automatically created on each record while the time cards are being entered. Code "1" in this field indicates that pay should be calculated for this employee.

It should be emphasized that, in order to fulfill government regulations, the source documents (time cards) must be kept in a safe place for at least three years.

PAYROLL UPDATE RUN

The system flowchart of this run is shown in Fig. 5-8. The inputs to this run are the Payroll Valid Transaction File and the Old Master File. The outputs of this run are the Updated Master File, Payroll Register, Pay Tape, and the Error File.

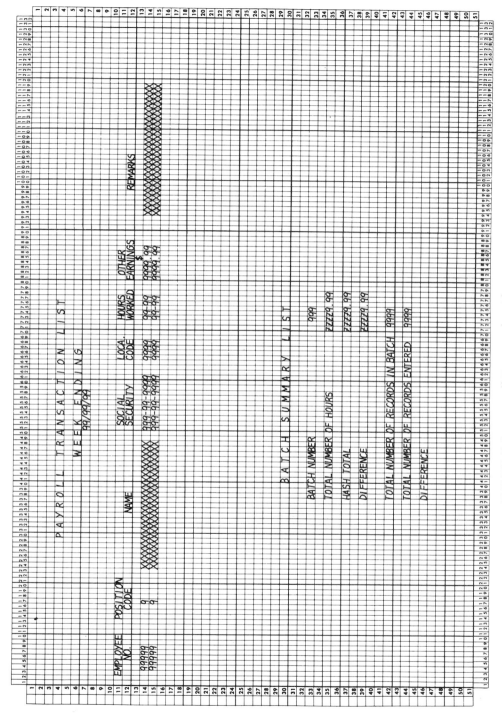

FIGURE 5-6 Payroll Transaction List

135

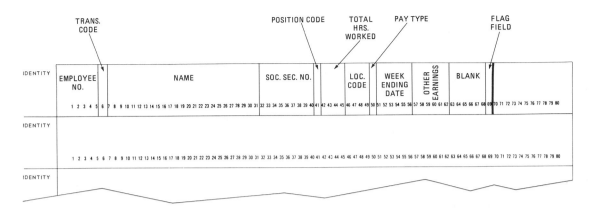

FIGURE 5-7   Layout of Valid Payroll Transaction File

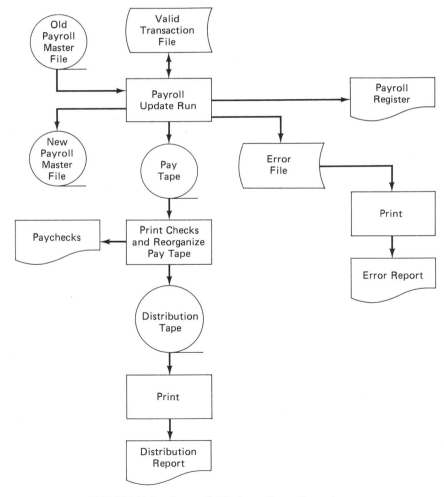

FIGURE 5-8   Payroll Update Run Flowchart

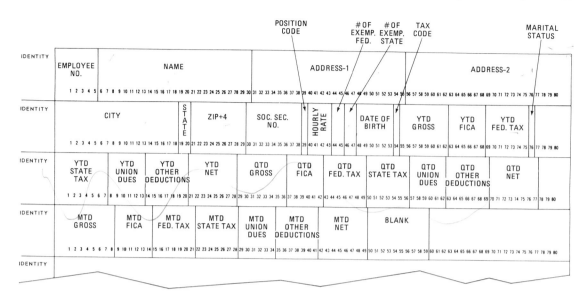

FIGURE 5-9 **Layout of Payroll Master File**

The Payroll Master File is organized sequentially on tape. The format of this file is illustrated in Fig. 5-9. The primary key for this fixed-length file is again the Employee Number field.

A Payroll Master Record is called into the main storage sequentially. If a transaction record for the same employee exists in the Payroll Valid Transaction File, the pay is calculated, the master file is updated, a Pay Record is created, and the Payroll Register is printed. A list of errors is also prepared on a disk file. Otherwise, the employee record is written on the Updated Payroll File without any change.

The layout of the Payroll Register, which is one of the outputs of this run, is shown in Fig. 5-10. The fields in this report are

1. Employee number
2. Employee name
3. Base rate
4. Hours worked
5. Regular pay
6. Overtime pay
7. Other pay
8. Gross pay
9. Social security tax
10. Federal tax
11. State tax

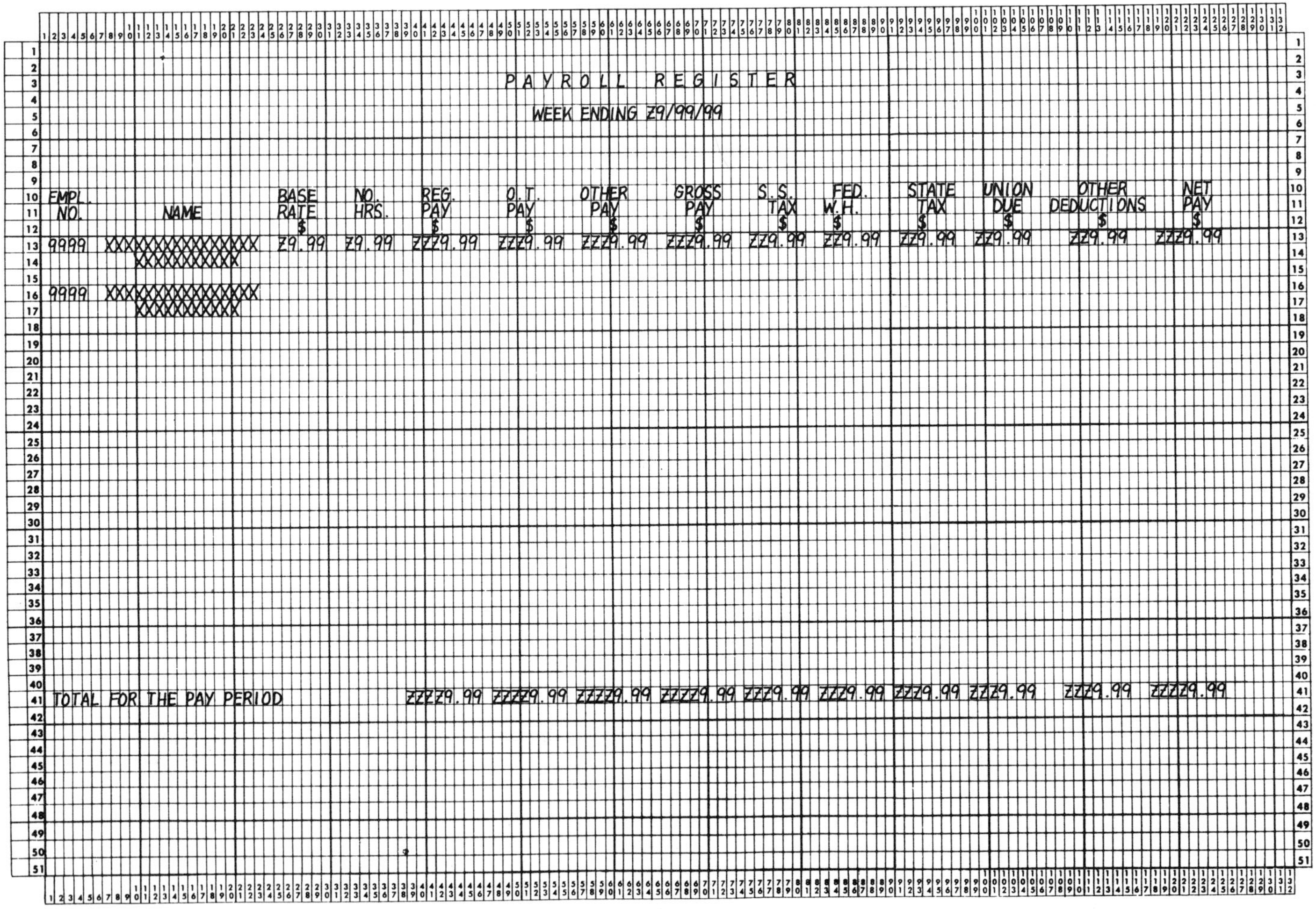

FIGURE 5-10 Layout of Payroll Register

12. Union dues
13. Other deductions
14. Net pay

The other output of this run is the Pay Tape. This tape is used for the preparation of checks and the Labor Distribution Report. The layout of this tape is shown in Fig. 5-11. This tape is used in future runs to print the paychecks and earnings statements. The earnings statement and paycheck layout is shown in Fig. 5-12.

The Labor Distribution Report is one of the most important tools for managerial cost control. In order to create this type of report, the Pay Tape is sorted on location code, position code, or other fields desired. For example, in order to evaluate the managerial effectiveness at each location, a report for total pay and breakdown of those paid could be generated.

The Edit Run might not be able to detect all the errors of the data entry step. Other errors that are detected in the Update Run on the Error File are printed later for required action. The layout of this report is shown in Fig. 5-13. Some examples of remarks in this report are

Master File Record Does Not Exist.   Referring to Fig. 5-7, Layout of the Valid Payroll Transaction File, notice a one-byte field called "Flag Field." As the transactions are recorded initially, nothing is recorded in this field. However, in the Update Run, as soon as the master record is located for a particular transaction and pay is calculated, a special character is recorded in this field. This process is called flagging. At the end of the Update Run, the unflagged records indicate that there were no Payroll Master Records for those transactions.

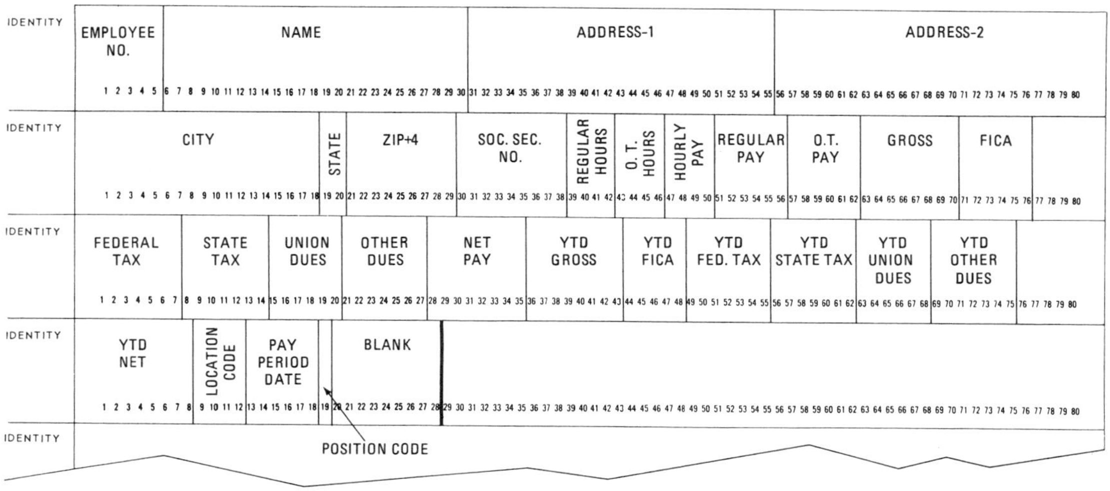

FIGURE 5-11   Layout of Pay Tape

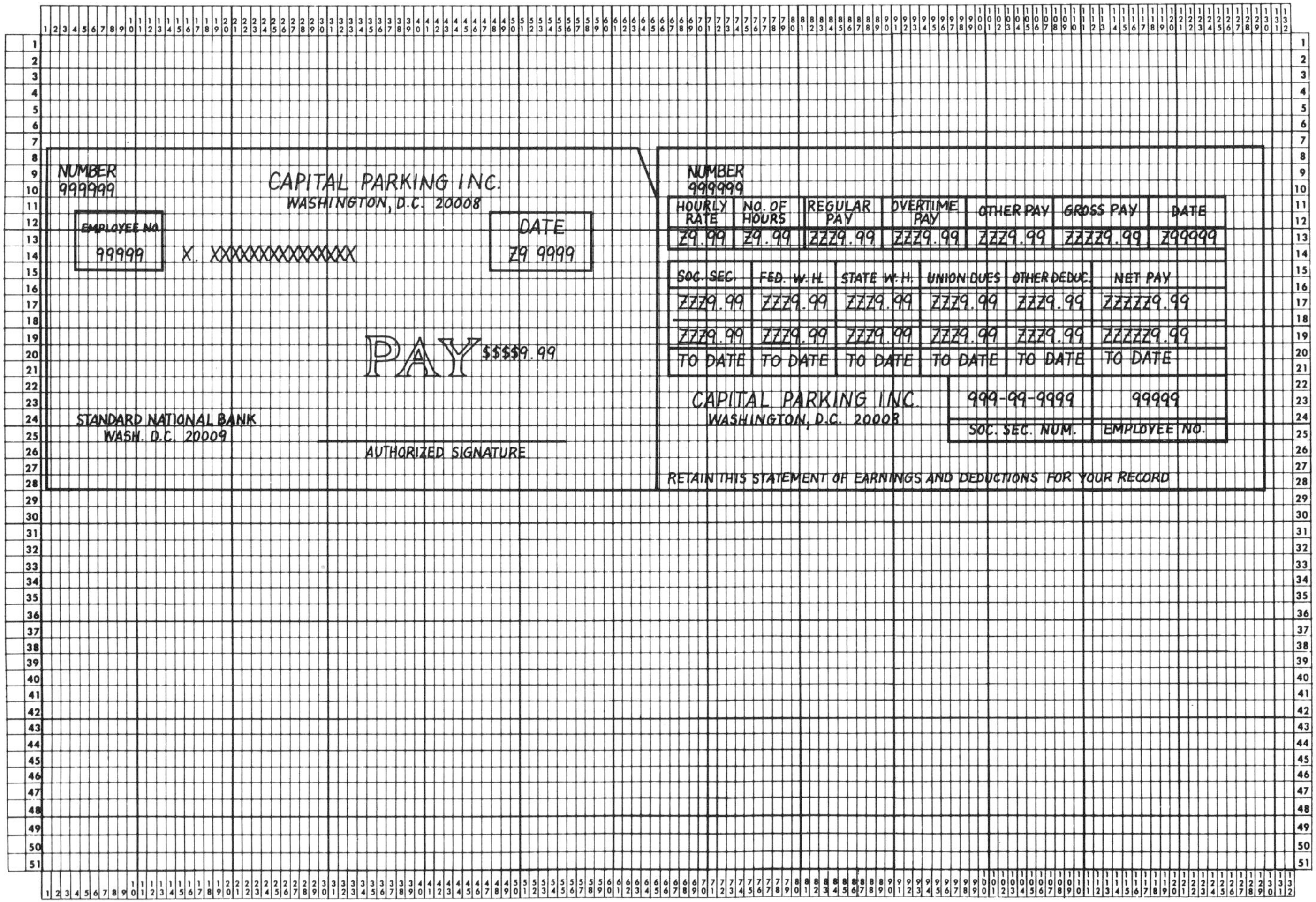

FIGURE 5-12 Layout of Paycheck

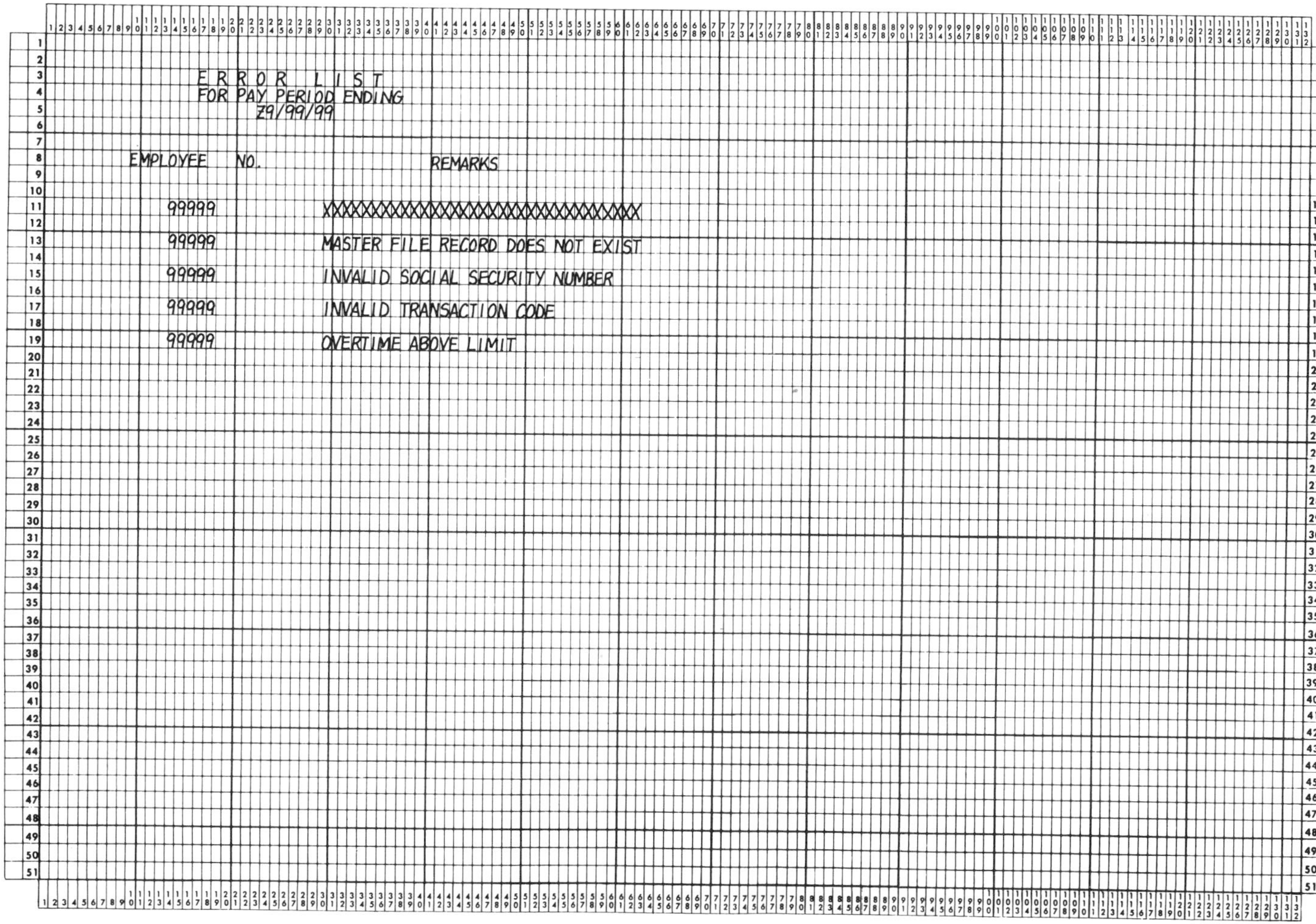
E R R O R L I S T
FOR PAY PERIOD ENDING
Z9/99/99
EMPLOYEE NO.
REMARKS
99999
XXXXXXXXXXXXXXXXXXXXXXXXXXXXXXXXXXXXXXXX
99999
MASTER FILE RECORD DOES NOT EXIST
99999
INVALID SOCIAL SECURITY NUMBER
99999
INVALID TRANSACTION CODE
99999
OVERTIME ABOVE LIMIT

FIGURE 5-13 Layout of Error List

Invalid Social Security Number. Social security number on the Payroll Master Record does not match with the social security number on the transaction record.

Invalid Transaction Code. Transaction code is not the Code "1" that indicates calculation of the pay and updating of the master file.

Overtime Above the Limit.   For those records where the overtime figure is above the prescribed limit. These records are processed in the next run.

Because of the likelihood of these and other errors, the old master file tape should be saved and kept in a secure place for a period not shorter than three pay periods. This procedure allows reconstruction of erroneous or invalid transactions and satisfies the company's policy of maintaining an adequate audit trail.

REPORT RUN

The payroll system requires the utmost attention because of various governmental requirements. The reports that are regularly needed are 941-A (quarterly earnings) and W-2 (yearly earnings). The master file contains monthly, quarterly, and yearly figures. After the preparation of, say, a monthly report, all the fields that show monthly accumulation of the figures should be set to zero for next month reporting. Similar steps are also taken for quarterly and yearly reporting. However, at the end of the year, the Payroll Master File is dumped and saved for a period of at least three years. The flowchart of these runs and the W-2 Form are shown in Figs. 5-14 and 5-15.

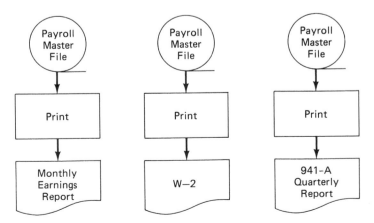

FIGURE 5-14   Print Runs Flowchart

1 Control number		OMB No. 1545-0008				

2 Employer's name, address, and ZIP code	3 Employer's identification number	4 Employer's State number

5 Statutory Deceased employee ☐	Legal rep. ☐	942 emp. ☐	Subtotal ☐	Void ☐

6 Allocated tips	7 Advance EIC payment

8 Employee's social security number	9 Federal income tax withheld	10 Wages, tips, other compensation	11 Social security tax withheld

12 Employee's name, address, and ZIP code	13 Social security wages	14 Social security tips

16		

17 State income tax	18 State wages, tips, etc.	19 Name of State

20 Local income tax	21 Local wages, tips, etc.	22 Name of locality

Form **W-2 Wage and Tax Statement**   **19XX**   Copy 1 For State, City, or Local Tax Department ☐
Employee's and employer's copy compared   ☐

FIGURE 5-15   W-2 Form

MAINTENANCE RUN

Because of high labor turnover in CPI, the maintenance run must be considered as one of the most important steps. A maintenance transaction file is created for this run. Different types of transactions are

Transaction Code[1]	Type
2	Deletion of a record
3	Change in position code
4	Rate of pay change
5	Change in number of exemptions
6	Change in state tax code
7	Change in marital status
8	Addition of a new employee record to the master file

The flowchart of the maintenance run is shown in Fig. 5-16. The inputs to this run are the Maintenance Transaction File and the Payroll Master File. The outputs of the run are the Maintained Payroll Master File and the Report of the Changes in the Master File.

In order to record the input transaction, a special form has been developed. This form should be properly authorized before being entered into the system. The layout of the Maintenance Run Report is shown in Fig. 5-17. For transaction type 8, a W-4 Form (Fig. 5-18) is used.

---

[1] Transaction Code 1 is used for calculation of pay and updating of the master file.

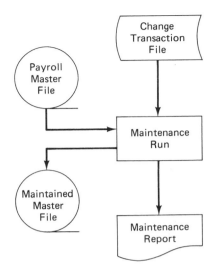

FIGURE 5-16   Maintenance Run Flowchart

The following controls are extremely crucial in this run.

1. Since the computer program will follow certain procedural steps as it encounters different transaction codes, checking the transaction code is crucial in the Edit Run.

2. All the changes must be authorized by a responsible person in the organization.

3. Both reports of "transaction listing" at the Edit Run level and "list of changes" at the Maintenance Run level must be reviewed and any deviation from the authorized changes must be investigated.

ASSESSMENT OF NEEDED STORAGE

The following discussion provides some calculated approximations of the storage needed to accommodate the various files of the system described in this chapter. (See the chapter appendix for details.)

Payroll Valid Transaction File

This file has a fixed-length record. From the file layout and by adding the number of bytes required; the size of the record is 59 bytes.[2] One record is established for each of the 400 employees each week. Therefore, the size of this file is 400 × 59 = 23,600 bytes.

---

[2] The number of bytes required will seldom agree with the number of bytes or characters shown in a file layout; *numeric* fields employ the "packed decimal" format, where two digits can often (but not always) be "packed" into one byte.

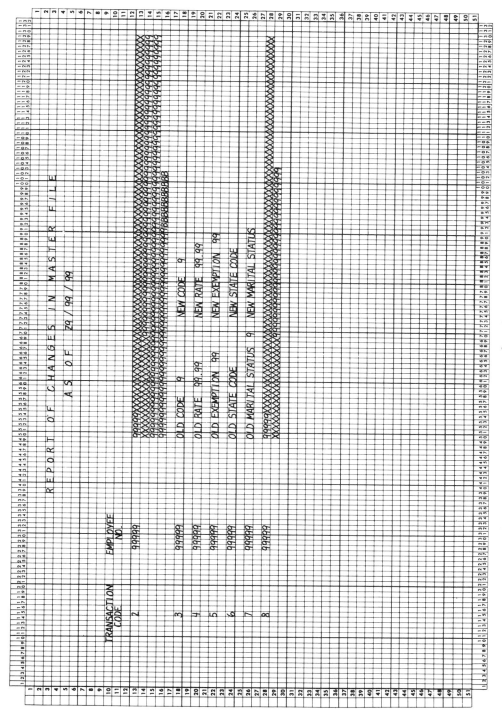

FIGURE 5-17 Layout of Maintenance Run Report

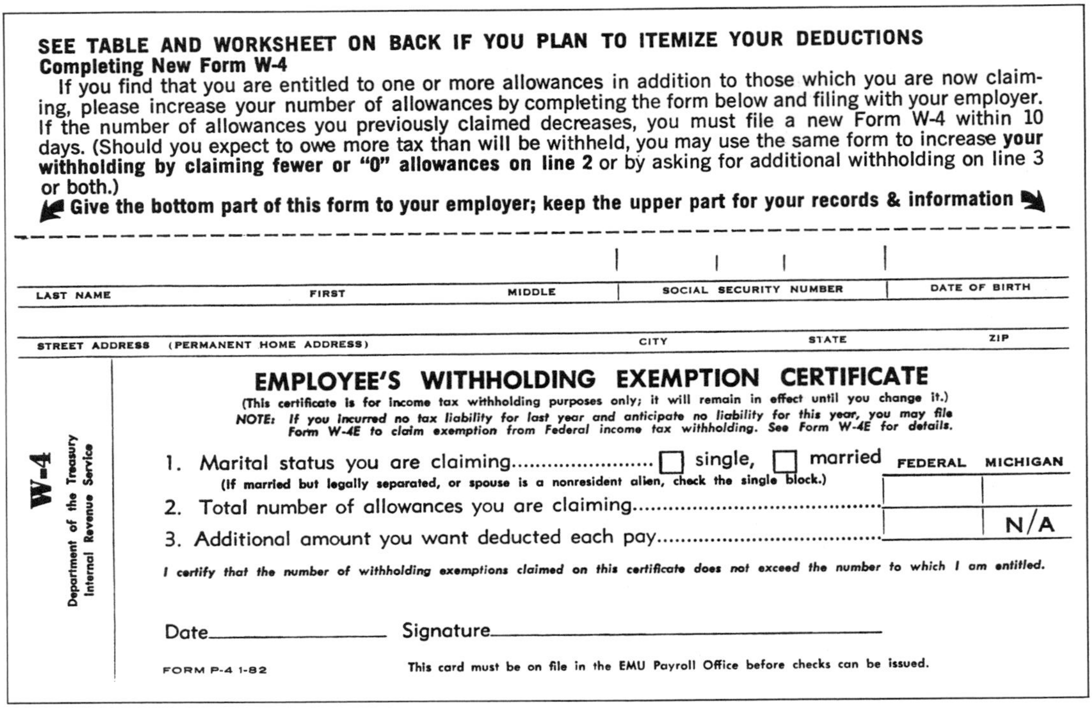

SEE TABLE AND WORKSHEET ON BACK IF YOU PLAN TO ITEMIZE YOUR DEDUCTIONS

Completing New Form W-4

If you find that you are entitled to one or more allowances in addition to those which you are now claiming, please increase your number of allowances by completing the form below and filing with your employer. If the number of allowances you previously claimed decreases, you must file a new Form W-4 within 10 days. (Should you expect to owe more tax than will be withheld, you may use the same form to increase **your withholding by claiming fewer or "0" allowances on line 2** or by asking for additional withholding on line 3 or both.)

Give the bottom part of this form to your employer; keep the upper part for your records & information

LAST NAME FIRST MIDDLE | SOCIAL SECURITY NUMBER | DATE OF BIRTH

STREET ADDRESS (PERMANENT HOME ADDRESS) CITY STATE ZIP

W-4

Department of the Treasury
Internal Revenue Service

EMPLOYEE'S WITHHOLDING EXEMPTION CERTIFICATE

(This certificate is for income tax withholding purposes only; it will remain in effect until you change it.)

NOTE: If you incurred no tax liability for last year and anticipate no liability for this year, you may file Form W-4E to claim exemption from Federal income tax withholding. See Form W-4E for details.

	FEDERAL	MICHIGAN
1. Marital status you are claiming........................ ☐ single, ☐ married (If married but legally separated, or spouse is a nonresident alien, check the single block.)		
2. Total number of allowances you are claiming..		
3. Additional amount you want deducted each pay.....................................		N/A

I certify that the number of withholding exemptions claimed on this certificate does not exceed the number to which I am entitled.

Date________________ Signature____________________________

FORM P-4 1-82

This card must be on file in the EMU Payroll Office before checks can be issued.

FIGURE 5-18 W-4 Form

Payroll Master File

This file has a fixed-length record. Adding up the number of bytes indicated in the file layout, each record is 228 bytes long. One record is established for each of the 430 employees. This results in 430 × 228 = 98,040 bytes being required to hold the file.

Pay Tape File

This file has fixed-length records. Each record is 207 bytes long. One record is established for each employee; therefore, 430 × 207 = 89,010 bytes are needed for the file. This can be accommodated by using one reel of magnetic tape.

In summary, the file storage requirements for this system are as follows:

1. Several reels of magnetic tape

2. 23,600 + 98,040 = 121,640 bytes or about 118 K bytes of on-line storage

PROBLEMS

1. Prepare the layout of a Labor Distribution Report assuming the objective is to minimize the overtime cost.

2. Prepare the flowchart of the Maintenance Run assuming the master file is on disk.

3. Prepare the flowchart of the Maintenance Run assuming the transaction file is on tape.

4. Redesign the payroll system given assuming the Payroll Master File is on disk.

5. Redesign the payroll system assuming that each employee is issued a magnetic card and the time-in and time-out are recorded by a machine similar to banks' automatic teller.

6. Prepare the layout of the Payroll Master File assuming the management wishes to monitor overtime payments to each employee.

7. Prepare the layout of the report for problem 6.

8. How often would the Maintenance Run be performed, as a rule? Would it, for example, be wise to perform this run right after the Payroll Update Run of Fig. 5-8?

APPENDIX

Payroll Valid Transaction File Layout

Data Element	Format	Number of Bytes	Notes
Employee Number	9(5)	3	
Transaction Code	9	1	
Name	X(25)	25	
Social Security Number	9(9)	5	
Position Code	9	1	
Total Hours Worked	9(4)	3	
Location Code	9(4)	3	Integer
Pay Type	9	1	Integer
Week Ending Date	X(6)	6	
Other Earnings	9(6)	4	
Blank	X(6)	6	Filler
Flag Field	X(1)	1	
		59 bytes	

Payroll Master File Layout

Data Element	Format	Number of Bytes	Notes
Employee Number	9(5)	3	
Name	X(25)	25	
Address—1	X(25)	25	
Address—2	X(25)	25	
City	X(18)	18	
State	X(2)	2	
ZIP+4	X(9)	9	
Social Security Number	9(9)	5	
Position Code	9	1	
Hourly Rate	9(4)	3	
No. of Exemptions—Fed.	9(2)	2	
No. of Exemptions—State	9(2)	2	
Date of Birth	X(6)	6	
Tax Code	X(1)	1	
YTD Gross	9(8)	5	
YTD FICA	9(6)	4	
YTD Fed. Tax	9(7)	4	
Marital Status	X(1)	1	
YTD State Tax	9(7)	4	
YTD Union Dues	9(6)	4	
YTD Other Deductions	9(7)	4	
YTD Net	9(8)	5	
QTD Gross	9(8)	5	
QTD FICA	9(6)	4	
QTD Fed. Tax	9(7)	4	
QTD State Tax	9(7)	4	
QTD Union Dues	9(6)	4	
QTD Other Deductions	9(7)	4	
QTD Net	9(8)	5	
MTD Gross	9(8)	5	
MTD FICA	9(6)	4	
MTD Fed. Tax	9(7)	4	
MTD State Tax	9(7)	4	
MTD Union Dues	9(6)	4	
MTD Other Deductions	9(7)	4	
MTD Net	9(8)	5	
Blank	X(10)	10	Filler
		228 bytes	

Pay Tape File Layout

Data Element	Format	Number of Bytes	Notes
Employee Number	9(5)	3	
Name	X(25)	25	
Address–1	X(25)	25	
Address–2	X(25)	25	
City	X(18)	18	
State	X(2)	2	
ZIP+4	X(9)	9	
Social Security Number	9(9)	5	
Regular Hours	9(4)	3	
OT Hours	9(4)	3	
Hourly Pay	9(4)	3	
Regular Pay	9(6)	4	
OT Pay	9(6)	4	
Gross	9(8)	5	
FICA	9(6)	4	
Federal Tax	9(7)	4	
State Tax	9(7)	4	
Union Dues	9(6)	4	
Other Deductions	9(7)	4	
Net Pay	9(8)	5	
YTD Gross	9(8)	5	
YTD FICA	9(5)	3	
YTD Fed. Tax	9(7)	4	
YTD State Tax	9(7)	4	
YTD Union Dues	9(6)	4	
YTD Other Deductions	9(7)	4	
YTD Net	9(8)	5	
Location Code	9(4)	3	Integer
Pay Period Date	X(6)	6	
Blank	X(10)	10	Filler
		207 bytes	

6 | Design of a System for Fixed Assets and General Ledger

In this chapter, two subsystems, one designed for fixed assets and one for general ledger, are discussed. These systems are less complicated than the other systems discussed in earlier chapters. However, the impact of the information generated by these two systems on decision making is much more far-reaching.

The first system discussed is a fixed-assets subsystem. The importance of the valuation of fixed assets is ever increasing. Statement of Financial Accounting Standard 33 (SFAS 33) by FASB and Accounting Release Series 190 issued by the Securities and Exchange Commission are the two most important pronouncements that affect valuation of property, plant, and equipment. Although the disclosures required by these pronouncements encompass only large corporations, smaller entities could also benefit by these types of disclosures.

The second system is a general ledger system. The information generated by this system is the main input to the decision models of stockholders, creditors, government agencies, and others. This may be due to the fact that, in most cases, general ledger information, as published in annual reports, is the only information available to so-called outsiders.

FIXED-ASSETS SYSTEM: MANAGEMENT INFORMATION REQUIREMENTS

The main objectives of management in this area are physical control of the property, inclusion of the most accurate figures in the publicly available financial statements, payment of the fair share of property tax, and utilization of the maximum amount of investment tax credit.

Fixed assets may be classified into several groups. This classification may be based on physical substance of the assets (tangible or intangible), type of the assets (building, plants), or any other classification useful to an organization. No matter how the assets are classified, management's information needs are related to the acquisition, utilization, and retirement of these assets. These needs vary. That is, information needs regarding plant and equipment are different from information needs regarding office furniture. Because of the diversity of needs, it is very difficult for the analyst to design an all inclusive multipurpose system. Therefore, it is possible the users may turn to other information systems such as cost accounting or production to acquire more information about the assets. For instance, if information about down-time or repair cost of each machine were required, the user might have to go to the production information system to get this information.

The following areas of the organization may be considered as the major users of the fixed-assets subsystem.

Operations

The main objective of the operations or production department is the efficient utilization of the resources assigned to them. The types of decisions in this area relate to the replacement of old assets and the purchase of new assets. Maintenance is another area of decision making for the production department.

Custodian

This department is charged with the physical security of the assets. In fact, one of the most important areas of internal control is the safeguarding of assets and prevention of misuse. In order to accomplish the above objective, the custodial department needs to know the

- Location of each asset
- Description of each asset
- Department or division that uses or has custody of the assets
- Insurance company that insures the asset

Physical Plant

This department is normally charged with maintaining the assets and keeping them in proper working condition. The information used by this department includes

- Description of each item
- Location of each item
- Physical details of each item, such as
  Measurements
  Manufacturer
  Model
  Useful life
  Specifications
  Other technical data such as horsepower, watts

Treasurer

This office is charged with providing adequate insurance coverage for the assets. If this functional area does not carry out this mission, consequences in a time of catastrophe (such as fire) would be devastating. Therefore, the objective of this department is to provide adequate insurance with minimum cost. The information usually required by this department is

- Location of each asset
- Physical details
- Historical cost
- Net book value
- Current replacement cost
- Insurable value based on net book value and current replacement cost
- Current amount of insured value

Corporate Planning Staff

The function of this group is strategic planning. One of their main objectives is to forecast future asset acquisition and resource requirements. They are mainly interested in the economic useful life of assets and possible replacement costs of those assets.

Corporate Accounting

Preparation of accurate and fair financial statements is the most important objective of the corporate accounting group. Financial statements must be prepared according to the Generally Accepted Accounting Principles. Therefore, the assets ought to be classified into proper categories and reported net of depreciation or amortization or depletion.

In order to satisfy the additional disclosure requirements of large enterprises, as specified in SFAS 33, the system should be capable of generating information about current cost, constant dollar accounting, lease accounting, and tax information about timing differences or investment tax credits.

INTERNAL CONTROLS AND AUDIT IMPLICATIONS

One of the objectives of an internal control system is to safeguard assets, especially fixed assets. Establishing an effective control system in this area is extremely important. The computer-related controls that are discussed in the case are of two kinds.

General Controls

The general controls are

- Procedure for maintenance of the fixed-assets master file and review of the report of master file changes
- Procedure for review of the exceptions report such as "accumulated depreciation exceeds net book value" or "life exceeds the economic useful life"
- Separation of duties among individuals who are in custody of the assets and those who maintain computerized records
- Separation of duties for purchasing the fixed assets, recordkeeping, and custodianship functions
- Procedure for maintaining an audit trail and maintaining backup and recovery steps

Applications Controls

These tests are built into the computer programs prepared for fixed assets. The controls are

- Self-checking digit for Item Identification Number: a check is performed on a modulus 11 basis, ensuring proper transformation of the source data into machine-readable form
- Batch and hash total for checking the input data
- Validity check for transaction code field
- Self-checking digit on location field
- Completeness test on several selected fields

These tests are explained in the case study.

CASE: Fixed-Assets System

Capital Parking Incorporated is a company which operates parking lots in the Washington, D.C. area. (See Chapter 5 for CPI's payroll system.) Although the company runs a successful parking operation, it experiences a great number of difficulties in management information areas.

The director of operations always complains about the lack of information about asset condition, location, and custodianship. Moreover, no information for replacement decisions is provided to him.

CPI's executives are well aware of the current tax law and the implication of the investment tax credit. However, they are not able to disseminate this information in a useful form. It is the general feeling among the corporate executives that the company is wasting its resources in the area of asset acquisitions and utilization.

They eventually decided to seek professional help. This was accomplished through hiring a management consultant. The consultant has recommended the computerization of the fixed assets after a thorough study of the existing system. Initially, the consultant divided the assets into the following categories:

- Parking structures
- Parking lots
- Leasehold improvements
- Machinery and vehicles
- Office furniture and equipment

Some of the facilities used by CPI are leased. In order to make those facilities operational for the intended use, some improvements have to be made. These improvements are classified under the caption "Leasehold Improvements."

The consultant's report consists of four segments. These segments are (1) generating the Fixed-Assets Master File, (2) the procedures for updating the Fixed-Assets Master File, (3) the procedures for maintaining the master file, and (4) generating ad hoc reports. Each of these segments is discussed on the following pages.

GENERATING THE MASTER FILE

The process of generating the Fixed-Assets Master File is similar to creation of a payroll master file. A clerk is assigned to the task of collecting the source documents by going through the past records. The past records include the invoices or other types of source documents that are considered as the evidence of ownership.

In order to facilitate transcribing the hard copy data into a machine-readable form, a data sheet is designed. For every item of asset one sheet is prepared. This form is shown in Fig. 6-1. All the necessary data for completing this form are provided through intensive research (in some cases engineering studies). This step is vital, since the company is attempting to create the Fixed-Assets Master File for the first time. However, for the newly acquired assets and those that will be purchased in the future, this step should not pose any major difficulties.

The data sheets for each group of assets are batched and a Batch Control Slip is prepared. In the Batch Control Slip (Fig. 6-2) the total number of asset data sheets and total cost are recorded.

The collected data sheets must be entered into the computer. This is done by calling an appropriate menu used for entering fixed-assets data. The layout of the screen for the data entering routine is similar to the layout of other data entering screens discussed in earlier chapters. The data entry and edit process

Capital Parking, Incorporated
Fixed-Assets Data Sheet

Date ☐☐☐☐☐

Item Number ☐☐☐☐

Description ☐☐☐☐☐☐☐☐☐☐☐☐☐☐☐☐☐☐☐☐☐☐

Location ☐☐☐☐☐☐☐☐☐☐☐☐   Location Code ☐☐☐☐

Manufacturer ☐☐☐☐☐☐☐☐☐☐☐☐☐☐☐

Manufacturer Serial No. ☐☐☐☐☐☐☐☐☐☐☐☐   Model ☐☐☐☐☐☐☐☐☐

Condition Code ☐   Economic Useful Life ☐☐

Date Acquired ☐☐☐☐☐☐   Tax Life ☐☐   Depreciation Code ☐

Cost ☐☐☐☐☐☐☐☐   Percent Declining Balance ☐☐☐

Current Replacement Cost ☐☐☐☐☐☐☐☐

Estimated Residual Value ☐☐☐☐☐☐☐

Insured Value ☐☐☐☐☐☐☐☐☐

_____
Prepared

_____
Reviewed

_____
Approved

FIGURE 6-1   Fixed-Assets Data Sheet Form

Batch Control Slip
Date _____
Batch No. _____   Asset Group _____
Total Number of Asset Data Sheets _____
Total Cost _____
Clerk _____

FIGURE 6-2 Batch Control Slip

(Fig. 6-3) contains various types of checks. The errors are corrected immediately as the data are entered into the system. The tests that are performed on different fields are as follows.

Test	Field
1. Validity	Item number
2. Consistency	All data fields
3. Validity	Location code
4. Completeness	All records
5. Validity	Condition code
	Code 1 = Poor
	2 = Adequate
	3 = Moderate
	4 = Good
	5 = Excellent

Test	Field
6. Self-checking digit	Item number
7. Self-checking digit	Location code
8. Limit test	Useful life and tax life
9. Validity	Depreciation code
	Code 1 = Straight-line
	2 = Sum-of-the-years'-digits
	3 = Declining balance
	4 = Other

The outputs of the edit process are the List of Transactions (including Batch Summary Report) and the Fixed-Assets Valid Transaction File.

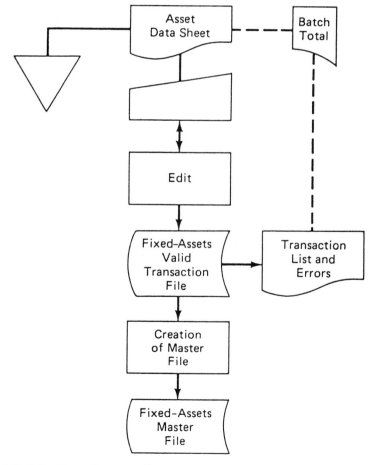

FIGURE 6-3   Data Entry, Edit Process, and Creation of Master File

The List of Transactions (Fig. 6-4) is produced on the printer and contains the following.

A. A detailed listing of data for each Asset Data Sheet consists of the following items
1. Item number
2. Description
3. Location
4. Location code
5. Manufacturer
6. Manufacturer serial number
7. Model
8. Condition code
9. Data acquired
10. Economic useful life
11. Tax life
12. Depreciation code
13. Percent declining balance
14. Cost
15. Current replacement cost
16. Estimates residual value
17. Insured value

B. Batch Summary Report (shown at the bottom of Fig. 6-4)
1. Batch number
2. Asset group
3. Total number of records entered
4. Total number of records on Batch Control Slip
5. Difference
6. Total cost of all the records entered
7. Total cost from the Batch Control Slip
8. Difference

This List of Transactions is called an "audit list" when used for audit trail purposes.

The Fixed-Assets Valid Transaction File is the other output of this run. This file, which resides on disk, is a random-access file with a fixed-length record format. Fig. 6-5 shows the format of this file. The primary key for this file is the Item Number. The first digit of the Item Number field is used for identification of each asset class. That is, all assets are classified into the five groups mentioned earlier in this chapter and each group is identified by a code. For example, all the parking structures Item Number start with 1(1----) and all the parking lots start with 2(2----), and so forth. This method of classification facilitates further sorting and classification of the assets for financial reporting purposes.

The Fixed-Assets Valid Transaction File is processed further through the Master File Creation Run as shown in Fig. 6-3. As a result, the Fixed-Assets Master

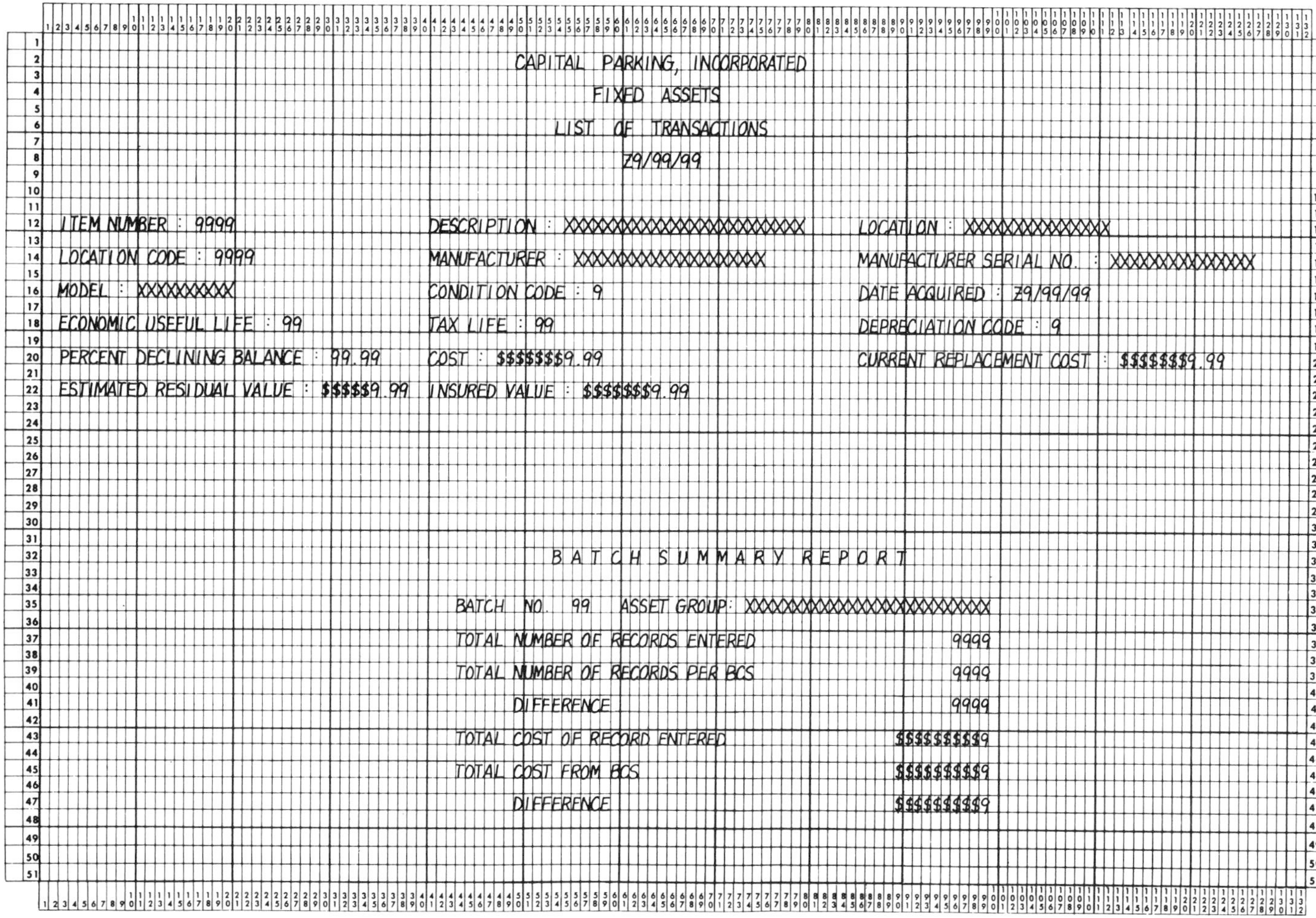
CAPITAL PARKING, INCORPORATED
FIXED ASSETS
LIST OF TRANSACTIONS
Z9/99/99
ITEM NUMBER : 9999
DESCRIPTION : XXXXXXXXXXXXXXXXXXXXXXXXX
LOCATION : XXXXXXXXXXXXXXX
LOCATION CODE : 9999
MANUFACTURER : XXXXXXXXXXXXXXXXXXXX
MANUFACTURER SERIAL NO. : XXXXXXXXXXXXXXX
MODEL : XXXXXXXXXX
CONDITION CODE : 9
DATE ACQUIRED : Z9/99/99
ECONOMIC USEFUL LIFE : 99
TAX LIFE : 99
DEPRECIATION CODE : 9
PERCENT DECLINING BALANCE : 99.99
COST : $$$$$$$9.99
CURRENT REPLACEMENT COST : $$$$$$$9.99
ESTIMATED RESIDUAL VALUE : $$$$$9.99
INSURED VALUE : $$$$$$$9.99
B A T C H S U M M A R Y R E P O R T
BATCH NO. 99 ASSET GROUP: XXXXXXXXXXXXXXXXXXXXXXXXX
TOTAL NUMBER OF RECORDS ENTERED 9999
TOTAL NUMBER OF RECORDS PER BCS 9999
DIFFERENCE 9999
TOTAL COST OF RECORD ENTERED $$$$$$$$$9
TOTAL COST FROM BCS $$$$$$$$$9
DIFFERENCE $$$$$$$$$9

FIGURE 6-4 Output Layout of Fixed-Assets Transaction List and Batch Summary Report

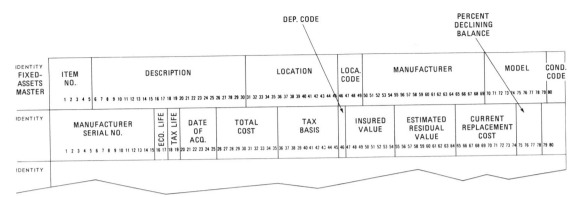

FIGURE 6-5   Layout of Fixed-Assets Valid Transaction File

File is created. This file is a variable-length format as shown in Fig. 6-6. The difference between this file and the Fixed-Assets Valid Transaction File is expansion of records in the former, as time goes on. That is, after calculation of the depreciation charge for each period, the corresponding amounts are stored or added to the appropriate fields of the Fixed-Assets Master File.

UPDATING THE MASTER FILE

One of the routine jobs at the end of each period is the calculation of depreciation. The program that performs this task is quite lengthy. It could calculate the depreciation charge on each item according to straight-line, sum-of-the-years'-

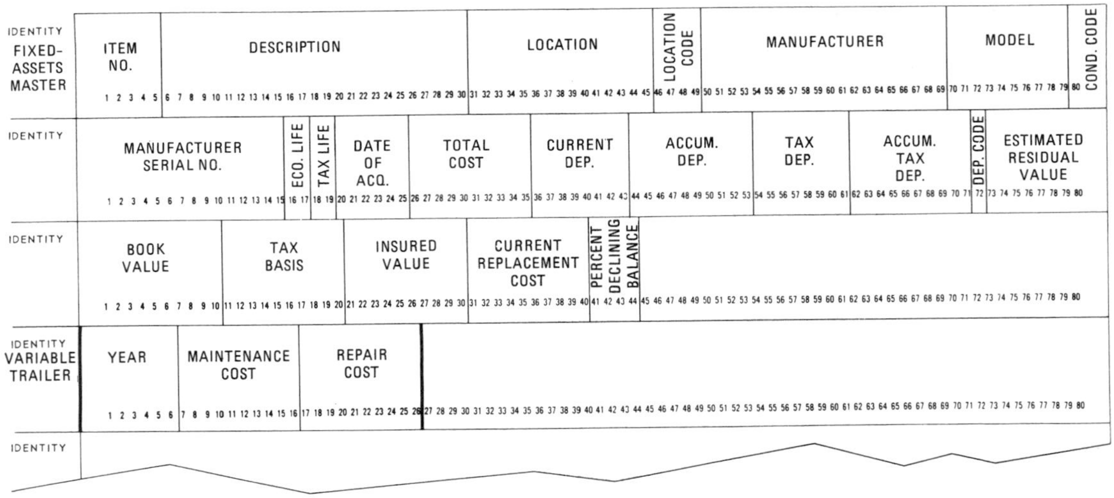

FIGURE 6-6   Layout of Fixed-Assets Master File

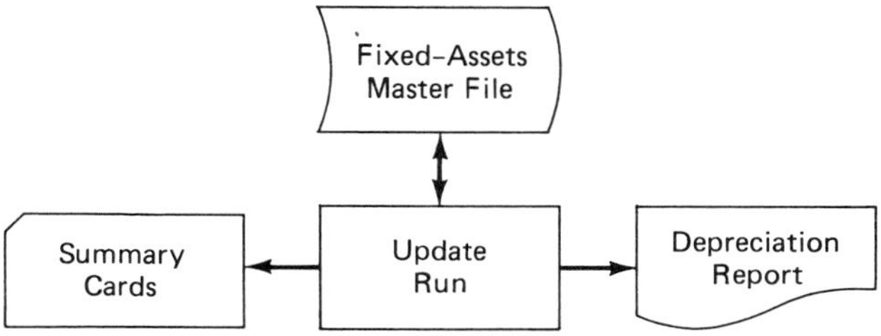

FIGURE 6-7   Update Run Flowchart

digits, declining balance, or some other specified method. In the calculation process, established service life and salvage value are taken into consideration. After the calculation process, all appropriate fields such as the accumulated depreciation are updated and the field is saved for the generation of ad hoc reports or maintenance runs. A backup copy of this file is prepared and kept in a safe location.

As depicted in Fig. 6-7, the input to this run is the Fixed-Assets Master File and the outputs of this run are the Updated Fixed Assets Master File, the Depreciation Report, and the Summary Cards of Depreciation Run.

The updated Fixed-Assets Master File contains all the updated fields (Fig. 6-6). The Depreciation Report shows the results of the calculation process (Fig. 6-8). The data included in this report are

1. Item number of each asset
2. Description of each asset
3. Location code
4. Estimated useful life
5. Residual value
6. Cost
7. Current depreciation charge
8. Accumulated depreciation
9. Book value
10. Date acquired
11. Summary total of each group of assets

As the title of this report indicates, the depreciation is calculated for financial accounting purposes. Another report with a similar format may be prepared for depreciation for tax accounting.

The third output of this run is summary cards prepared for the General Ledger Run.[1] For each group of assets, two cards are punched having the following contents.

1. Reference number (for identifying each transaction)
2. Date

---

[1] This run is discussed in the second part of this chapter. Diskettes could be used instead of punched cards.

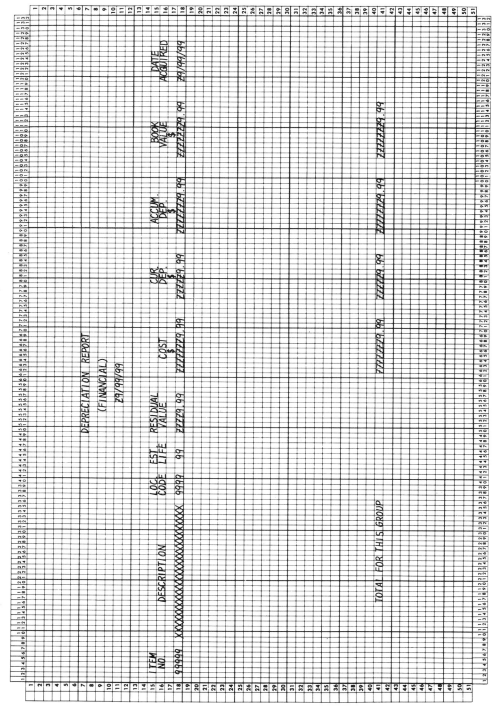

FIGURE 6-8 Output Layout of Depreciation Report

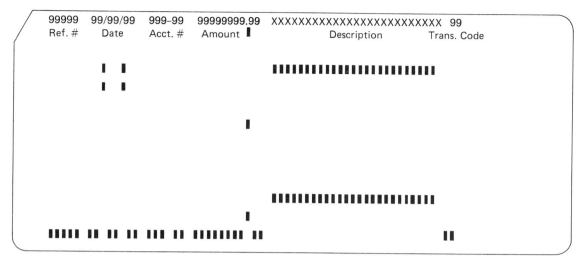

FIGURE 6-9 **Depreciation Summary Card**

3. Account number
4. Amount
5. Description
6. Transaction code

The format of the summary card is shown in Fig. 6-9.

MAINTAINING THE MASTER FILE

A fixed-assets master file is created when an organization computerizes its recordkeeping procedures. However, subsequent additions to this file are handled through the maintenance run. The following are the most frequent types of transactions that are processed through the maintenance run.

- Deletion of an asset as a result of retirement or disposal
- Revision of the estimated useful life for tax and public reporting purposes
- Revision of the estimated residual value
- Change in the location of the asset
- Change in the current replacement cost of the asset
- Change in the insured value of the asset
- Change in the condition code of the asset
- Change in the value of any other field in the master file
- Purchase of new assets

The most important internal control procedure is the proper authorization of those changes. Usually a responsible person such as the controller authorizes the change. After the master file is modified, a record of these changes is sent to the internal auditing department for further evaluation.

In CPI, whenever a change is necessary, a special form is prepared to make this change effective. This form is shown in Fig. 6-10. By referring to the directory of procedures for changes, this form is prepared and after proper authorization it is sent to the data clerk. It should be noted that for the addition of a new asset a Fixed-Assets Data Sheet (Fig. 6-1) should be used. Moreover, when a given record has to be eliminated from the Fixed-Assets File, only "Item Number" and "Transaction Code" fields in the request form have to be entered.

Since the maintenance transactions are limited in number, it may not be

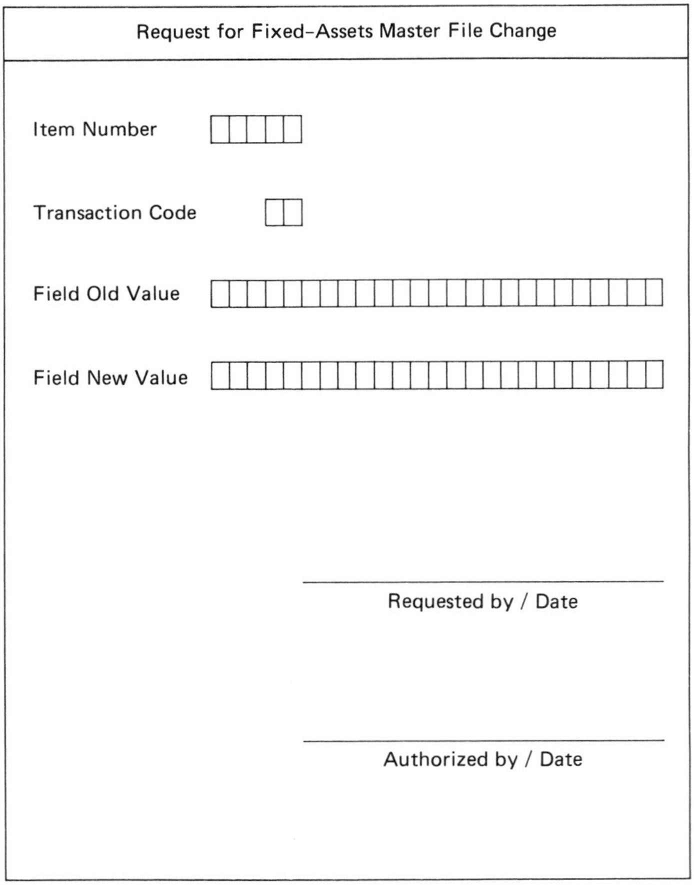
Request for Fixed-Assets Master File Change

Item Number

Transaction Code

Field Old Value

Field New Value

Requested by / Date

Authorized by / Date

FIGURE 6-10 Request for Fixed-Assets Master File Change Form

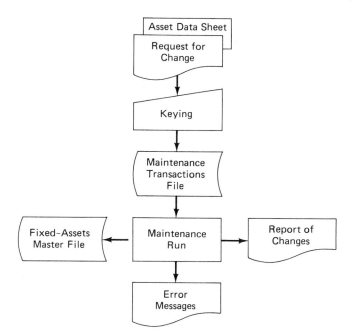

FIGURE 6-11 Maintenance Run Flowchart

economical to have a separate edit run for each. In this situation, an effective manual or visual check might be sufficient.

The data clerk calls the appropriate menu and types in the information into the system. A simple Edit Run consists of a check digit of the Item Number field and a validity check of the transaction code. These tests are performed automatically by the system at data entry. That is, an error is highlighted on the screen of the monitor as soon as it is discovered. The data clerk then has to make an attempt to correct each case. The Maintenance Run is shown in Fig. 6-11.

The output of this run is the Maintenance Transaction File. The layout of this file is shown in Fig. 6-12. This file is in a fixed-length format. The file is then

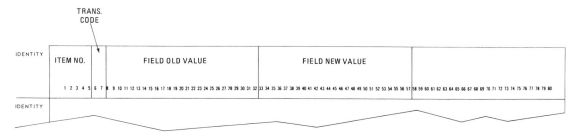

FIGURE 6-12   Layout of Maintenance Transaction File

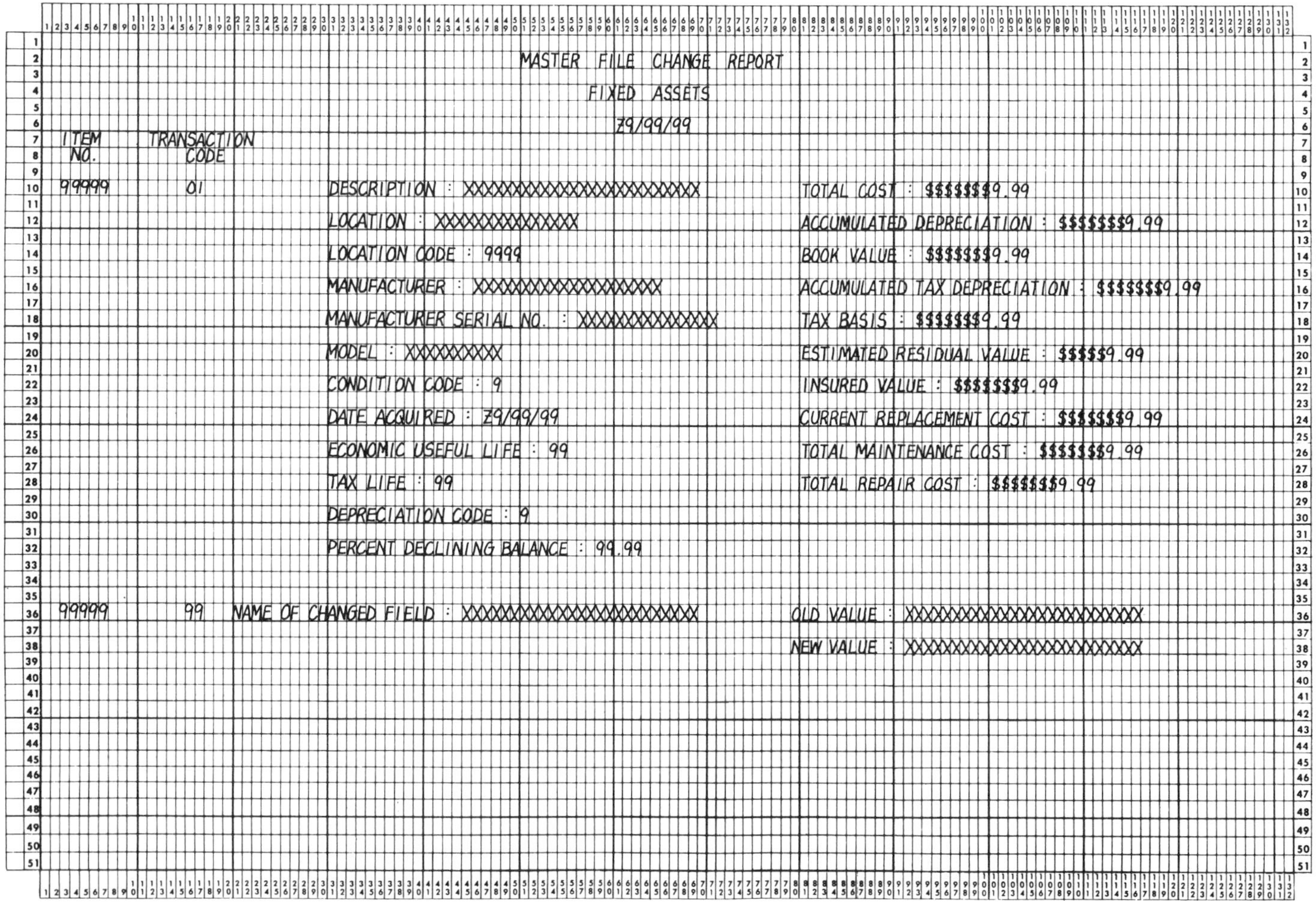

FIGURE 6-13 Output Layout of Master File Change Report

further processed according to Fig. 6-11. The outputs of this run are the Maintained Fixed-Assets Master File, the Report of Changes, and the Error List. The layout of the Fixed-Assets Master File has already been shown (Fig. 6-6).

The Report of Changes is an extremely important report. (See Fig. 6-13.) It contains information changes as they are classified according to their transaction code. Each transaction code represents a change in a particular field, adding a record or deleting a record. For instance, Code "1" deletes a record from the Fixed-Assets Master File. In this situation, a proper audit trail requires that the entire contents of that particular record be dumped on the report. However, in case a value of a field is changed, the report shows the name of the field, its old content, and the new data that has been stored.

When a new item has to be added to the master file, all the input data from the Fixed-Assets Data Sheet is printed after the Item Number and Transaction Code fields.

Occasionally some errors may occur in the system. In this case, the list of errors is printed on the hard copy terminal. Two types of errors are normally detected in this run: "Invalid Transaction Code" and "Invalid Item No." The transactions in error are eliminated from this run and are included in the next maintenance run. The layout of the error list is shown in Fig. 6-14.

Class No.	Ref.
99999	Invalid Transaction Code
99999	Invalid Item No.

FIGURE 6-14 Layout of the Error List

GENERATING AD HOC REPORTS

Because the Fixed-Assets Master File is designed to satisfy a variety of needs as stated in the earlier part of this chapter, many other reports could be generated that were not discussed in this section. Those reports could range from asset-utilization reports to preparation of constant dollar information for supplementing the financial information. The layout of these reports is not discussed in this section.

GENERAL LEDGER SYSTEM: MANAGEMENT INFORMATION REQUIREMENTS

Reports generated by a general ledger accounting system are useful to all areas of management. Indeed, it is difficult to pinpoint any specific interested party or group in this respect.

General ledger accounting is charged with the processing of all finance-related transactions. The relationships of this functional area with other functional areas is depicted in Fig. 6-15. In this illustration, the general ledger system is considered as the center of all information.

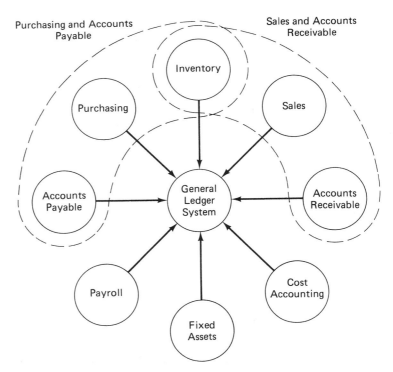

FIGURE 6-15 General Ledger Accounting System

This system can be designed with different degrees of sophistication. At one end of the spectrum, all the transactions related to an accounting event are captured on-line and stored into a common data base. Then the accounting reports are generated through segmentation of this data base.[2] At the other end, the results of each application run (such as Accounts Receivable, Accounts Payable, and so on) are summarized and punched into a few cards. These cards are processed further in the general ledger system and different reports are generated.

The objective of a general ledger accounting system is to provide relevant information for various interested parties, inside and outside. Outside parties include stockholders, creditors, customers, the Internal Revenue Service, the Securities and Exchange Commission, and the general public.

The primary concern of this system is to assure the recording and reporting of all relevant transactions based on the Generally Accepted Accounting Principles (GAAP).

This system at its lowest level of sophistication can generate the following reports.

- Trial balance
- Transaction register
- Detailed transactions for each account
- Balance sheet
- Income statement
- Current and year-to-date amounts

INTERNAL CONTROLS AND AUDIT IMPLICATIONS

The outputs of this system are probably the most important information that is available to outsiders. SEC and IRS normally put this information under scrutiny more than any other information available about the firms. Due to these facts, and also to the third-party reporting implication, the internal controls of this system play a major role. These controls are generally divided into two groups.

General Controls

The most important general controls of this application are

- Proper authorization of the accounting policies that govern the selection of alternative methods of applying GAAP
- Proper authorization of nonroutine journal entries including adjusting entries and protection of accounting forms
- Preparation of all the financial statements based on GAAP
- Separation of duties between the EDP personnel who are responsible for

---

[2] For further information, refer to Robert A. Leitch and K. Roscoe Davis, *Accounting Information Systems* (Englewood Cliffs, N.J.: Prentice-Hall, 1983), Chapter 14.

general ledger applications and those who work on other applications such as accounts receivable or payroll
- Proper review of the generated financial statements prior to their release
- Procedure for maintaining an audit trail

Application Controls

Four tests and control features are built into the programs of the general ledger application.

- Self-checking digits for General Ledger Account codes
- Batch total for checking input data
- Validity test on transaction type codes
- Completeness tests on the validity of the amount and date fields

---

CASE: General Ledger

This case is designed for Capital Parking, Incorporated (CPI). The firm has computerized most of its operational areas. Therefore, the results of the operations are summarized into several punch cards. These cards provide a basis for the general ledger transaction file. However, other aspects of the system need discussing.

GENERAL ACCOUNTING

This department is charged with the function of maintaining the records of all the economic events within CPI's operating environment. This recordkeeping function is based on GAAP. In order to comply with GAAP, specified accounting policies must be established in order to assure uniform and consistent recordkeeping.

Based on the general objectives of financial accounting and the informational needs of outsiders, a chart of accounts is prepared. This allows CPI to report the results of the transactions for each organization's function or unit. Each account in the chart is identified by a five-digit code. The first three digits are used for the classification of the accounts found on the balance sheet and income statement. The other two digits are used for details of each account. For example, since CPI deals with 20 suppliers, the code 01 through 20 is used to identify them.

999–99

Main   Sub-
class   class

Some of the transactions may not be summary results of a computer run. Since this type of transaction occurs infrequently, a system has to be established to capture and record them. A "Journal Voucher" is prepared for each line of transactions. This indicates that for each simple transaction at least *two* journal vouchers are prepared. Naturally, the combined journal entries would require more than two journal vouchers. These vouchers, after being authorized, are used as source documents for the general ledger system. A sample of this form is shown in Fig. 6-16. In order to protect the integrity of this system, the journal vouchers are serially prenumbered.

This document is prepared in three copies. The crucial data that must be coded in this form are

1. Journal voucher number (prenumbered)
2. Date

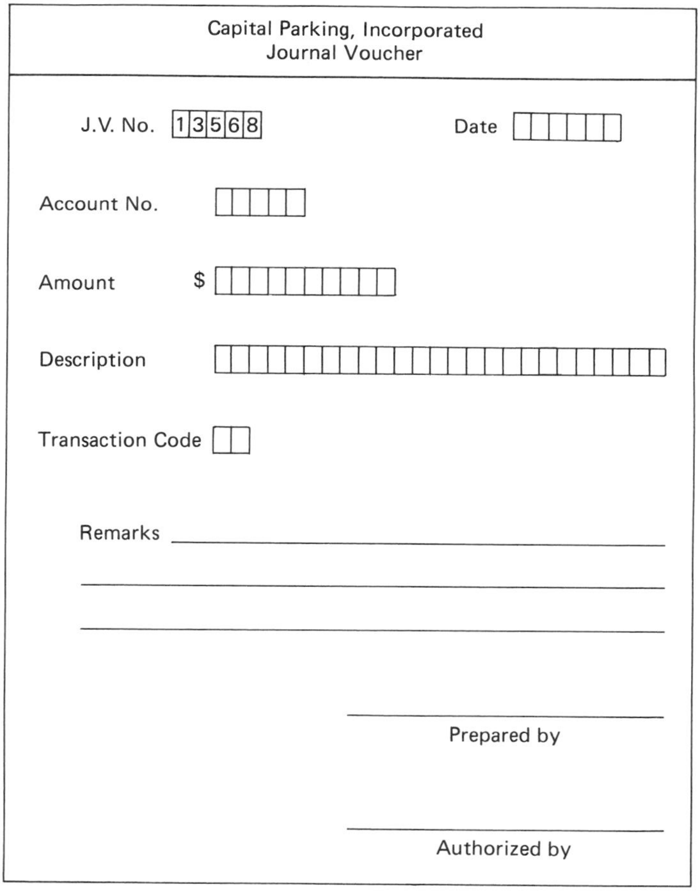

FIGURE 6-16 Journal Voucher Form

3. Account number
4. Amount
5. Description of transaction
6. Transaction code

The account number is determined by referring to the Chart of Accounts Manual. A short description of the transaction is abbreviated in the appropriate field of this form. However, a complete version of this description is written in the Remarks section of this form. The transaction code field is used to indicate the debit or credit effect of each line of transaction.

The first copy of the form is sent to the computer processing division for data entry purposes. The second copy is attached to the original source document, such as invoices, and the third copy is filed according to the journal voucher number.

All the transactions entered into the system pass through an edit run. The flowchart of this section is shown in Fig. 6-17.

EDIT PROCESS

Editing is on-line and automatic at data entry. Each error is detected immediately while the data are being entered into the system. The following tests are used in this application.

Test	Item
1. Sequence check	Journal voucher number
2. Validity check	Account number
3. Validity check	Transaction code
	Code 01 = Debit
	02 = Credit
4. Consistency	Amount
5. Completeness	All the records

The outputs of this run are the List of Transactions and the General Ledger Accumulated Transaction File.

The List of Transactions serves as a journal listing. It merely lists each line of transaction according to the journal voucher number. The layout of this report is shown in Fig. 6-18. The out-of-sequence transactions are highlighted by an asterisk in the Remarks column.

The General Ledger Accumulated Transaction File is a cumulative file of all the transactions from the beginning of the fiscal period. This file is random-access, fixed-format and may be sorted using almost any field as a key. The primary key of this file is the "Account Number" field. However, other fields such as Date, Code (transaction code), and J.V. No. (journal voucher number)

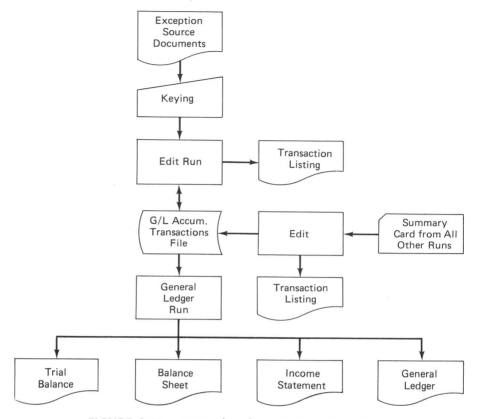

FIGURE 6-17   General Ledger System Flowchart

may be used as secondary keys for generating different types of reports. The layout of this file is shown in Fig. 6-19.

SUMMARY OF OTHER APPLICATION RUNS

The summary cards from all the other computerized applications such as payroll and fixed assets are edited and merged into the General Ledger Accumulated Transaction File (Fig. 6-17). The edit process is less sophisticated because the other computerized applications are already benefiting from an effective control process. Nevertheless, validity checks of the account number fields and completeness of each record are essential. The outputs of this run are similar to the outputs described for the previous run, that is, a General Ledger Accumulated Transaction File and a Transaction Listing.

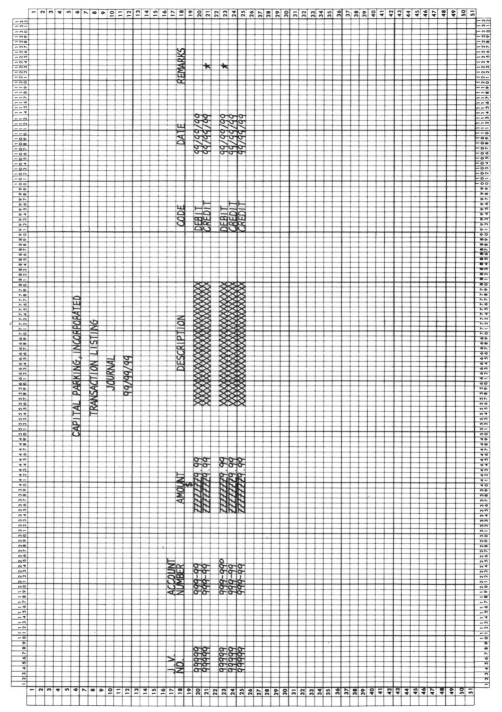

FIGURE 6-18 Output Layout of Transaction Listing Journal

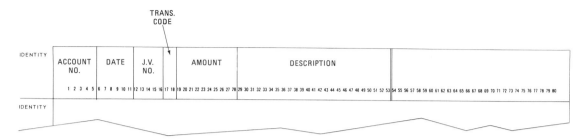

FIGURE 6-19   Layout of General Ledger Accumulated Transaction File

GENERAL LEDGER RUN

As depicted in Fig. 6-17, this run generates various types of reports for the users of this system. The reports are

- Trial balance
- Balance sheet
- Income statement
- General ledger

Because the General Ledger Accumulated Transaction File is a random-access file, the creation of the required reports is done by merely sorting this file for different purposes. For example, the information about individual accounts is sorted according to the account number. The transactions are also sorted according to their date, journal voucher number, and transaction code within each account. The output of this segment of the process is a general ledger listing as shown in Fig. 6-20.

The General Ledger Accumulated Transaction File also could be used to generate the Trial Balance (Fig. 6-21), the Income Statement (Fig. 6-22), and the Balance Sheet (Fig. 6-23).

You have noticed that in Fig. 6-17 these reports are shown as the outputs of a single run. However, there might be a time lag between generation of each of the reports. It may be possible, according to the systems analyst's recommendation, that these reports are to be generated in a single run and be stored on a disk or tape unit. Then, this newly created file could be used to print the requested reports.

The Income Statement and Balance Sheet's year-to-date column is a cumulative amount of each account up to the last transaction processed. In this particular case, it is assumed that CPI's fiscal year ends on August 31. The Income Statement program in the CPI also provides the vertical analysis of the Income Statement—that is, the percentage of each line to the bottom line. It is also

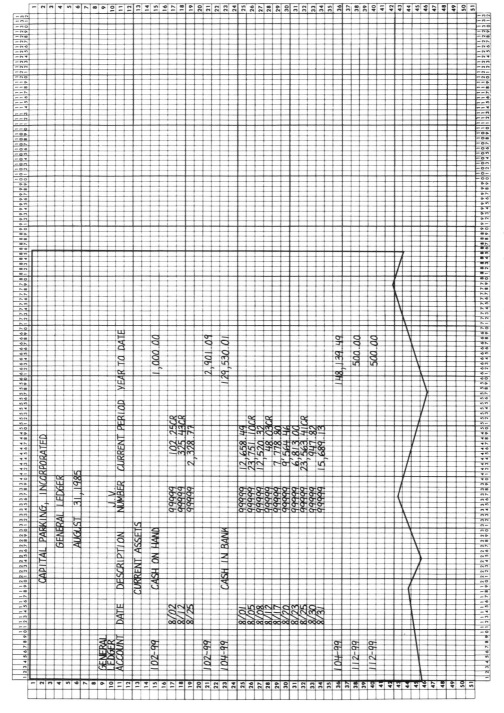

FIGURE 6-20 Output Layout of General Ledger

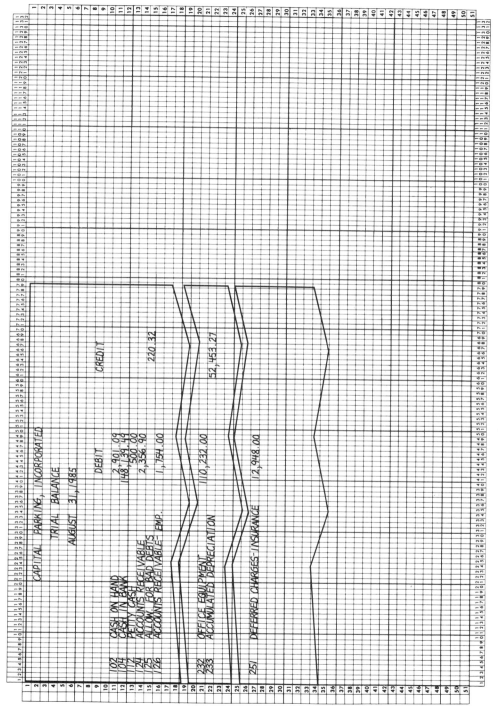

FIGURE 6-21 Output Layout of Trial Balance

177

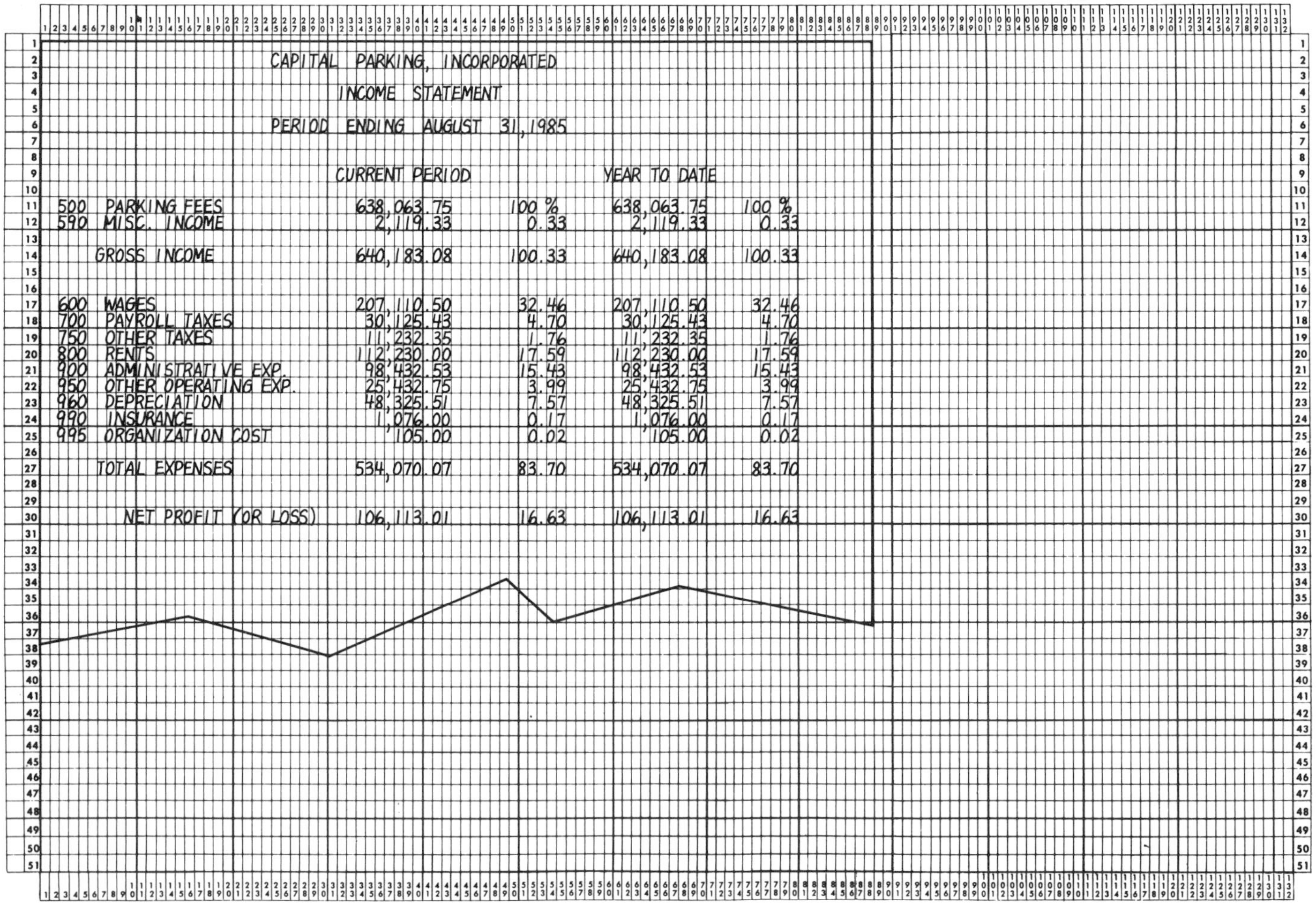
CAPITAL PARKING, INCORPORATED
INCOME STATEMENT
PERIOD ENDING AUGUST 31, 1985
CURRENT PERIOD
YEAR TO DATE
500 PARKING FEES 638,063.75 100 % 638,063.75 100 %
590 MISC. INCOME 2,119.33 0.33 2,119.33 0.33
GROSS INCOME 640,183.08 100.33 640,183.08 100.33
600 WAGES 207,110.50 32.46 207,110.50 32.46
700 PAYROLL TAXES 30,125.43 4.70 30,125.43 4.70
750 OTHER TAXES 11,232.35 1.76 11,232.35 1.76
800 RENTS 112,230.00 17.59 112,230.00 17.59
900 ADMINISTRATIVE EXP. 98,432.53 15.43 98,432.53 15.43
950 OTHER OPERATING EXP. 25,432.75 3.99 25,432.75 3.99
960 DEPRECIATION 48,325.51 7.57 48,325.51 7.57
990 INSURANCE 1,076.00 0.17 1,076.00 0.17
995 ORGANIZATION COST 105.00 0.02 105.00 0.02
TOTAL EXPENSES 534,070.07 83.70 534,070.07 83.70
NET PROFIT (OR LOSS) 106,113.01 16.63 106,113.01 16.63

FIGURE 6-22 Output Layout of Income Statement

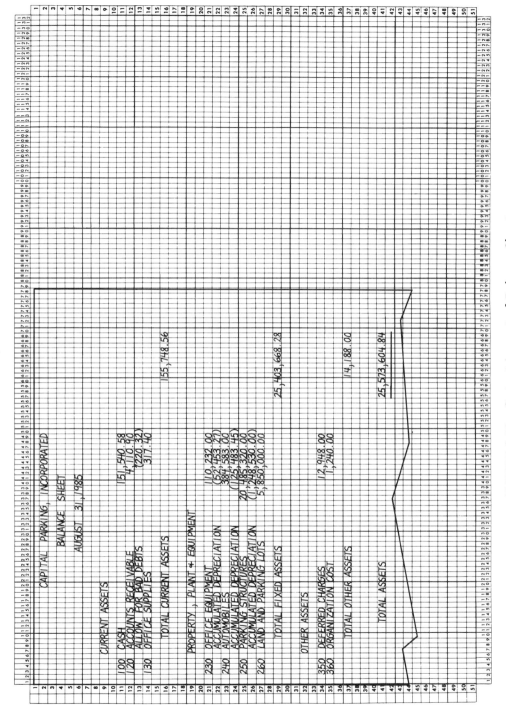

FIGURE 6-23 Output Layout of Balance Sheet

179

possible to create a comparative financial statement assuming the file is properly organized.

ASSESSMENT OF NEEDED STORAGE

The fixed-assets system has three files; moreover, the general ledger system uses an additional file. All these files are random accessed and reside on magnetic disk storage units. The following are approximations of the storage needed to accommodate these files. (See the chapter appendix for details.)

Fixed-Assets Valid Transaction File

This file has fixed-length record format. From the file layout and by adding the number of bytes needed to store the various items, we find that the size of the record is 135 bytes. One record is established to describe each asset. CPI's management estimates that no more than 2,000 individual fixed assets will be on hand at any given time. Therefore, the file requires $2,000 \times 135 = 270,000$ bytes.

Fixed-Assets Master File

Each record of this file has two components; a fixed part, and a variable part. The fixed part requires 136 bytes of storage. The size of this component of the file is therefore $2,000 \times 136 = 272,000$ bytes. The variable-length part results from including a fixed number of bytes (16 bytes) a variable number of times. Suppose that, on the average, each asset is subjected to 10 maintenance operations during its economic life. This results in $10 \times 16 \times 2,000 = 320,000$ bytes being required for the variable part of the file. Hence, the total number of bytes needed to accommodate this file is $320,000 + 272,000 = 592,000$ bytes.

Maintenance Transaction File

The purpose of this file is to hold maintenance transactions temporarily until an edit run for them is economical. Assume that 100 records are allocated for this file. Each record is 55 bytes long; therefore, $100 \times 55 = 5,500$ bytes are needed to accommodate this file.

General Ledger Accumulated Transaction File

This file is created to keep records of all economic events within CPI's operating environment. Suppose that, on the average, there are 30 such events per day, or about 10,000 events per day. Each transaction record is 45 bytes in length; this results in $45 \times 10,000 = 450,000$ bytes being needed to accommodate the file.

The total requirement of file storage for this application is 270,000 + 592,000 + 5,500 + 450,000 = 1,317,500 bytes or about 1,100 K bytes.

PROBLEMS

1. Design a screen layout for menu-driven fixed-assets data entry, showing all the possibilities that you could have in your menu.

2. Design a layout of a report that could be used for managerial decision making. The report should include constant dollar information.

3. How should the Fixed-Assets Master File be changed in order to be able to produce the above report?

4. Design a layout of a report which highlights the custodianships of assets by reporting the asset and its type for each location.

5. Design a layout of a report which facilitates replacement and retirement decisions.

6. Design a layout of a report to highlight the maintenance and repair costs of each asset.

7. Refer to the general ledger system and redesign this system in such a way that comparative financial statements can be generated. Your design should include a new master file and a new layout for all the output reports.

8. Redesign the general ledger system by eliminating punched cards from the system.

9. Draw a flowchart for a general ledger accounting system that utilizes all the individual transactions that are recorded in the computer data base rather than using the summary transactions. Assume that all transactions, including adjusting entries, are immediately recorded into the corporate data base.

10. Develop a computerized chart of accounts for a manufacturing operation. The sales level of the firm is approximately $50 million.

11. The journal voucher described in the case may not be considered efficient since one voucher should be prepared for each line of transaction; that is, each simple transaction should have two J.V.'s to indicate the debit side and credit side of the transactions. Redesign the system in such a way that only *one* J.V. is used for each transaction. Your design should include all aspects of the system from data capturing to final output.

APPENDIX

Fixed-Assets Valid Transaction File Layout

Data Element	Format	Number of Bytes	Notes
Item No.	9(5)	3	
Description	X(25)	25	
Location	X(15)	15	
Location Code	9(4)	3	
Manufacturer	X(20)	20	
Model	X(10)	10	
Condition Code	9	1	
Manufacturer Serial No.	X(15)	15	
Economic Life	99	2	
Tax Life	99	2	
Date of Acquisition	X(6)	6	
Total Cost	9(10)	6	
Tax Basis	9(10)	6	
Depreciation Code	9	1	
Insured Value	9(8)	5	
Estimated Residual Value	9(10)	6	
Current Replacement Cost	9(10)	6	
Percent Declining Balance	9(4)	3	
		135 bytes	

Fixed-Assets Master File Layout

Data Element	Format	Number of Bytes	Notes
Item No.	9(5)	3	
Description	X(25)	25	
Location	X(15)	15	
Location Code	9(4)	3	
Manufacturer	X(20)	20	
Model	X(10)	10	
Condition Code	9	1	
Manufacturer Serial No.	X(15)	15	
Economic Life	99	2	This is the fixed part of each record.
Tax Life	99	2	
Date of Acquisition	X(6)	6	
Total Cost	9(10)	6	
Current Depreciation	9(8)	5	
Accumulated Depreciation	9(10)	6	
Tax Depreciation	9(8)	5	
Accumulated Tax Dep.	9(10)	6	
Depreciation Code	9	1	
Estimated Residual Value	9(8)	5	
		136 bytes	(fixed part)
Year	9(6)	4	
Maintenance Cost	9(10)	6	This is a variable trailer
Repair Cost	9(10)	6	
		16 bytes	(variable part)

Maintenance Transaction File Layout

Data Element	Format	Number of Bytes	Notes
Item No.	9(5)	3	
Transaction Code	99	2	
Field Old Value	X(25)	25	
Field New Value	X(25)	25	
		55 bytes	

General Ledger Accumulated Transaction File

Data Element	Format	Number of Bytes	Notes
Account No.	9(5)	3	
Date	X(6)	6	
Journal Voucher No.	9(5)	3	
Transaction Code	99	2	
Amount	9(10)	6	
Description	X(25)	25	
		45 bytes	

7 | Design of a System for Management Planning and Control

The basic function of a manager is decision making. A manager may decide to plan or to control. The process of planning and control has been divided into strategic planning, management control, and operational control.[1]

Strategic planning is defined as the process of deciding on objectives of the organization, on changes in the objectives, on the resources used to obtain these objectives, and on the policies that are to govern the acquisition, use, and disposition of these resources.[2] Strategic decisions are normally made by top management, and generally involve defining the goals of organizations. Strategic planning decisions are very complex and are usually identified as unstructured (nonprogrammable) decision problems. However, sophisticated models can be used to predict and evaluate the outcome of the various strategic plans.

Management control refers to the process by which managers assure that resources are obtained and used effectively and efficiently in the accomplishment of the organization's objectives.[3] Most of management's efforts in this area are directed toward efficient use of the resources and effective performance of the objectives. The source of decisions in this area is generally financial information.

The third level is *operational control,* which refers to the process of assuring that specific tasks are carried out effectively and efficiently. The decision models used in this level are structured (programmable). These three levels of managerial activities and their associated decision-making processes are shown in Fig. 7-1.

Lucas[4] has added a fourth category of decisions. This new level is *transaction*

---

[1] Robert N. Anthony, *Planning and Control Systems: A Framework for Analysis* (Boston: Division of Research, Harvard University Graduate School of Business Administration, 1965). Used with permission.

[2] Ibid., p. 24.

[3] Ibid., p. 27.

[4] Henry H. Lucas, Jr., *Why Information Systems Fail* (New York: Columbia University Press, 1975), Chapter 1.

Four Levels of Managerial Activities

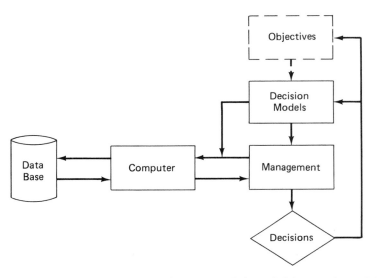

FIGURE 7-1   The Four Levels of Managerial Activities and Decision Framework of an Organization

processing, which involves limited or no decisions at all. Examples of transaction processing are computer applications which process bills, checks, or any similar function. This level is referred to as paper processing systems.

MANAGEMENT INFORMATION REQUIREMENTS

The three levels of managerial activities and the decision-making process for all the levels are shown in Fig. 7-2. The first three levels each deal with some form of decision model. Depending upon the organizational structure and the nature

	Operational Control	Management Control	Strategic Planning
Structured	Accounts Receivable	Budget Analysis— Engineered Costs	Tanker Fleet Mix
	Order Entry	Short-Term Forecasting	Warehouse and Factory Location
	Inventory Control		
Semi-Structured	Production Scheduling	Variance Analysis— Overall Budget	Mergers and Acquisitions
	Cash Management	Budget Preparation	New Product Planning
Unstructured	PERT/COST Systems	Sales and Production	R&D Planning

Source: G. Anthony Gorry and Michael S. Scott Morton,'' A Framework for Management Information Systems,'' *Sloan Management Review,* Fall 1971, p. 62, by permission of the publisher. Copyright © 1971, by the Sloan Management Review Association. All rights reserved.

FIGURE 7-2   The Degree of Structure Associated with Managerial Activities

of the decision, the complexity of decision models varies. At the highest level of organization for strategic planning decisions, the models are very unstructured and complex, whereas at the operational control or transaction processing levels, the models are trivial and structured.

Strategic Planning

Decisions about introducing a new product, exploring a new market, introducing a new production technique, acquiring new capital assets, creating a new employee training program (to enhance the capabilities of the work force), and implementation of a new policy are all *strategic* decisions.

Generally, the decision models are complex and unstructured and the source of information for this type of decision is predominantly external. Although the communication of the information in this area is relatively simple, the information available is rather scanty and inaccurate. Simulation and "what if" models are two types of models used in this area. The major obstacle to computerization of these types of models is the lack of coding techniques for capturing and processing of strategic data.

At the outset, efforts toward computerization of these models were made at the corporate level by creating custom-made models. An example of this situation is the corporate financial model developed by Sun Oil Company.[5] However, as this area of management endeavor became known to commercial software firms, several packages became available. Some of these packages are System W, Interactive Financial Planning System (IFPS), EXPRESS, the Combs Unangst Financial Forecasting System (CUFFS), SIMPLAN, and XSIM.

Because of the inability of the strategic decision models to provide management with the exact answer to management's problems, they are normally referred to as *decision support systems* (DSS). As mentioned earlier, most of the sources of information for this area of decision making are external. A few examples of the external information used are costs of resources and their trends (raw material, energy, and alternatives for them), costs of funds and capital, trend analysis of risks, laws, and regulations, and trends of changes in foreign currencies.

Internal information used in this area includes: cost of resources manufactured, costs of selling and administrative activities, different margins (for example, contribution margin and gross margin), cash flows, acquisition cost of assets, breakeven analysis, and so forth. The accounting department is the major source and provides this information in such forms as cost analyses, fund flow analyses, and financial ratios.

Management Control

This area is mainly concerned with the efficient use of resources and effective measure of performance. Middle management is normally involved with this type of decision. The decision models used in this area are relatively more structured than strategic planning; thus the information used in the models is expected to be more accurate.

Examples of these types of decisions are

- Budget analysis of engineered costs (manufacturing budget)
- Short-term financial forecasts (pro forma statements)
- Short-term cash flow (cash budget)
- Operational budgets (sales, production, selling, and administrative and variable costs)
- Performance reports (variance analysis of overhead, finished goods, utilization of production facilities, and exception reports on work orders)
- Responsibility reports

The major source of information needed for such decisions is the managerial accounting system.

---

[5] George W. Gershefski, "Building a Corporate Financial Model," *Harvard Business Review,* July–August 1969, pp. 61–72.

Operational Control

Effective and efficient performance of an individual task is within the domain of operational control. Decisions about scheduling an individual job or an order entry are two examples of this type of decision. The sources of information for operational control decisions are internal. The models utilized are structured and unsophisticated. Information used in this type of model is precise.

The impact of computerization on this area has been the greatest. This is mainly due to the nature of the decision problems, which can be defined easily, and the corresponding decision rules that lend themselves to programming. Signaling the out-of-stock inventory item or automatically printing purchase orders are two common computer applications of operational control decisions. Most of the operations research (OR) models such as economic order quantity (EOQ) are used in this area of management.

Transaction Processing

Transaction processing is a routine decision-making function that is usually programmed. The decision about classification of thousands of transactions that occur daily is one example of this type of decision.

INTERNAL CONTROL AND AUDIT IMPLICATIONS

Since this application utilizes the files that are created at other stages (such as the Inventory Master File), the internal controls are discussed only for files that are created for this case. It should be noted that in certain areas of strategic planning, the only available control is management's judgment.

The controls are divided into the two categories of general and application controls.

General Controls

General controls used for this application are

- Procedures for review of the policies set by top management
- Procedures for review of production schedules in order to prevent unauthorized production orders
- Procedures for periodic review of the chart of accounts, to allow for accurate classifications of each transaction and creation of responsibility reports
- Separation of functions of personnel in production and inventory handling
- Separation of duties between production staff and recordkeeping staff
- Establishment of passwords so that only authorized individuals are allowed to access the system
- Procedures for maintaining audit trail and safeguarding the files

Application Controls

These are the tests and control features that are built into the computer programs. These controls are

- Validity checks on customer number, trailer status code, and direct material item number fields
- Limit tests on unit requested, scrap rate, overhead rate, time, cost/hour, and number of units required fields
- Completeness tests on several selected fields

CASE: Manufacturing

Gyrocircuits, Incorporated is a manufacturer of circuit boards for military and commercial applications. The company was started in 1972 by Richard (Dick) Lemieux, an electrical engineer who believed in incorporating the latest technological advances into his products.

Dick started his operations from his garage. His firm rapidly grew to 100 employees and annual sales of more than $10 million. His success was due to two factors: first, the possession of two patents for circuits layout and, second, the ability to fill emergency orders and expedite orders in process. The company is still closely held, and Dick exercises complete control.

Gyrocircuits normally gets its contracts through a competitive bidding process in response to a specific request for proposal (RFP). Circuit-board layouts are designed and cost-projected by the technical marketing team consisting of Lemieux and Ray Karam, his only salesman. Necessary components are ordered immediately upon award of the contract. Photomasks are produced from the original blueprints, and the boards are punched and printed on the premises before electrical components are attached. Quality control is assured through computer-assisted testing of all circuit elements on the completed boards.

The scrap rate has been close to 2 percent. This rate is considered very good by industry standards for this type of operation.

In 1982 Lemieux completely converted Gyrocircuits' shop to the use of a new technology known as direct application of components. The old method required the insertion of component pins into holes drilled in the board and the soldering of the pins to circuits printed on the "verso" side of the board. The production layout of the old method is shown in Fig. 7-3.

The new method allows the circuit to be printed on the "recto" side. The components, according to this method, are laser spot-welded directly to the circuit path. This new technology allows the creation of faster, more compact circuit paths. Moreover, it produces lighter, smaller, and more reliable boards. In short, the new production layout combines two processes of "drilling" and

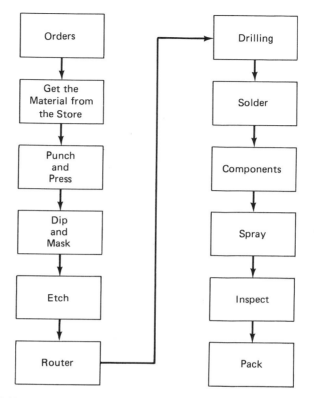

FIGURE 7-3 Production Layout of the Old Method

"soldering" into one process of laser welding. The production layout of the new method is shown in Fig. 7-4.

The new process has been an immediate success. Sales have increased more than 50 percent in 18 months. There is every indication that the sales will continue to increase and possibly accelerate. The past 10 years' data are shown in Fig. 7-5.

Much to Lemieux's surprise, however, the profits that he expected the new technology to generate have not materialized. Although sales have increased, the profit margin is down. In fact, the profit is only slightly more than it was before conversion.

Management of Gyrocircuits has attempted many times to pinpoint the cause of this failure, but has been unable to reach any conclusions. They also have noticed that the scrap rate is high and labor productivity is down. They feel that they have lost track of direct labor and scrap costs. Furthermore, they have noticed considerable difference between estimated and actual materials costs, irrespective of scrap costs.

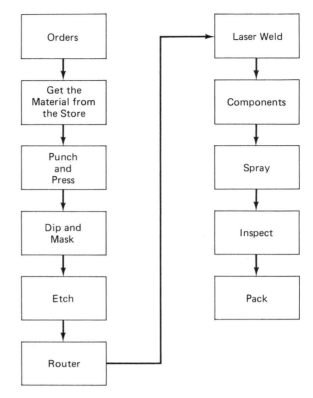

FIGURE 7-4   Production Layout of the New Method

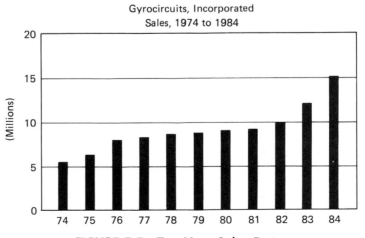

FIGURE 7-5   Ten-Year Sales Data

After considerable deliberation, Lemieux decided to hire a professional consultant to look into this situation. The following is extracted from the consultant's report.

PROBLEM DEFINITION

The consultant has identified the problem as lack of control over costs of labor and materials. The symptoms of the problems are

- Increase in sales, yet decrease in profit margin
- Increase in the cost of materials in excess of expectations
- Increase in direct labor costs in spite of elimination of one of the steps from the old production method
- Increase in scrap costs beyond the standard development for the new system
- A survey of similar production layouts suggests that the standards are attainable

The consultant has collected some historical data from April 1983 through August 1984. Figure 7-6 shows direct labor variance per unit of the product for the said period. Figure 7-7 shows the scrap deviation from the standard for the period April 1983 through August 1984.

The consultant has come to a conclusion: Since the timing and quality of orders are satisfactory, the lack of an adequate cost accounting system has

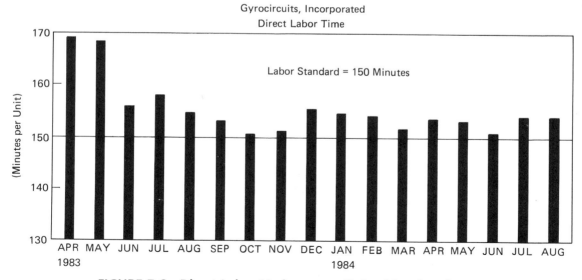

FIGURE 7-6   Direct Labor Variance per Unit of Product from April 1983 to August 1984

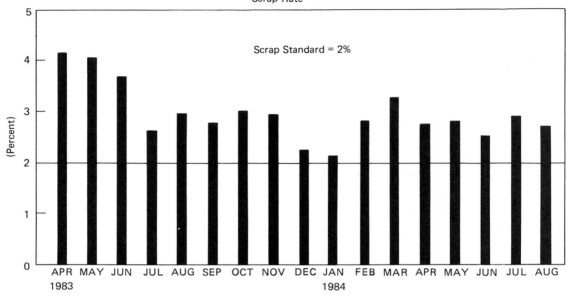

FIGURE 7-7 Scrap Variance of Products from April 1983 to August 1984

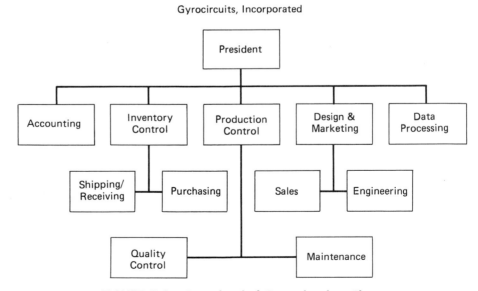

FIGURE 7-8 Gyrocircuits' Organization Chart

caused all the problems. In addition, lack of long-range planning has made Gyrocircuits volatile to environmental factors.

Based on the organization chart presented in Fig. 7-8, the consultant has proposed a cost accounting system to facilitate management planning and control in the short run and a decision support package to assist the management in its long-range decisions.

INFORMATION SYSTEMS FOR SHORT-RUN PLANNING AND CONTROLS

The matrix of information needs by various departments is shown in Fig. 7-9. An X in each cell suggests the necessity of particular types of information for specific departments. This matrix simply matches the "sources" of information

		Sources					
		Labor	WIP	Finished Goods	RM	Scrap	Overhead
Uses	Accounting	X	X	X	X	X	X
	Inventory Control		X	X	X	X	
	Shipping/ Receiving			X			
	Purchasing				X		
	Production Control	X	X	X	X	X	
	Quality Control and Standards	X				X	
	Maintenance					X	
	Design and Marketing	X				X	X
	Sales		X	X			X
	Engineering					X	X
	Data Processing	X	X	X	X	X	X
	Top Management	X	X	X	X	X	X

FIGURE 7-9   Matrix of Departmental Information Needs

with the "uses" of information. As you may have noticed, some of this information is reported in monetary units (dollars in this case) and some is reported merely on the basis of the number of units. Nevertheless, some decision-making areas (such as top management) may require the information according to both dollars and units.

This matrix, which is a system analysis tool, facilitates the design process by defining the users' need in a more efficient manner and helps to standardize reporting.

The system designed to satisfy the short-run information needs attempts to encompass all phases of the operations. However, in this chapter, only those segments that interact with the cost accounting system are presented.

Development of Bids

Since most of the sales contracts are acquired through competitive bidding, a systematic method has been designed to process bids at Gyrocircuits. The flowchart of this part of the process is shown in Fig. 7-10.

As the customer's request for proposal arrives, the Design and Marketing Department evaluates the request to see whether it is worthwhile or falls within the domain of Gyrocircuits' activities. If the project does not seem worth pursuing, the customer is informed of Gyrocircuits' intention. Otherwise, the design process will continue.

At this stage, the Bid-in-Process File is scanned in case the company had prior experience with this type of product. The design and blueprints of these types of products are already available; therefore, only cost information must be retrieved from the Bid-in-Process File.

The Bid-in-Process File is a multifunction file. At this stage it is used to scan the historical information; it also is considered the main input to other phases of the operation. For example, the material and labor variances are calculated by comparing the actual results with the standards that are stored in this file.

This file is an on-line file on a disk unit. It has a fixed section and several trailers. The format of this file is shown in Fig. 7-11. The fixed portion of the file is used to record the following information:

1. Bid number and part number
2. Part name
3. Date
4. Customer name
5. Customer number
6. Units requested
7. Scrap rate
8. Overhead rate
9. Flag
10. Number of trailers

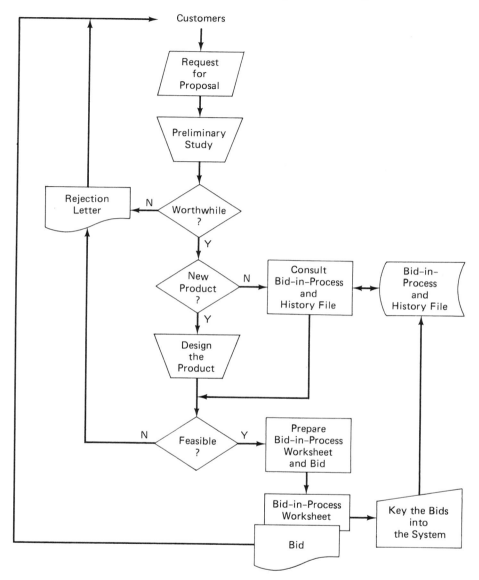

FIGURE 7-10   Development of a Bid

The bid and part number is a six-digit field. The first two digits are assigned to the bids. The last four digits are used to identify each unit within a given bid. The field "Units Requested" represents the number of units requested by customer. The field scrap rate is a two-digit field, and is used to reflect the scrap rate up to one decimal. It should be mentioned that the 2 percent standard

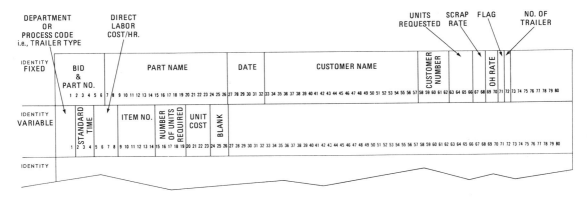

FIGURE 7-11   Layout of Bid-in-Process File

scrap rate which is set by Lemieux is an average figure. Therefore, depending on the complexity of the design of products, the rate could be higher or lower than 2 percent.

Overhead rate is a fixed rate which is developed as a result of analysis of Gyrocircuits' historical information. Currently this rate is developed as a result of correlation between overhead costs and direct labor cost. Therefore the overhead rate is expressed in terms of percentage of direct labor cost.

The flag field is a single-digit field which is used to reflect various states of each bid. There are four possible states for this field and are represented by the following codes:

Code	State of the Bid
1	Submitted
2	Accepted (in process)
3	Completed
4	Rejected by customer

The historical portion of the Bid-in-Process File basically includes the completed bids and rejected bids. Furthermore, as the bids go from one state to another state, this code is also changed to reflect the situation.

The variable portion of the file represents different stages that a given product must go through (Fig. 7-11). One trailer is created for each stage and the following data are stored in each trailer.

1. Department or process (status code)
2. Standard time (for state)
3. Direct labor cost/hour
4. Direct material item number

5. Number of units required
6. Direct material cost/unit
7. Blank fields

In the current production layout each product must pass nine stages. Therefore, for each bid, nine trailers are created and each represented by a unique code. These codes and stages are

Code	Production Stage
A	Punch, press
B	Dip and mask
C	Etch
D	Router
E	Laser weld
F	Components
G	Spray
H	Inspection
I	Packing

The contents of each trailer record consist of standard prime cost components of each stage of production. By combining the costs of all stages, the total prime costs of the production could be easily figured. Furthermore, the computer program could apply the overhead rate to direct labor cost and calculate the overhead cost of each stage of the production. Thus the contents of this record are extremely important for calculation of the direct material and direct labor variances.

It should be noted that if a product does not have to go through all the stages, a trailer for that particular stage should not be included.

Sometimes, a request for proposal requires development of a new product. In this case, this new product must be designed before any costs estimate. However, both new and old design must go through an economic feasibility study. If the production is considered unfeasible, the customer is notified of Gyrocircuits' intention. The bids are submitted only for those products that are economically acceptable. Therefore, as part of the process, a Bid-in-Process Worksheet is prepared.

The worksheet is a preprinted form and must be completed manually. Most of the data on this form was discussed earlier when the contents of Bid-in-Process File was explained. This form is shown in Fig. 7-12. Based on the estimates provided, this form is completed and the total costs of the products are determined. This information is used as a benchmark for bidding on the products. As soon as the bid is prepared and sent, the data in the bold section of this form is entered in the Bid-in-Process Master File. The status code of the record at this stage is "1" indicating that the bid has been submitted for customer consideration.

Gyrocircuits, Incorporated

Bid-in-Process Worksheet

Bid No. ☐☐☐☐☐☐   Units Requested ☐☐☐   Date (Mo. Day Yr.)

Customer Name & Address

Customer No. ☐☐☐☐☐

Scrap Rate ☐☐

Overhead Rate (% of DL Cost) ☐☐

Department	Code	Time	Cost/Hr $	Total	Direct MTL Item No.	Units Required	Unit Cost	Total	Dept. Labor & Materials
Punch & Press	A								
Dip & Mask	B								
Etch	C								
Router	D								
Laser Weld	E								
Components	F								
Spray	G								
Inspection	H								
Packing	I								
Total									
Overhead									
Total Cost of the Bid									$

FIGURE 7-12   Bid-in-Process Worksheet

During the edit process at data entry, the following tests are performed.

Test	Field
1. Limit test	Unit requested
2. Validity	Customer number
3. Limit test	Scrap rate

Test	Field
4. Limit test	Overhead rate
5. Validity	Trailer status code
6. Limit test	Time
7. Limit test	Cost/hour
8. Validity	Direct material item number
9. Limit test	Number of units required
10. Limit test	Cost/unit

Data entry at this stage involves calling the appropriate menu.

Acceptance of Bids

Customer responses to Gyrocircuits' bids are in the form of either acceptance or rejection of the bids. In either case, the status code of the Bid-in-Process record must be changed. Remember that the status code for the record at the time being is "1". If the customer accepted the bid, the status code should be changed to "2". By the same token, customers' rejections of bids are reflected by changing the status code from "1" to "4".

When a bid is accepted, the production and material schedule must be prepared. Therefore, the Bid-in-Process File is run against the Inventory Master File to assure the availability of the materials. This run is shown in Fig. 7-13. The inputs to this run are the Bid-in-Process File and the Inventory Master File.

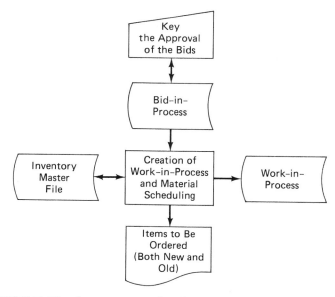

FIGURE 7-13   Acceptance of Bids and Material Scheduling

Record layout of the Inventory Master File is similar to Fig. 4-4 illustrated in Chapter 4. The outputs of this run are the List of the Items to Be Ordered and the Work-in-Process Master File.

To schedule materials availability, the Bid-in-Process File and Inventory are matched. A report of out-of-stock materials and the number of units to be ordered is prepared. Since some of the circuit board designs may require new materials that normally have not been carried by the company, in this report a Remarks column is provided to identify this fact. The information in this report is useful to the Purchasing Department for preparation of purchase orders. Output format of this report is shown in Fig. 7-14 and the report includes the following items.

1. Bid number
2. Item number
3. Description of item
4. Number of units to be ordered
5. Name of the supplier
6. Supplier number
7. Remarks

It should be noted that if new materials are to be ordered, the Remarks column highlights this fact by printing the phrase "New Item." Naturally, in this case, no information is printed in the columns 5 and 6 (supplier's name and number).

The other output of this run is a Work-in-Process Master File. For every part (unit) that is produced, one record is created in the Work-in-Process Master File. This file is a random-access file on disk. The layout of this file is rather simple and shown in Fig. 7-15. The fields provided in each record include bid and part number, status, and date a given status occurs.

The "Bid & Part No." field is a unique identifier of each unit to be produced. The first two digits of this field are used to identify each particular bid and the last four digits are used to identify each part within each bid. For instance, if bid number 49 requires production of 500 units of a given board (refer to Fig. 7-12, the Bid-in-Process Worksheet), in the Work-in-Process Master File the first part is identified by a unique key of 490001 and the last part is identified by the key of 490500. Therefore, each of the parts to be produced is uniquely identified. It should be mentioned that having a 2 percent scrap rate will require Gyrocircuits to produce roughly 500 units plus 2 percent: 510 units. Therefore, the number of work-in-process records created is equal to the number of units to be produced plus 2 percent. The scrap rate is considered in determining the number of items of the inventory that are to be ordered.

Status code is a single-digit field that indicates the status of a given unit. As each unit of product moves from one department to another department, this status code changes. There are ten acceptable codes for this field. Nine of the codes are used to identify nine departments or processes that each unit must

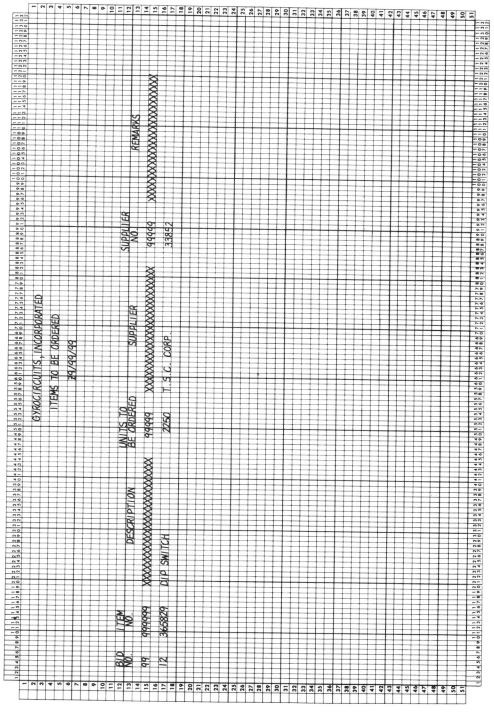

FIGURE 7-14 List of Items to Be Ordered

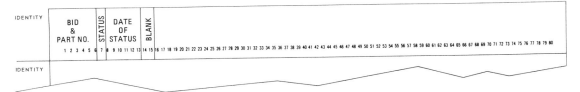

FIGURE 7-15   Layout of Work-in-Process Master File

pass through. The tenth code is used to identify scrapped parts: Code "S". For example, if a given part passed the Dip & Mark process and is scrapped in the etching process, the status code for this part is changed from "B" to "S". This method of file organization allows the determination of the standard costs of work-in-process as they are needed.

The process of changing the status codes is discussed later in this chapter. However, it must be mentioned that the last field of a work-in-process record is a date field. The date is crucial for control purposes. Anytime that a status code is changed, this date is also changed, denoting the date of completion of each process.

Issuance of Materials

As soon as the production schedules are prepared, the materials used at different stages must be sent to the shop. Most of the materials used are sent to the Component Department. The inputs of this run which is shown in Fig. 7-16 are the Bid-in-Process File and the Inventory Master File.

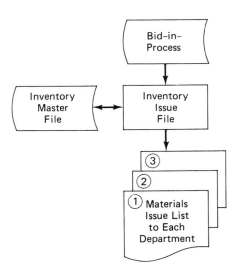

FIGURE 7-16   Issuance of Materials

The records of the Bid-in-Process File which are identified by the status code "2" (bids accepted) are run against the Inventory Master File. The materials are issued and the status code of bid records is changed to "3", indicating that as far as the materials are concerned this bid is complete.

The materials issued generally include a 2 percent scrap rate for normal operation. Therefore, if the materials were in excess of the needs of a particular bid, a special form is filled out and signed by the production supervisor. This, in a sense, is a favorable material variance. Contrary to this situation, if the scrap rate is in excess of the 2 percent standard set up by the company, the production supervisor must authorize the issue of those materials on a special pink form. This clearly indicates an unfavorable material usage variance. The form is shown in Fig. 7-17.

The outputs of this run are the Updated Inventory Master File and the Material Issue List. Updating of the Inventory Master File has already been discussed in Chapter 4.

The Material Issue List is prepared in three copies. The first copy of this report is sent to the Accounting Department and includes the following information:

1. Department name
2. Bid number
3. Part number for each bid
4. Item number
5. Item description
6. Number of units
7. Cost per unit
8. Total cost for each department
9. Total cost of materials for each bid

Copy numbers 2 and 3 of this report are lacking the unit cost and total cost information. This is made possible by carboning only those columns that are essential in materials handling. Both copies are sent along with the materials to the production line. The production supervisor signs the third copy and returns it to the store indicating that the materials have been delivered to the production departments. The output layout of this report is shown in Fig. 7-18.

Production of the Parts

The production process in Gyrocircuits is labor-intensive. Therefore, monitoring the labor cost is crucial. The standard direct labor time for production of one part is 150 minutes. In order to achieve this goal, Gyrocircuits has installed special time-recording devices on various strategic locations. The function of this device is similar to the function of automatic tellers installed in many banks throughout the country.

Each employee is provided with a plastic identification card similar to the bank card. The CRT screen on this recording device reflects various questions as

	Gyrocircuits, Incorporated				

From: Department

To: Store

Please Issue the Following

Item No.	Description	Units Needed	Bid & Part No.	Department	Remarks

Requested by / Date

Authorized by / Date

FIGURE 7-17   Request Form for Excess Materials

soon as a card is inserted into a slot. The answers to the questions on the screen (in addition to the data already magnetized on the employee identification card) causes the creation of the Employee Transaction File. For instance, the card is inserted into the machine when an employee enters the shop. The screen asks "Time-in?" and the employee enters the time in by pressing the keys on the machine. The time-out is also entered in a similar manner. The difference be-

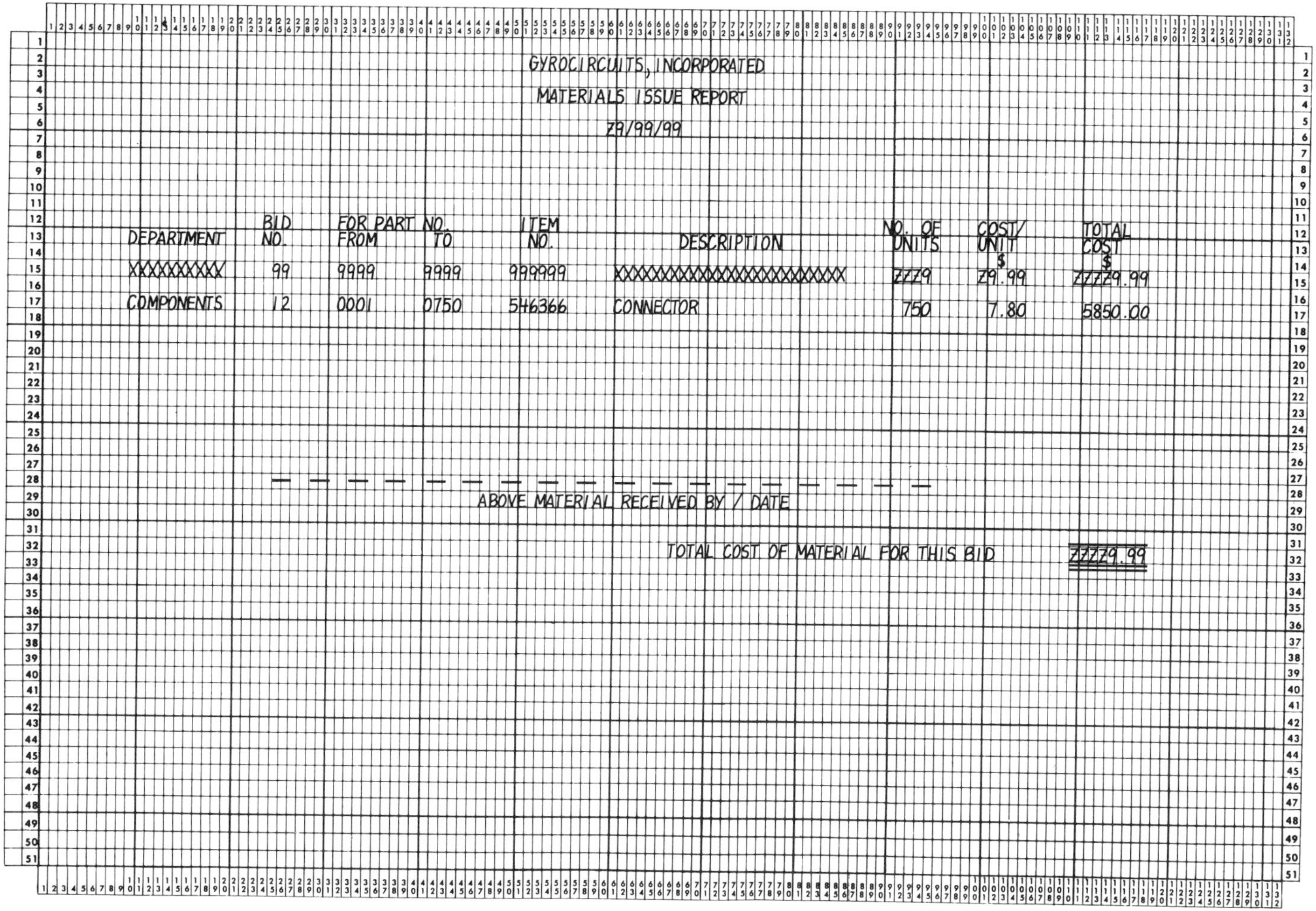

GYROCIRCUITS, INCORPORATED

MATERIALS ISSUE REPORT

Z9/99/99

DEPARTMENT	BID NO.	FOR PART NO. FROM	TO	ITEM NO.	DESCRIPTION	NO. OF UNITS	COST/ UNIT $	TOTAL COST $
XXXXXXXXX	99	9999	9999	999999	XXXXXXXXXXXXXXXXXX	ZZZ9	29.99	ZZZZ9.99
COMPONENTS	12	0001	0750	543366	CONNECTOR	750	7.80	5850.00

ABOVE MATERIAL RECEIVED BY 7 DATE

TOTAL COST OF MATERIAL FOR THIS BID   ZZZZ9.99

FIGURE 7-18   Output Layout of the Materials Issue Report

207

tween the time-in and time-out will determine the period of time that each employee should be compensated for.

The same device is also installed in each of the production departments. As soon as a unit is completed in each department, the employee records this fact on the Employee Transaction File. This is done by inserting the employee identification card into the recording device. The screen by way of default asks "Bid & Part No.?" The employee enters the number. The next question is "Status?" The employee enters the letter which is representative of completion of a given process. For example, letter "C" indicates that etching process is completed. At this time, the status code of each Work-in-Process File is updated. This phase of the process is shown in Fig. 7-19.

System security is preserved by using a two-tiered password. Each user has a sign-on code composed of five characters that allows access to a set of inquiry functions prescribed by a job. This is accomplished by inserting the plastic identification card. To alter information, a user must then enter an alphanumeric six-character verification code. Any unauthorized attempt to access a file is reported on a Daily Security Summary Report. Any unauthorized attempt to change any file is triggered by alerting the console operator.

The password is run against the personnel file on a daily basis and the password of any employee not in active status is deleted. The passwords file is also run to determine the age of the password. In the event that an employee has not changed the password in the past month, an on-line request is made upon the employee's next sign-on to change the password before access to the system is permitted.

The outputs of this process are the Updated Work-in-Process File, the Employee Transaction File, and the Work-in-Process Status Change Report.

The format of the Work-in-Process File was discussed earlier. The Employee Transaction File is a variable-length file organized on disk. The format of this file

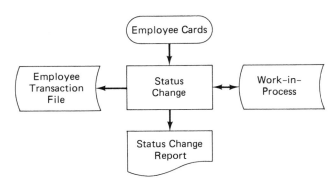

FIGURE 7-19   Flowchart of Employee Interaction with the System

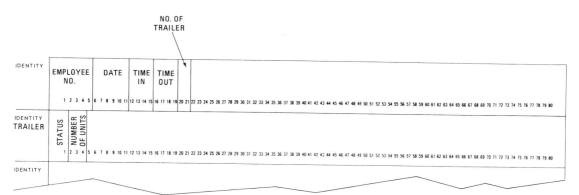

FIGURE 7-20   Layout of Employee Transaction File

is shown in Fig. 7-20. The primary key of this file is the "Employee Number" field. The fixed portion of each record includes

1. Employee number
2. Date
3. Time-in
4. Time-out

The variable section of this record represents the number of units that is completed by each employee. Since one employee may work in several operations, the number of trailers for each record could vary. There is one trailer for each operation. It should be noted that the number of scrapped units is also recorded for each employee and identified by Code "S" in the Employee Transaction Record.

The last output of this run is the Work-in-Process Status Change Report. Layout of this report is shown in Fig. 7-21 and includes the following information.

1. Bid and part number
2. Change of status from
3. Change of status to
4. Employee who caused the change
5. Remarks

In case the status of a part is changed to "S" (scrap), the cause must be entered by the employee into the terminal.

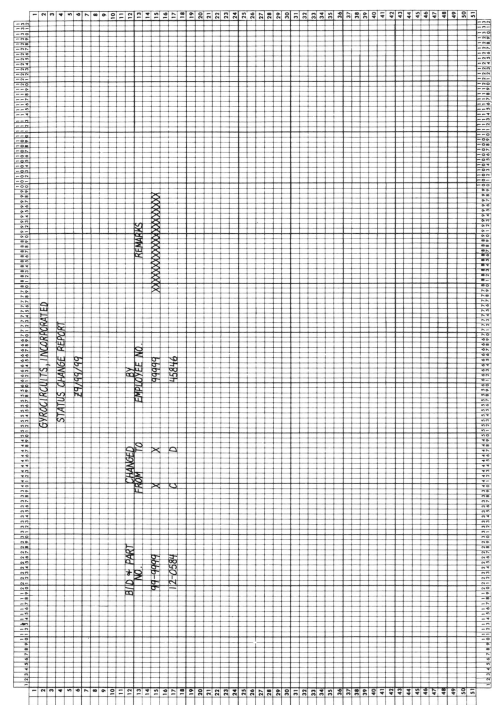

FIGURE 7-21 Output Layout of the Work-in-Process Status Change Report

210

FIGURE 7-22   Layout of the Finished Goods/Cost of Goods Sold File

Completion of the Production

When the production of a bid is totally completed, the Bid-in-Process File and Work-in-Process File are matched. This is necessary in order to create the Finished Goods/Cost of Goods Sold File. As discussed earlier, the cost information is stored in the Bid-in-Process File. Therefore, in order to create finished goods records, cost and customer information are extracted from the Bid-in-Process File, and bid and part numbers are retrieved from the Work-in-Process File.

As it is shown in Fig. 7-22, the inputs to this run are the Bid-in-Process File and the Work-in-Process File. The outputs of this run are the Finished Goods/Cost of Goods Sold File and Listing of Completed and Scrapped Orders.

The format of the Finished Goods/Cost of Goods Sold File is shown in Fig. 7-23. This file is organized on disk and has a fixed format. The information in this file is

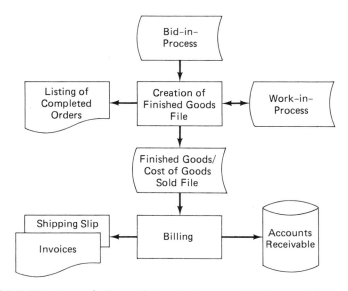

FIGURE 7-23   Completion of Production and Billing of the Product to the Customers

1. Bid and part number
2. Date
3. Customer number
4. Customer name
5. Cost per unit
6. Status code

The cost per unit field is calculated by adding three elements of the costs (direct labor, direct material, and overhead) from the Bid-in-Process File. This is necessary due to the fact that the cost of goods sold in Gyrocircuits is based on standard costs of the resources used.

The status code is also necessary for this file. This field is a single character field and accepts two status codes of "Y" and "Z". Code "Y" indicates the goods are completed and should be delivered to the warehouse. Code "Z" replaces the code "Y" when the goods are, in fact, billed to the customers and the title on goods has changed.

The other output of this run is the list of orders completed and must be sent to the warehouse. The layout of this report is shown in Fig. 7-24 and contains the following information:

1. Bid and part number
2. Customer number
3. Customer name
4. Standard costs/unit
5. Total cost of goods manufactured

This report is prepared in several copies and the copy which is sent to the warehouse does not include any cost information.

As you have observed, the list of the scrapped parts, the department causing the damage and cumulative costs to the scrap point are reported at the lower part of Fig. 7-24.

Reporting the Variances

One of the main problems that Gyrocircuits is faced with is control of the labor costs. The key to this control is labor variance reports. These variances are traditionally divided into two categories of rate and efficiency variances. With the help of the data collected at different phases of the process, the variance reports are calculated on a daily, weekly, monthly, and yearly basis. It should be noted that the key file for generating these types of reports is the Employee Transaction File. The daily transactions for each employee are accumulated on a weekly basis. The daily file is kept in a secure place for a period of seven days. The weekly transaction file is used for two purposes. First, weekly paychecks of

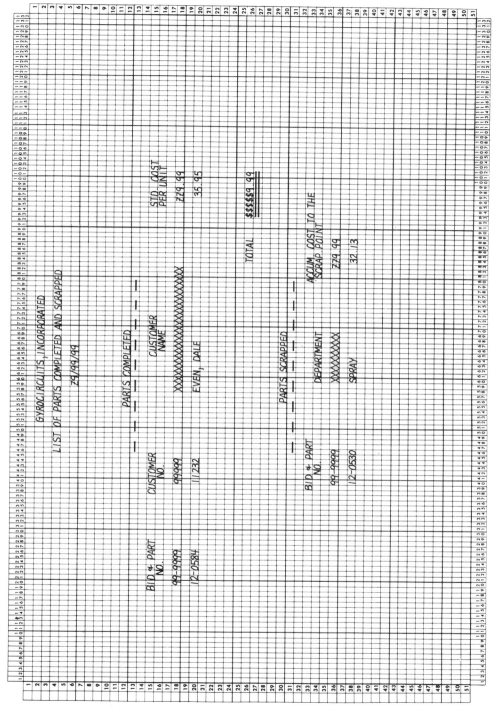

FIGURE 7-24 Output Layout of Parts Completed

213

the employees are prepared by use of this file; and, second, the weekly labor variance report can be generated.

The daily transaction file is also accumulated to create a monthly transaction file and a yearly transaction file. These files in their turn are used to generate monthly and yearly variance reports. Both processes of calculating the variances and processing of the payroll are shown in Fig. 7-25.

In Fig. 7-25, the inputs for the variances reporting run are the Employee Transactions File, the Employee Master File, and the Bid-in-Process File.

The Employee Transactions File is the source of all the events. The actual pay rates are extracted from the Payroll Master File and standard labor rates and times are retrieved from the Bid-in-Process File. The output of this run is the Daily Labor Variances Report, which is shown in Fig. 7-26. The format illustrated is for calculation of the daily variances. The formats of the weekly, monthly, and yearly variances are similar to the daily report, except the heading which may state, for example, Weekly Variances Report for the week ending Z9/99/99.

Direct materials and overhead variances, as stated earlier, are prepared off-line. The reporting of the materials variances is rather simple. For additional

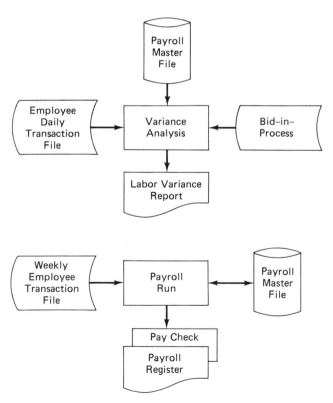

FIGURE 7-25 Variance Reporting and Payroll Process

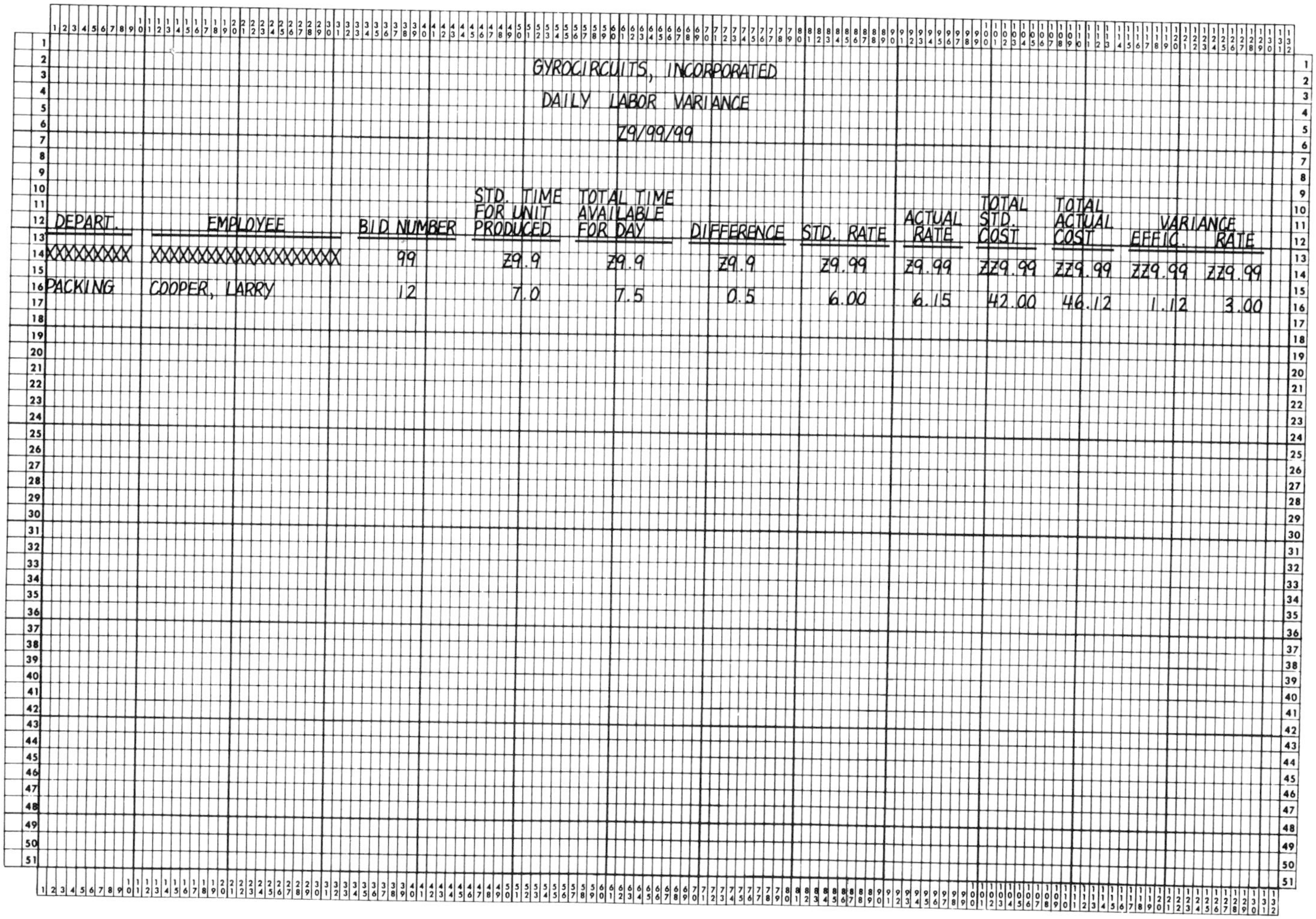

GYROCIRCUITS, INCORPORATED

DAILY LABOR VARIANCE

Z9/99/99

DEPART	EMPLOYEE	BID NUMBER	STD. TIME FOR UNIT PRODUCED	TOTAL TIME AVAILABLE FOR DAY	DIFFERENCE	STD. RATE	ACTUAL RATE	TOTAL STD. COST	TOTAL ACTUAL COST	VARIANCE EFFIC.	VARIANCE RATE
XXXXXXXX	XXXXXXXXX	99	Z9.9	Z9.9	Z9.9	Z9.99	Z9.99	ZZ9.99	ZZ9.99	ZZ9.99	ZZ9.99
PACKING	COOPER, LARRY	12	7.0	7.5	0.5	6.00	6.15	42.00	46.12	1.12	3.00

FIGURE 7-26 Output Layout of Daily Labor Variances

materials used in each process, and excess materials at each process, the production supervisor has to create special forms. A copy of these forms is used by the accounting staff to prepare the favorable and unfavorable material variances.

Reporting of overhead costs is done in a similar manner. The overhead costs absorbed by the products are easily calculated through matching of the Bid-in-Process File with the Work-in-Process File. The overhead absorbed is then matched with the accounting books to calculate overabsorbed and underabsorbed overheads.

The last operation of this case is processing the payroll. The process of payroll in Gyrocircuits is to a certain extent different from the payroll application discussed in Chapter 5. Since most of the data entry activities are done through the employee plastic card reading terminals, the possibility of errors is far more remote. At the end of each week, the Weekly Employee Transactions File is run against the Payroll Master File, and the necessary reports and the paychecks are created.

INFORMATION SYSTEMS FOR LONG-RANGE PLANNING

Long-range planning normally falls under the domain of strategic planning, which is defined as the formulation of long-range plans that span both goal establishment and guiding policies, and the means for reaching the goals. Decisions are made about the acquisition and disposition of major facilities, new market channels, organization structure, and research and development activities as the examples of the strategic decisions.[6]

Characteristics peculiar to strategic planning require specific design consideration. Some of these characteristics that have major impact on the information systems are[7]

- They focus on one aspect of a plan at a time.
- They are complex and include many variables.
- They produce *expected* results.
- They are creative and analytical.
- Their appraisals are extremely difficult.

In order to satisfy the informational needs of strategic planning, both computer-based information systems and operations research models have been

---

[6] Robert N. Anthony, John Dearden, and Norton M. Bedford, *Management Control Systems* (Homewood, Ill.: Irwin, 1984), Chapter 1.

[7] Ibid.

developed to support the decision-making process. These models have been classified into three categories of descriptive, predictive, and normative models based on the function that they perform. The descriptive models, as the name suggests, merely describe a situation and do not predict or recommend any course of action. A plant layout diagram is an example of this type of model. The predictive models on the other hand propose that "if this occurs, then that will follow." They provide a means for "what if" questions by finding relationships between dependent and independent variables. An example of this type of model is a sales prediction model. The third type are normative models that suggest a recommended course of action or the "best" answer to solve problems. An example of this type of model is an advertising budget model.[8]

Almost all of the models discussed above are generally classified under the title decision support systems. Gyrocircuits uses three types of DSSs in its planning process.

Simulation

Gyrocircuits, a high-technology firm in a fast-moving market, faces a relatively short planning horizon. Economic conditions and technology are constantly changing, the competitive environment is in continual flux, and customer needs change almost daily.

Simulation helps to streamline Gyrocircuits' planning. However, sufficient care must be taken not to oversimplify the system to mathematically describable components only. In this context, the simulation technique allows Gyrocircuits to model the system and study its behavior under changed circumstances, both internally and externally. The firm uses simulation as a means of prediction and development in the following areas.

- Design of new production systems
- Design of new operating systems
- Creation of novel board designs
- Training in design and in production management

Furthermore, design of a capital budgeting model based on discounted cash flow techniques is under consideration by Dick Lemieux. This model is supposed to aid considerably in making decisions about the resources to be spent on equipment. In addition to the discounted cash flows, the model also evaluates the project based on Internal Rate of Return, Payback Period, and Accounting Rate of Return. The process of building a simulation model is shown in Fig. 7-27.

[8] Robert G. Murdick, Joel G. Ross, and James R. Claggett, *Information Systems for Modern Management* (Englewood Cliffs, N.J.: Prentice-Hall, 1984), p. 387.

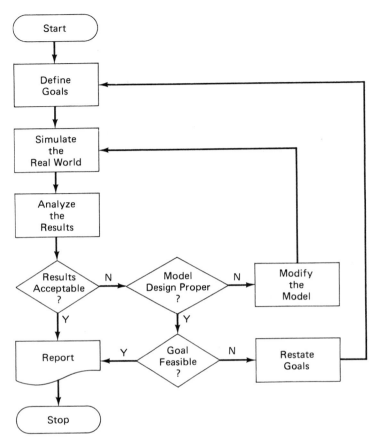

FIGURE 7-27   Simulating the Operations in Gyrocircuits

Corporate Planning Model

Gyrocircuits, following their consultant's recommendation, has adapted a formal corporate planning philosophy. In order to implement the corporate model, they have selected one of the commercial packages available in this area. The package selected is System W,[9] which integrates data management, data analysis, modeling, reporting, and graphics. System W is designed to handle large, complex problems, consolidations, allocations, and multiple-currencies situations. Gyrocircuits does not utilize all the capabilities of System W to the fullest

---

[9] System W is a Decision Support System designed by COMSHARE®, 3001 South State Street, Ann Arbor, MI, 48104, a pioneer firm in timesharing and decision support software. The discussion of this example which follows is adapted with COMSHARE® permission.

extent. The system's fundamental building blocks are time periods and variables, with rules for combining them. Adding a third dimension is dimension viewpoint.

The first dimension of a System W model is *time*. This software can handle up to 500 time periods. Half of these time periods can be classified as history and other half as forecast. The history periods store previous years' results for analysis and comparison. Forecast periods are for planning and projection. In this environment, there is no need to create extra variables for opening balances and exceptions. Furthermore, the time periods can be weeks, months, years, or combinations thereof.

The second dimension of the software is *variables*. The variables are defined in a way that is meaningful to the users—for instance, unit price, revenue, profit. There are 2,000 such variables that can be defined for System W. New variables can be inserted at any position in the variable list without causing an error in the calculation sequence or requiring reorganization.

Rules in System W define the relationships between variables of the model. For instance,

$$REVENUE = VOLUME \times PRICE$$
$$or$$
$$ALLOCATION = OVERHEAD \ OF \ COMPANY \ TOTAL \times$$
$$(SALES/SALES \ OF \ COMPANY \ TOTAL)$$

In System W the sequence of calculations need not be defined. It detects and solves simultaneous equations automatically.

The third dimension of the system is *viewpoint*. When the model describes multiple products, multiple markets, and multiple divisions, there is a need to incorporate all the relevant factors, such as organizational structure of the company, its products, and its markets into the model and into the rules. This task is made possible by expressing each dimension of the data set as a viewpoint.

The three dimensions of the model and three possible viewpoints are shown in Fig. 7-28.

The process of model building is quite simple. This is possible through the Model-by-Example™ feature of the system.[10] The model building process is done visually, merely by filling in the blanks, going from one field to the next. In this mode, 5 currencies, 36 forecast periods, 36 history periods, and 15 variables are available. Three additional dimensions of products, markets, and versions of the data (budget, actual, and forecast) are also available.

This model is used in Gyrocircuits for corporate planning and other less structured types of decisions. It allows the executives to evaluate the outcomes of various courses of action.

---

[10] A product of COMSHARE®.

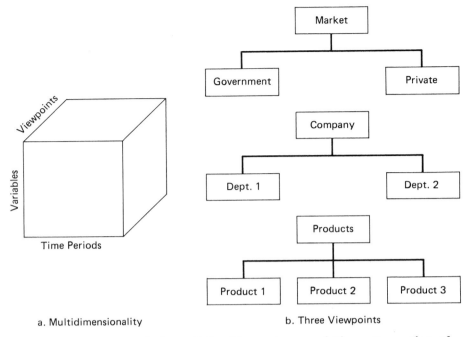

a. Multidimensionality

b. Three Viewpoints

FIGURE 7-28 **Description of the Dimensions and Three Examples of the Viewpoints**

Microplanning Models

To satisfy the corporate and financial managers' need for fast information processing, Gyrocircuits has acquired several copies of TARGET FINANCIAL MODELING.™[11] This package is generally known as a spreadsheet which calculates and recalculates multiple rows and columns by allowing the users to duplicate a situation, project hypothetical developments, and analyze their options instantly. It helps Gyrocircuits in simple sales forecasting, budget analysis, and material and labor planning. It offers two approaches to manipulating numbers. The first approach formats the monitor's screen much like other spreadsheets shown in Fig. 7-29.

Section 1.   The *Guideline,* contains four pieces of information:

1. Model name, the name of recalled or saved model
2. Memory, the approximate amount of computer memory remaining (hundreds of cells)

---

[11] This package is also a product of COMSHARE®.

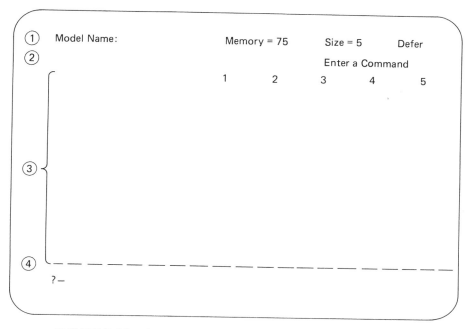

FIGURE 7-29   **Screen Layout of Target Planning Model™**

3. Size, the number of columns defined in a model
4. Defer, the calculation mode

Section 2.   The *status line* indicates processing during calculation, displays error messages and gives the current mode of operation (for example, "Enter a Command").

Section 3.   Displays either the spreadsheet results of your commands or the model summary.

Section 4.   The *cursor line* is used as a constant display of data, logic, or commands.

The second approach, called "command file," operates in a manner similar to mainframe and timesharing systems. It provides a complete listing of all terms, definitions, calculations, and variables that the user has typed in, which simplifies subsequent review and analysis of data. An example of this approach is shown in Fig. 7-30. In this illustration, a profit plan program which prepares income statements based on a direct costing model of managerial accounting is displayed.

Gyrocircuits makes heavy use of this package for projecting day-to-day operations.

```
Model Name:                    Memory = 60      Size = 5       Immediate
                                                             Enter a Command
     Line  1.0   SALES = 2000., GROW BY 6.%
     Line  2.0   AVE'PRICE = 85., 90. FOR 2, 92.,
     Line  3.0   REVENUE = SALES * AVG'PRICE
     Line  4.0   RAW'MAT'COST = 64., 67., 69. FOR2,
     Line  5.0   LABOR'COST = 4.FOR4, 16.
     Line  6.0   DISTRIBUTION = 4.FOR3, 5.,
     Line  7.0   UNIT'COST = SUM OF RAW'MAT'COST THRU DISTRIBUTION
     Line  8.0   TOT'VAR'COST = SALES * UNIT'COST
     Line  9.0   CONTRIBUTION = REVENUE-TOT'VAR'COST
     Line 10.0   FIXED'COST = 30000., 11000., 11500., 12000.,
     Line 11.0   GROSS'PROFIT = CONTRIBUTION-FIXED'COST
```

FIGURE 7-30   Example of a Command File

ASSESSMENT OF NEEDED STORAGE

In this section the storage needed to accommodate each of the files is computed. These computations are at best approximations of the actual storage needed when a real system is implemented. However, this discussion provides a procedure that may be used as is or modified for assessing needed storage of similar systems. Furthermore, these approximations are usually improved when better performance data is made available. (See the chapter appendix for details.)

Bid-in-Process File

This file has variable-length records. Each record is composed of a fixed-length part, 67 bytes, and a variable-length part. The variable-length part is the result of including a fixed number of bytes (representing the stage that a given product is in), 19 in total, a variable number of times (indicated by the value of the "No. of Trailers" field). Every record will use all nine stages that a product must go through. Therefore, every record is of size $67 + 19 \times 9 = 238$ bytes. Assume that there are 100 bids on file on the average; this results in $238 \times 100 = 23,800$ bytes being needed to accommodate this file.

Work-in-Process File

This file consists of fixed-length records. Each record is 13 bytes in length. One record is established for each unit produced and each unit scrapped. Suppose that no more than 500 units are in the system at any time. At a 2 percent scrap rate, 510 records make up the file. Therefore, the size of this file is $13 \times 510 = 6,630$ bytes.

Employee Transaction File

This file has variable-length records. Each record has a fixed-length part (17 bytes) and a variable-length part. The variable-length part is the result of including a fixed number of bytes (representing each unit a given employee has worked on during a day; 3 bytes in length) a variable number of times (indicated by the value of the "No. of Trailers" field). Assume that every employee works on 20 different parts per day. Therefore, on the average, the size of the variable part is $3 \times 20 = 60$ bytes. The firm has 100 employees resulting in 100 records being needed per day; or $(17 + 60) \times 100 = 7,700$ bytes. However, these records are kept for seven days, resulting in a file of size $7 \times 7,700 = 53,900$ bytes.

Finished Goods/Cost of Goods Sold File

This file consists of fixed-length records each of which is 42 bytes in length. One record is established for each unit of finished goods. Suppose that no more than 500 of these units are kept on file. This results in a file of 21,000 bytes.

In summary, the file storage requirements for this application are

1. $23,800 + 6,630 + 53,900 + 21,000 = 105,330$ bytes for the operations files.
2. 5,000 bytes of disk storage for historical data so variances in time, materials, and costs can be computed.

Therefore, the total size is 110,330 bytes or about 110 K bytes.

DECISION SUPPORT SYSTEM DESIGN CONSIDERATIONS

To assist in solving some of the semistructured and unstructured types of problems encountered by the management of Gyrocircuits, a DSS generator package is selected. Using this package a suitable DSS, or a number of DSSs, can be implemented and then used by management. Building a DSS using a generator package is simpler than designing, developing, and implementing one from scratch. However, the disadvantages of such a process are the limitations imposed by the generator, and sometimes the prohibitive cost of the generator if only a limited number of DSSs (one or two) are needed. Therefore, frequently a DSS needs to be built according to the needs of the organization and without the benefits of a DSS generator. Certain systems analysis and design, development, and implementation issues should be addressed as the process of building the DSS unfolds.

In the case of a conventional data processing system, the system's designers initially concentrate their efforts on systems analysis and logical design of the system. Following the completion of this phase, the designers focus attention on the development and implementation aspects, the physical design of the system, which detail the way in which the system becomes operational on the computer. In building a DSS the same tasks must be performed, but in a parallel fashion using a series of tightly coupled iterations of logical and physical designs. In other words, the design of the DSS tends to unfold; as parts of the system are developed and implemented, earlier components are modified to reflect the experience gained from the later ones. This evolutionary process of system design proceeds and progresses in a cyclical fashion through the following steps.

System's Scope

Analysis of the key decisions areas that the DSS is expected to handle is performed. As a result of this analysis, anticipated problem situations and the information needed to support decision making are identified.

Summary Report Specification

Summary reports such as averages, comparisons, projections, monitoring, summaries, and alert indicators are designed and the designs are carried out to meet the objectives of supporting the user in problem-discovery situations. Printed reports, video display terminals, graphics, display panels, and voice response devices are all appropriate forms for this type of reporting. However, the degree of usefulness of each of these media is dependent on the specific function of the report.

Detailed Report Specifications

In this step the designer should concentrate on the relevant functions and seek to provide output that meets reasonable forecasts of anticipated information needs. Reporting schemes to facilitate ad hoc inquiries, comparisons, finding and locating entities, projections, modeling, and detailed reports are all desirable. The forms that might be used to produce these reports are similar to those specified for summary reports. Again the usefulness of a specific form depends on the function of the report. The ad hoc inquiry scheme is most preferred by managers, even though response time might be slow.

User Interface

In this step the dialogue subsystem is specified. Factors such as ease of use, security, flexibility, and recovery after failure should be considered in great detail during this phase of design. Furthermore, the variety of devices supported by the dialogue system should be taken in consideration to accommodate the various input/output media that might be required to handle the individual reporting styles of decision makers.

Data Base Requirements

In this step the data base is specified. This process is similar to that of regular information systems design, except it is important to make sure that the structure, location, precision, and timing of data elements are appropriate for producing the required reports.

Input Design

In this step the necessary input data, edit rules, verification rules, security checks, input media, and timing considerations are specified. Usually the majority of data necessary for the DSS are obtained directly from the data base.

System Walkthrough

In this step the design is reviewed with the users of the DSS. During this process the objectives of the DSS are compared with the design to ensure that they are adequately met. The design should be flexible enough to accommodate future expansions and modifications without major rework.

As in other information systems, a programming language for implementation needs to be selected. The issues to be considered here are similar to those in other information systems implementations. Furthermore, postimplementation reviews are necessary to ensure a desirable level of performance. Because a DSS is usually constructed of a set of smaller systems, these reviews are conducted for each one of the component systems. Additionally, the objectives of these subsystems, the sequence and techniques used for their implementation, and the suitability of methods used to implement the reporting schemes are reviewed to determine if any need to be changed for future DSS modifications.

PROBLEMS

1. In the case discussed, in order to identify each bid, a two-digit code is provided. What kind of problem may Gyrocircuits face in the future? How would you correct the situation if you consider that there is a problem?

2. Gyrocircuits has designed its system based on the fact that only one component is introduced in each department. Redesign the system assuming that more than one component is used in each department.

3. Design the screen layout of the menu which is used for Bid-in-Process data entry.

4. Redesign the system and prepare the labor-efficiency variance report for each month.

5. How do you change the file structure in order to produce variance reports that also include year-to-date information?

6. In this case, the actual overhead accounts are kept in manual records. Redesign the system in a way that you can also produce a computerized overhead variance report.

APPENDIX

Bid-in-Process File Layout

Data Element	Format	Number of Bytes	Notes
Bid & Part No.	9(6)	4	
Name of Part	X(20)	20	
Date	X(6)	6	
Customer Name	X(25)	25	
Customer Number	9(5)	3	
Units Requested	9(4)	3	
Scrap Rate	9(2)	2	
OH Rate	9(2)	2	
Flag	9(1)	1	
No. of Trailers	9(1)	1	
		67 bytes	Fixed-length part
Department or Process	9(1)	1	
Standard Time	9(3)	2	
Direct Labor Cost/Hr.	9(4)	3	
Item No.	9(6)	4	
Number of Units Required	9(5)	3	
Unit Cost	9(4)	3	
Blank	X(3)	3	Filler
		19 bytes	Variable-length part

Work-in-Process File Layout

Data Element	Format	Number of Bytes	Notes
Bid & Part No.	9(6)	1	
Status	X(1)	1	
Date of Status	X(6)	6	
Blank	X(2)	2	Filler
		13 bytes	

Employee Transaction File Layout

Data Element	Format	Number of Bytes	Notes
Employee No.	9(5)	3	
Date	X(6)	6	
Time In	9(4)	3	
Time Out	9(4)	3	
No. of Trailers	9(2)	2	
		17 bytes	Length of fixed part
Status	X(1)	1	
Number of Units	9(3)	2	
		3 bytes	Length of variable part

Finished Goods/Cost of Goods Sold File Layout

Data Element	Format	Number of Bytes	Notes
Bid & Part No.	9(6)	4	
Date	X(6)	6	
Customer No.	9(5)	3	
Customer Name	X(25)	25	
Cost/Unit	9(5)	3	
Status	X(1)	1	
		42 bytes	

Suggested Readings

American Accounting Association. *A Statement of Basic Accounting Theory*. Evanston, Ill.: AAA, 1966.

————. "Report of the Committee on Management Accounting," *The Accounting Review Supplement,* 1970.

————. "Report of the Committee on Accounting and Information Systems." *The Accounting Review Supplement,* 1971.

American Institute of Certified Public Accountants. *Accounting Terminology Bulletin No. 1*. New York: AICPA, 1961.

————. "Codification of Auditing Standards and Procedures," *Statement on Auditing Standards No. 1*. New York: AICPA, 1972.

————. "The Effects of EDP on the Auditor's Study and Evaluation of Internal Control," *Statement on Auditing Standards No. 3*. New York: AICPA, 1974.

————. "Audit Approaches for a Computerized Inventory System." New York: AICPA, 1980.

Anthony, Robert N. *Planning and Control Systems: A Framework for Analysis*. Boston: Division of Research, Harvard University Graduate School of Business Administration, 1965.

Anthony, Robert N., and James S. Reece. *Accounting: Text and Cases* (7th ed.). Homewood, Ill.: Irwin, 1983.

Anthony, Robert N., John Dearden, and Norton M. Bedford, *Management Control Systems*. Homewood, Ill: Irwin, 1984.

Bodnar, George H. *Accounting Information Systems*. Boston: Allyn and Bacon, 1980.

Cushing, Barry E. *Accounting Information Systems and Business Organizations,* 3d ed. Reading, Mass.: Addison-Wesley, 1982.

Dearden, John. "How to Organize Information Systems," *Harvard Business Review,* March–April 1965.

Gershefski, George W. "Building a Corporate Financial Model," *Harvard Business Review,* July–August 1969.

Gillespie, Cecil. *Accounting Systems—Procedures and Methods* (3d ed.). Englewood Cliffs, N.J.: Prentice-Hall, 1971.

Gorry, G. Anthony, and Michael S. Scott Morton. "A Framework for Management Information Systems," *Sloan Management Review,* Fall 1971.

Hicks, James O., Jr., and Wayne E. Leininger. *Accounting Information Systems*. St. Paul, Minn.: West, 1981.

Horngren, Charles T. *Cost Accounting—A Managerial Emphasis* (5th ed.). Englewood Cliffs, N.J.: Prentice-Hall, 1982.

Hussain, Donna, and K. M. Hussain. *Information Resource Management.* Homewood, Ill.: Irwin, 1984.

Keen, Peter G. W. "Value Analysis: Justifying Decision Support Systems," *MIS Quarterly,* March 1981.

Leitch, Robert A., and Davis, K. Roscoe. *Accounting Information Systems.* Englewood Cliffs, N.J.: Prentice-Hall, 1983.

Li, David H. *Accounting Information Systems: A Control Emphasis.* Homewood, Ill.: Irwin, 1983.

Lindhe, Richard, and Steven D. Grossman. *Accounting Information Systems.* Houston: Dame Publications, 1980.

Lucas, Henry H., Jr.. *Why Information Systems Fail.* New York: Columbia University Press, 1975.

Mair, William C., Donald R. Wood, and Keagle W. Davis. *Computer Control and Audit.* Altamonte Springs, Fla.: The Institute of Internal Auditors, Inc., 1978.

Moscove, Stephen A., and Mark G. Simkin. *Accounting Information Systems: Concepts and Practice for Effective Decision Making* (2d ed.). New York: John Wiley and Sons, 1984.

Murdick, Robert G. *MIS Concepts and Design.* Englewood Cliffs, N.J.: Prentice-Hall, 1980.

Murdick, Robert G., Thomas C. Fuller, Joel E. Ross, and Frank J. Winnermark. *Accounting Information Systems.* Englewood Cliffs, N.J.: Prentice-Hall, 1978.

Murdick, Robert G., Joel E. Ross, and James R. Claggett. *Information Systems for Modern Management.* Englewood Cliffs, N.J.: Prentice-Hall, 1984.

National Association of Accountants. *Statement on Management Accounting No. 1A.* New York: NAA, 1981.

Nash, John F., and Martin B. Roberts. *Accounting Information Systems.* New York: Macmillan, 1984.

Page, John, and Paul Hooper. *Accounting and Information Systems* (2d ed.). Reston, Va.: Reston Publishing, 1982.

Porter, Thomas W., and William E. Perry. *EDP: Controls and Auditing.* Boston: Kent, 1984.

Senn, James A. *Analysis and Design of Information Systems.* New York: McGraw-Hill, 1984.

Sprague, Ralph H. "A Framework for the Development of Decision Support Systems," *MIS Quarterly,* December 1980.

Watne, Donald A., and Peter B. B. Turney. *Auditing EDP Systems.* Englewood Cliffs, N.J.: Prentice-Hall, 1984.

Weber, Ron. *EDP Auditing—Conceptual Foundations and Practice.* New York: McGraw-Hill, 1982.

Wilkinson, Joseph W. *Accounting and Information Systems.* New York: John Wiley and Sons, 1982.

Wu, Frederick H. *Accounting Information Systems—Theory and Practice.* New York: McGraw-Hill, 1983.